David Covington has given us a remarkable window onto the Bible's take on aesthetics. He gently but firmly deflates adages such as "beauty is in the eye of the beholder" and other subjective judgments, but without demeaning the spirit from which they are generated. A thoroughly elevating read.

—*William Edgar,* professor of apologetics,
Westminster Theological Seminary

I have long wished that somebody would write a Bible-centered study of art, applying to aesthetics the trinitarian three-perspective approach that Vern Poythress and I have developed. This book fulfills my wish. I recommend it not just to artists but to anyone who seeks to know God as he truly is.

—*John Frame,* professor of systematic theology and
philosophy, Reformed Theological Seminary

This book is the hinge book that transforms the entire field of aesthetics, art, and human delight through the reality of God, manifest in the work of Christ. We have needed it, and now it exists, a legacy for generations.

—*Rev. Dr. Vern Poythress,* professor of New Testament
interpretation, Westminster Theological Seminary

Covington approaches the complexity and transcendence of aesthetics and the arts the way only a sensitive creator can. His love for art, imagination, and creation, combined with his excitement about God's intention for these things, lends a unique and vibrant shimmer to his words and thoughts on the subject.

—*Daniel Goans,* singer-songwriter; member of Lowland Hum

Covington's love for God and music fires his conviction that truth and beauty, mind and passion, belong together. His keen eye for the brokenness of all things in and around us fires his conviction that the healthy reintegration of these gifts depends on God's healing power, mediated to us by his Word and gospel. Join him in his searching exploration.

—*Charles D. Drew,* singer; author; founding pastor,
Emmanuel Presbyterian Church, Manhattan

Covington joins generations of creative minds in engaging not only with culture but with the beauty of God's truth through the eyes of an aesthetic practitioner. A deeply caring and good read. I recommend it wholeheartedly for artist and hearer alike.

—*Jerry Eisley,* founder and director, Washington Arts
Group; founder and director, Eisley Fine Art

Covington asks the questions worth asking about how beauty, ugliness, pleasure, passion, and meaning all filter into our everyday lives, and what the Bible has to say about it. I appreciate his gentle tone, his vivid prose, his grasp on theory without letting it get too abstract. But what stands out to me is his God-centered and biblical approach. This is a book worth reading and reflecting on.

—*Dr. Ted Turneau,* Global Scholars Teaching Fellow, Cultural and Religious Studies School of Humanities and Social Sciences, Anglo-American University, Prague

Written with both intellectual integrity and artistic sensitivity, which is hard to find. Covington has given us a wonderful and needed contribution to the discussion on beauty, art, and faith. He cares deeply about both art and theology, and leads us to reexamine how our desires and passions in life and art can lead us back to God.

—*Rev. Joel Pelsue,* president, Arts and Entertainment Ministries

Art that reveres the divine is more than shuffling around labels of adoration. Calling for a sincere and authentic expression of love, this book is a heartfelt reminder to seek out the redemptive quality in everything we do.

—*Noel Paul Stookey,* member of Peter, Paul, and Mary

If you are an artist, or know one, or have ever wondered how to appreciate or evaluate or understand the purpose of art in any form as a follower of Christ, you need to read this book. This is the fraternal twin of *Coram Deo*. Liberating, refreshing, and worshipful!

—*Elizabeth Groves,* lecturer in biblical Hebrew, Westminster Theological Seminary

Covington is a musician, a husband, and a true lover of Scripture. The decades he has spent integrating those callings makes this book a masterpiece. He equips those of us who want to take to heart God's aesthetic preferences, even as we read the more jarring passages of the Old Testament and our lives.

—*Anna Shea,* guest lecturer on the intersection between science, theology, and poetry, Pepperdine University and Evangelical Seminary

# A REDEMPTIVE THEOLOGY of ART

# *A* REDEMPTIVE
# THEOLOGY
# *of* ART

## RESTORING GODLY AESTHETICS
## *to* DOCTRINE *and* CULTURE

## DAVID A. COVINGTON

ZONDERVAN

*A Redemptive Theology of Art*
Copyright © 2018 by David A. Covington

This title is also available as a Zondervan ebook.

Requests for information should be addressed to:
Zondervan, *3900 Sparks Dr. SE, Grand Rapids, Michigan 49546*

ISBN 978-0-310-53436-5

*Cover design: Tammy Johnson*
*Cover photo: Viad G. / Shutterstock*
*Interior design: Kait Lamphere*

*Printed in the United States of America*

18 19 20 21 22 23 24 25 26 27 28 /DHV/ 15 14 13 12 11 10 9 8 7 6 5 4 3 2 1

*To my mother, Miriam Bruff Covington,*
*who cultivates my love of learning;*

*To David and Nan Powlison,*
*who welcomed these two attic mice for five lovely years*
*and who live the gospel to us;*

*To Vern Poythress,*
*who encourages me with devout glee.*

# CONTENTS

# Detailed Contents

# ACKNOWLEDGMENTS

This work explores biblical aesthetics on a scale grander than I could have tackled alone. It took a combination of nearsightedness and procrastination—call them focus and reflection, if it reads smoother—and much good help. Great help I have enjoyed. Dick Keyes of L'Abri Fellowship in Massachusetts first showed me that word and image go together in Christian theology, through his message "The Theology of the Imagination." He sent me in search of Dr. William Edgar of Westminster Theological Seminary, who patiently encouraged me that the Bible dealt with aesthetics in a way that could map onto the passions and experience of a real artist—he himself plays an energetic jazz piano—and he guided me through five years of full-time study at WTS.

The entire Westminster faculty inspired me to look more deeply to the Bible for the roots, defacement, and restoration of beauty. Dr. Vern S. Poythress pulled me out of more than one slough of despond and set a high bar of clarity, cogency, and profundity that I still hope to recognize on the street someday. He taught many of us how to think triadically and perspectivally, and I am deeply indebted. Dr. David Powlison and his wife, Nan, graciously hosted, encouraged, taught, supported, and prayed with and for us through years of study and many more of friendship.

The Fellows of the Trinity Forum Academy classes of '10, '11, and '12 improved my reflections on these matters with their questions, earning my lasting thanks.

I enjoyed the privilege of consulting on technical matters with really smart people who are also friends. Dr. Dan McCartney, Mrs. Elizabeth "Libbie" Groves, and Dr. Peter Wallace have helped and encouraged me in this project, though neither they nor any other friends or consultants bear responsibility for anything unwelcome here.

I wrote this with the present assurance that people were praying for me.

God has helped me in answer to the prayers of scores of friends and neighbors. I invite the reader to join me in thanking God for their faithful partnership; they have also prayed for you!

Roger Freet, beloved nephew and dear friend, patted my sweating hand through the stages of this labor, then generously introduced me to his friends at Zondervan, midwives whose kindness, vision, and wisdom brought this swaddled noisemaker into your hands.

Daughter Joy, beloved counselor and professional vocalist, whose aesthetic sensibilities are more intuitively infused with sound theology than any others I know, contributed patiently to these reflections. She also asked repeatedly, "So, Dad, how's the book coming?" Here it is, thanks in large part to her. Son Jesse, who sharpens iron with me continually on these and many other themes, merits lasting thanks for good questions, hearty encouragement, and the special friendship of a beloved son.

No one but Sharon, my wife, could have supported me and spoken so patiently, so faithfully to me, especially when the necessary became impossible. She read, wrote, argued, and prayed over this with me. She pulled this project and me out of dozens of digital ditches. She is my first and best colleague, discussing every insight during decades of sweet partnership. If you can profit from what follows, or even understand it, she deserves your thanks as well as mine.

God has shepherded me faithfully through the discipleship of writing this; he is unfathomably good, true, and beautiful. May he be glorified in this as in all things!

# INTRODUCTION

Everyone leans toward beauty in some form. You may lean toward beauty in painting, cooking, acting, hiking, or poetry. This book started in my leaning toward beauty in music.

## I Searched for Passion through Beauty

Where do you spend more money, on your music collection or on your books? I have been a singer-songwriter for many years. My lovely collections of vinyl, tapes, CDs, and MP3 files, of instruments, hymnals, sheet music, and paper and digital chord charts keep requiring creative new storage solutions. I love to make music, to listen to it, to worship God musically in church and with friends, and to write music. It gets me juiced, motivated.

Loveliness of all kinds stirs my passions and has from earliest memory: oranges from our orchard that we peeled and ate, ocean waves that foamed about Prisoner Rock below my favorite childhood home, the classical music my folks sent down the hallway as my sister and I listened in our bedrooms. The ugliness of an abandoned, condemned house and a playmate's meanness stirred revulsion.

Folk music featured large in our family, and I grew to appreciate it. I heard no big band or jazz until later because my parents didn't go in for them. My cousin played the Everly Brothers on the radio, and I heard early Beach Boys with real pleasure. Peter, Paul, and Mary's music made the fun of music more physical when I discovered I could play along on my guitar. A college friend led me enthusiastically to something new: Simon and Garfunkel were actually saying something in their music. I learned guitar by copying all their early songs. My friends and I began to discover that cultural influence wasn't all one-way: we could play and sing along. Then we turned off the records. We could write and sing songs, accompanying, entertaining, and influencing others as we had been influenced. Solitary pleasures in nature and culture became shared pleasures. We enjoyed the pleasure, also a little power.

My folks had long limited the amount of TV my sister and I could watch and turned down the volume during most commercials, so I learned that they thought images and media can seduce, leading unwary people to do unwise things. Songs came in, charged with ideas and emotions, from idealism to satire, from propaganda to marketing, stirring violent passions and deeds, sometimes nearby. You can't trust everything attractive, it seems.

## Passions Serving God?

Friends and I played and sang together to a growing circle of friends, and found that better music got a better response. As our faith and skills grew, we began to hope we could use music to affect people for good, for the gospel. We imitated, modified, and wrote songs and performed them for evangelistic musical programs. We expressed our faith in the popular music we loved. Audiences responded well, so we concluded that the musical form suited the evangelistic content.

The good folks at our church wondered whether hymn-style music might be better suited to the gospel, but we had our doubts. We wanted to use upbeat, contemporary music. We asked, as Larry Norman put it, "Why should the devil have all the good music?" We did not wonder long about this good music, "Good to whom?" We assumed good is objective, readily recognizable to everyone, Christian or not.

Our church tolerated our music, but they apparently believed, like we did, that good music is objectively good. They hired trained soloists to supplement the volunteer choir. These four professionals had learned their skills not at church during the weekly sermons, in a Sunday school class, or even during choir rehearsals. They learned music in conservatories and music schools, open to all, Christian or not. It made sense to us: the church teaches the truth about God, and music experts teach music. Truth and aesthetics run on parallel but independent tracks.

The church's separation of doctrine from aesthetic standards seemed to fit our experience; we were being well taught in the Bible, our musical skills were improving, and people were growing under our ministry. We tried to marry the good theology we learned in church to the good music we found outside the church. Then things started to get complicated.

Sharing the stage with other Christian musicians at youth rallies, concerts, and coffeehouses, we noticed that some musicians coordinated truth with beauty better than others. I particularly remember one young singer who, after passionately delivering an artistically tepid song, announced to the applauding audience, "God wrote that song, not me!" We were generally patient with each other in those days—my own musical efforts called for a good deal of patience—but still, I couldn't help wondering, "Couldn't God do any better than that?" We noticed that many songs with pretty good theology seemed musically shallow, weak, and tacky, while others with no deliberate theology or mistaken theology stirred us deeply. Why didn't theological accuracy and aesthetic excellence always go together? We pursued excellence in theology and in artistry along parallel tracks, but we had trouble keeping our theology and music coordinated.

## Can Truth Alone Lead Us to God?

Two schemes for coordinating artistic excellence with the gospel scrabbled for dominance. A train with three cars labeled Fact, Faith, and Feeling, pictured on a widely circulated evangelistic tract,[1] caught our eye. The Fact locomotive pulled the Faith car, and the Feeling caboose brought up the rear. The author meant facts to stand for God's utterly reliable revelation in all its fullness, and feelings to stand for our emotions as an unreliable gauge of truth. We were college students trying to sort out music's role in the Christian life while cramming for classes; our culture leaned anti-establishment, anti-intellectual, but the tract sounded just like our teachers. We took it wrong, but it seemed that the authorities wanted our feelings to take a back seat and let reason drive. That didn't sound like the solution; it sounded like part of the problem. The tract's authors meant to establish the reliability of biblical revelation over personal responses, and that sounded fine to us. But this train went off the tracks when it hit our music; we knew we had plenty of godly feelings riding in the Faith car—we were singing about them—as well as the less wholesome ones that belonged in back. Could our reason handle the facts to protect us against emotionalism? Did this train have any good feelings onboard, feelings that didn't always have to tag along in the caboose? We weren't sure. And why, we wondered, did facts about God fail so often to fit with beauty or to lead to God?

## Or Can Beauty Alone Lead Us to God?

We switched the train onto a siding, and I wondered about an emerging scheme for coordinating the truth about God with aesthetic excellence: "Follow beauty; it will never lead you astray and can even bypass intellectual roadblocks

---

1. Bill Bright, *Have You Heard of the Four Spiritual Laws?* (Peachtree City, GA: Campus Crusade for Christ, 2007).

to gospel teaching and make us more human." Embracing this second schema, we asked, "Why do we hunger for beauty?"[2] believing that our hunger for beauty was really a hunger for God. We never asked, "Beauty in whose eyes?" or "What god?" These ideas infused the air we breathed. We had all heard sermons full of truth *and* passion. The Bible too seems as full of feelings as of the articulated good news, and creation itself sings God's glories. Occasionally, a song would achieve a tantalizing blend of truth and beauty.

Soon I was married to a talented singer, and my wife and I eventually took our music and two kids on the road. We had a great opportunity to test this second schema, using evocative music to draw people to the gospel and to challenge thinking, believing, and living. Sometimes it worked.

This story is bigger than one musician, his family and friends. Aesthetics permeate our lives, understood in art, music, media, passion, beauty, all things affectional. All of us feel beauty's tug and the repelling force field of ugliness. Sometimes these come in disorganized clusters, and we wrestle with attraction and revulsion and with connecting them to our Christian faith. We have guessed that passions work predictably from given stimuli: we like this sort and not that. Still, people respond differently, even neighbors. Cultures differ more the farther we get from home, all around the world. Maybe, we wonder, beauty and the passions it stirs in us are neither good nor bad, neither inclined to lead us to God nor inclined to lead us away from him, but are ethically and religiously neutral. According to the popular wisdom, feelings are neither good nor bad; they just are. That might explain how feelings seem to follow patterns but remain unpredictable.

Understanding feelings as neutral also seems powerful, opening the possibility of control. First, self-control: although we can be slaves of our passions, we can also be their masters. Then we can use feelings to influence others. If music and other aesthetic media impact us according to predictable patterns of stimulus and response, we might master these patterns and use them to draw people to Christ, even to disciple them. These high goals might be accessible to us if we master the media that stir people's feelings, always being careful to stay away from abuses.

The feelings question became personal to this passionate Christian. I wanted to use my gifts and grow them, to help people come to faith in Jesus through good music that would draw them with their feelings for beauty and repel them from darkness. But how? The Bible spoke directly to me in other areas, and I wondered, "What does the Bible say about the power of music, about all beauty,

---

2. Jim Croegaert, "Why Do We Hunger for Beauty?"

all passions?" I longed to lead one life rather than two separate ones, one in music and one in theology. After years of touring, reading, reflecting, and questioning anyone who would talk about it, I determined to tackle the question head-on. In spite of warnings—"You'll never write another song"—I enrolled in a seminary I thought could help me find Bible answers to my questions about music and the power of passion.[3] Seminaries intend to train pastors, not musicians, so I had to adapt most of my studies to these questions. The professors befriended, challenged, and helped me.

I began these studies hoping to write better songs. The Bible shifted my questions to encompass all the arts and, eventually, all aesthetics. I broadened my questions to probe the Bible about affections. Instead the Bible probed me, changed me, and changed my questions again. We do not master songwriting or beauty or aesthetics; the Beautiful One masters us. And it's a bigger job than we thought.

Thus began the fuel-injected, turbocharged academic-devotional ride of a lifetime. The Bible answers the questions of our experience better than we ask them. These answers brought me enormous delight. Since this wonderful beginning, years of study, music, conversation, and students' questions have confirmed and enriched these early, tentative answers. The Bible teaches not only why music works but also an entire theology of aesthetics and passions, revealing God's glory. His glory is beautiful! His mercy is strong! His judgments are terrible! His love is overwhelming!

## The Bible Leads to Eternal Delight

The Bible's teachings about passions, private and shared, are not new. Still, the development of a system of these teachings—the topic of this book—has long produced mixed, incomplete results. The system I propose advances the theological discussion of aesthetics and passions in three respects: first, we connect previously unconnected familiar teachings about aesthetics; second, we connect this system to systematic theology; third, this system makes these doctrines more accessible for discipleship.

I speak from inside the orthodox, historic Christian tradition, broadly considered, with fondness for its Reformed expression. While I make what may seem unfamiliar connections, the framework arises not from any departure from Christian orthodoxy but from adherence to it. I intend not to innovate but rather to mine eternal riches to meet the need of our aesthetically driven cultural moment. I contribute to discussion, long in progress, toward an

---

3. Westminster Theological Seminary in Philadelphia, 1993–2000.

orthodox, systematic, and practical theology of aesthetics that by faithfulness to the Scriptures maintains consistency with the best traditions of the church.

## Premises

### Trust the Scriptures

As I mined with premises, so I lay out these nuggets for your eye with the same premises. My exploration of the biblical roots of aesthetics and of the glorious framework to which it belongs assumes biblical authority. Others have argued this premise better than I can, so if you find it necessary, read them first. No other book speaks as this Book speaks.

My experience of the Bible, like that of many others, bubbles with feelings. Joy keeps me company; song lifts my heart; weeping groans for sorrow and leaps with bliss; eyes sting from horror and awe. I can smile and sigh as I read; dance or crumple with Scripture sung. I can wince at misapplications or goofy worship lyrics. My sin troubles me more and more, but the guilt of my sin troubles me less and less. Self-loathing is in retreat. My spirit answers that God's Spirit lives and overflows in me, in spite of remaining sin. I often find my heart burning when I hear the Bible read aloud, its truth taught or preached. I can find comfort in God's church. Joyful hope in God crops up in me. Of course I have many other less creditable experiences, yet these remain and grow. How did I get this way? I can attribute these experiences only to the Bible and its God.

Assuming biblical authority—the Fact and Faith of the train metaphor, rightly understood—can help us avoid finding, if we assume culturally defined concepts and categories, that our conclusions and our system don't comfortably fit the Scriptures. Unnecessary tweaking or complexity or a structure lacking elegance often suggest careless definitions or premises. One's conclusions gestate in one's definitions and premises, so here we will ask Scripture to probe our assumptions.

### Seek the Origins

To understand aesthetics, we need to seek its deepest roots. That's why I went to seminary to study songwriting. We must know: Does aesthetics originate in creation? Or does it arise first in human cultivation of creation? Or is God himself aesthetic? Is beauty in the eye of the beholder as subjectively as the proverb says? Or does it arise from something above the cause-and-effect rules of human objectivity and the infinite variations of human subjectivity? Answering these initial questions has enormous practical implications. By exploring these roots first, we can hope to answer these questions and then apply the answers in ways that fit and help.

## *Use Biblical Concepts and Definitions*

Instead of asking our questions using categories and concepts borrowed from our culture—beauty, art, aesthetic objectivity—and then asking what Scripture has to say about them, we will, after some preliminaries, ask Scripture to develop its own definitions and categories. Honesty, at least, necessitates this approach: I began my studies intending to take an aesthetic look at the Bible, but the Bible had another idea. My studies became a biblical look at aesthetics—a change for the better.

## *Apply to Experience*

To make sense of aesthetics for real people, not just philosophers, we need to see how the Bible's aesthetic concepts and categories explain people's experience, comfort people, and strengthen God's folk in faithful, holy, fruitful living. Having worked top down, we will also work bottom up. Calvin begins his *Institutes* saying that we can seek knowledge of God from knowing ourselves or seek knowledge of ourselves through knowing God.[4] We will do a bit of both. We would love to discover that our assessment of roots can fit the church's historic creeds and confessions, also make sense of our experience, and finally suggest a hopeful path for other Christians. The best systematic theology is necessarily practical. Believing this, we will use biblical concepts and categories to arrange, explain, and interact with samples from culture and the arts, letting the Bible make sense of our experience. We will see God's goodness more clearly as we articulate a vision for aesthetic discipleship.

## *Seek a Biblical Theology*

This is a Bible study and a biblical theology, not a review of literature. Through the centuries, many Christians have noted aspects of the Bible's teachings on aesthetics. Modern Christians—Catholic, Orthodox, Protestant—have recently taken up a fruitful exploration in a surge of books and articles. They note similarities between aesthetic experience and Christian theology and intuitively grasp benefits for and dangers to the church posed by the culture. Few thinkers, though, have attempted a systematic theology of aesthetics, or to locate aesthetics within systematic theology. I have selected a few representatives from the major threads of contemporary Christian thought on aesthetics to illustrate key points and to illumine the need.

Our biblical theology of aesthetics must interact with the best of systematic

---

4. John Calvin, *Institutes of the Christian Religion*, ed. John T. McNeill, trans. Ford Lewis Battles, Library of Christian Classics XX (Philadelphia: Westminster, 1960), 1.1.1–2.

theology as well as with human experience. We can tell this story of aesthetics in one chapter or in four. If we deal with aesthetics as if it were objective and static, our work is complete in one chapter: follow the culture leaders, because they're working with common grace and they're generally better at it than the Christians are. Or if we unpack the story of aesthetics along the Bible's redemptive narrative of creation, fall, redemption, and consummation, we can see ourselves and our aesthetic experiences more clearly woven into God's purposes for the whole world, with even better to come.

## This Work's Distinctives

### Personal

This effort has also become a biblical look at an artist: this one. Like many, I have taken on personal and culture-wide habits of thought, including imbalances, errors, even sins. This attempt to think consistently about the role, meaning, and power of aesthetics and its relation to theology proper arises from my hunger to find God's unity for the apparently parallel tracks of theology and aesthetics. Call it housecleaning in pursuit of discipleship. I hope it will be so for the reader. Further, this work bears some of the character of a devotional memoir. Responsible diligence requires a certain candor.

### God-Centered

Evangelical Christians and many others, when asked, say they believe that God is supreme in everything, but we're a little puzzled to articulate this supremacy in the aesthetical dimension. We hardly know what that means in detail. Let's start with the obvious. It means, first, that the same Bible that may have stirred our hearts to repent and believe the gospel also guides the stirring of our hearts in aesthetic pursuits. It means that the proper approach to aesthetics is itself God-centered. How does God approach aesthetics? Or is God aesthetic? If so, how does he approach himself? He could never approach his own aesthetics or those of his creation as an abstract principle or in isolation from other aspects of his glory. So this work concludes with a call to think God's aesthetic thoughts after him, even share his feelings, by taking a God's-eye view of aesthetics.

### Practical

Once we have hammered out a quick outline of this field, we will map it onto the contemporary discussion between Christianity and the arts, between theologians and artists. The resulting systematic theology of aesthetics displays symmetry, coherency with the gospel, practicality for discipleship, and a capacity for nuance that challenges, enlightens, refreshes, and gratifies. By this means, we hope to find a biblical path to thinking and working wisely in aesthetic undertakings, from the arts to pop culture to favorite foods, to the end that God's people be more like him and that his glory should fill the earth.

Some lovers of beauty respond with suspicion, even anger, to the suggestion that aesthetic properties may be qualified by faith in God or its absence. The reader who finds this indignant swelling in his bosom has been warned. Yet to the curious I say read on; you may find a coherent answer here.

## *Argument by Analogy*

While logical argument plays a major role in constructing this case, my method includes more argument by analogy than customary for theological discussion. Analogical argument has, for some of us, more power to persuade intuitively than has logic alone, and my use of it may help readers familiar with picture thinking and with literary, typological approaches to Scripture to find themselves at home. I hope to show here that logical and analogical arguments pull most powerfully when yoked.

When one sees a theme or connection that corresponds to another in Scripture, one follows the common thread to its source. "Why is this like that? Where else does this theme show up? Where does it start? Where is it leading? Why?" Readers accustomed to the solely syllogistic may find themselves on new turf, though I have done my best to mark the path clearly. Readers who, like me, find picture thinking a bit more comfortable may find that this work unfolds for them with refreshing ease. I hope so.

These explorations, both of the biblical roots of aesthetics and of the paradigm for interacting biblically with culture, have burned a hole in my heart. I have ached to share these riches with my friends that we may see more and more through the eye of the Beholder.

# Chapter 1

# STORYBOARD

*Why do we hunger for beauty?*
—JIM CROEGAERT

## Math 101, Meet Rock 'n' Roll

The day I got back my first college math exam—I failed—I was crushed. My career plans were blocked, and I had no plan B. I pedaled home, nestled the LP carrying my favorite song onto the turntable in my folks' living room, and dialed their Heathkit amp to full throttle to get the most out of the big Lansing speakers. I threw myself on the floor and let the rock 'n' roll soothe my soul from the grief of a bad grade. Music weaves through my life like a vein of gold through coarse rock, embedded fitfully in the surrounding stone, brightening and enriching. You too? Even if it's not music, something calls aesthetic passion from everyone. I use this term to collect aesthetics and passions in all their definitions. I use many synonyms and include all the forms, images, and stories that evoke them.

## Aesthetics and Passion

Aesthetic passion—what am I talking about? We know what we mean, but conventions help us know what others mean. Since people use *aesthetics* and *passions* in several ways, we should specify which meanings we use here and which we exclude. I will use *aesthetics* in the broader sense of the consideration of beauty to form judgments. In this I include the properties of objects together with viewers' responses. I exclude aesthetics' narrower and technical sense as one of the five branches of philosophy. Aesthetics' philosophical sense, an ongoing conversation of scholars and artists across the ages and around the world, gives little attention to two key considerations—the unbeautiful, and God as viewer—which we will consider here.

*Passion*, likewise, I use in a general sense of strong emotion rather than in its technical, even archaic senses of the sufferings of Christ or the ability of being acted on by something or someone else. This latter meaning of passion seems to be that used to describe God in the Westminster Confession of Faith: ". . . without body, parts, or passions . . ."[1] Those two senses of passion I exclude from use here. The use of passion I intend here has been contrasted with reason (a helpful distinction) and often set in opposition to reason (unhelpful). By passion we mean emotions, feelings, and affections, especially in the classical sense.

The power of beauty is, it's fun. Beauty delights us. Beauty gives pleasure, and we want pleasure, enjoyment, fun, comfort. So we pursue it. Of course, beauty is ennobling; but if ennoblement were unpleasant, who would seek it? I know this equation blurs the distinction between beauty, which sounds classy, and fun, which sounds cheap, but that distinction hasn't helped us much. I know we also risk blurring the difference between objective beauty and subjective enjoyment, but that difference works like a fuzzy sliding scale. It has bred confusion and argument. Yet we haven't figured out how to dodge it, so most of us shrug and go on, saluting first one uniform and then the other as occasion suits.

Pursuing fun drags in lots more besides beauty. Much that we love isn't exactly beautiful, in the classical sense. "The pursuit of happiness" seems to validate almost every pursuit. We avoid pain: physical, emotional, and public. When avoiding pain gives us a moment to draw breath, we avoid the absence of pleasure, a.k.a. boredom. This broad category of human life includes what we call comfort and discomfort, coloring every experience. Though we call it by many names, we all swim and flounder in one enormous aesthetics ocean that flavors our whole life.

Our pursuit of fun—good feelings—and avoidance of pain and other bad feelings seems always to drag in other aspects of life: truth and lies, integrity and affectation, effectiveness and futility. And every field of work too: medicine, home-making, entertainment, politics, business, manufacturing, missions, communications, agriculture, craft, marketing, church, education. We seek comfort for ourselves and for others, according to objective standards or following individual tastes.

Other language catches this same power of the aesthetic. Where do we take *comfort*? What *experiences* do we pursue, buy, and sell? What do we say we *need*

---

1. Westminster Confession of Faith II, I, from *The Trinity Hymnal*, rev. ed. (Suwanee, GA: Great Commission, 1990), 849.

or don't need? What do we *feel*? What *appeals* to us? What do we *like*? What's your *taste* in books or foods? What's your *pleasure*? Your *preference*? Your *favorite*? In every case, we're talking about aesthetics.

## What's the Biblical Idea?

When I began theological studies, I was looking for what the Bible had to say about art, in order to apply that to the more specific area of songwriting. The more I studied, the broader the studies became. The Bible said little about art per se but a fair amount about craft and design and forms. It said very little about songwriting—while giving me many examples of the craft—but much about beauty, picture language, and images. When I sought out beauty per se, I found more about affections in general—the good, the bad, and the ugly.

The more I looked, the more I noted that forms and images, art and beauty, distortion and ugliness always appeared in context; they always had an observer, a seer. And that was God himself. He spoke into existence a beautiful creation, and he evaluated it as good. He directed in intimate detail the material and design of his craft and orchestrated with intention its proliferation by his people. He set the stars in space and commanded and conducted their song, for a purpose: to show and sing his own glory. He defined ugly, repulsive, and crude, responding with a turned back, a hot face, and crushing judgment. He came as a man—the very image of God—with no form or beauty that *we* should desire him, but pleasing to the Father in every way.

I was looking for art and found instead the full range of affections springing from the Creator of all things. I looked to write better songs and found instead the One in whose eyes all is measured. I looked for beauty and found it only one of a robust expanse of affectional aspects of the Father of lights. I looked for aesthetics and discovered the headwaters.

While I write about aesthetics, I depart from the historical branch of philosophy which studies the principles of art, beauty, and taste; I find I need a different starting point. I start with Scripture. I do this out of loyalty—Jesus has forgiven my sins and answered a lot of other questions—and also in pursuit of simplicity; the Christian literature on aesthetics, alone, is dizzyingly broad and complex, and the writings of the secular philosophers offer a lifetime of reading. Without a simple, guiding center, one approaches each classic work on aesthetics with the suspicion that it is impossible to understand anything without having read everything. Simplicity, if it can be found, has a certain aesthetic appeal of its own. Since I entered the discussion of aesthetics through my interest in songs, which consist of music and words, the conjunction of beauty and truth, particularly theological truth as taught in the Bible, has long fascinated me—what works, what doesn't, and why. Finally, having returned to school later in life for this reason—to learn the Bible's take on aesthetics—I noticed a hole in the literature, a real need.

## Conversation with the Bible: Whose Terms?

For these reasons, I have first written a Bible study, in which I have been asking God to redefine my subject and even reframe my questions, the language I bring to the discussion. Then I developed some theological constructions, with an attempt to locate them in the larger theological project. Finally, I have suggested some practical applications. All this derives from my unorthodox approach of going first to Scripture to set the terms and scope for study.

I have seen fruit of this approach taken to the care of souls. I discovered in studying biblical counseling that the terms and questions I take to the Bible determine whether it has something to say on a subject. As in a job interview, the one who asks the questions has power to guide the outcome. In wondering what light the Bible can shine on schizophrenia, I can search a concordance for *schizophrenia* and find the Bible silent. Yet if I listen to the Bible's own terms and ideas, I find it speaks richly of fear through stories and teaching. The Bible seems silent at first only because my questions need correction.

Similarly, in songwriting, art, even aesthetics, when I brought my terms (not to mention the imprint of my culture and era), I found the Scriptures thin and anemic, not the robust and comprehensive lens of life I have come to expect. I had set the parameters, I asked the questions, but my conceptual grid was the narrow one.

We are pleasure people, even the most dispassionate of us. Pursuing happiness and avoiding pain and anxiety form a single premise of our shared lives. Advertisers traffic delights; many charitable fundraisers package suffering to maximize donations; businesses market experiences; educators promise self-satisfaction; religions offer inner peace; politicians, outer. We just want our children to be happy; we bid them, "Have fun!" as they head off. We plan retirement to maximize personal fulfillment. Give to worthy causes so you will feel good about yourself. We invite unbelievers, "Commit your life to Christ because he will satisfy your longings better than sin does," assuming that the pursuit of personal satisfaction is always right. Personal pleasure also tantalizes us with personal power, the power to repeat it.[2] The appeal of this power penetrates every human endeavor.

---

2. C. S. Lewis notes this appeal in *Perelandra* (New York: Macmillan, 1944), 42–43.

Pleasure and truth, though, do not go always hand in hand. When they seem to separate, what shall we do? Find the truth, and feelings will follow? Or go with your gut because your heart knows better than your head? We usually take our first step with our feelings, then later with our thought and our will. Ads for ocean cruises lead with pictures and descriptions of luxurious accommodations and exotic ports, not with spreadsheets showing how we might afford them. We eat, drink, work, play, speak, listen, buy, sell, marry, divorce, raise children, give, receive, vote or abstain as our feelings stir us.

## Opening Terms: Models and Morals

Still, motive isn't everything, even if it may be the first thing. I heard Dick Keyes explain our common experience that *models* (by which he means pictures, stories, all aesthetic media) motivate us as *morals* (rules, truth, logic, and reason) never can.[3] His illustration gripped me in the mid-1980s, so I retell it here: Imagine that you're poring over your tax return late at night, falling asleep with weariness. Unable to continue the drudgery, you decide to go to bed and finish in the morning. On the nightstand sits the novel you've been reading, and you say, "Just a page or two to get the hero through this awkward bit." Three hours later you're wide awake, still reading. The story has engaged your imagination, keeping you up when the power of numbers or even the hope of a refund failed. The story delivered pleasures, giving you what you needed to stay awake.

This models-morals framework could sound like the "right brain–left brain" paradigm, but there's more going on here than human physiology. This *more* connects our basic, common humanity to reality as a whole. If we were just following the inner impulses of our own bodies, we wouldn't believe with such fervor in what we do or pursue it with such energy.

And believe we do! We pursue beauty and comfort for ourselves and for others; just as avidly, we avoid aesthetic disruptions, displeasure, or pain. We step across the room to straighten a crooked painting; we pick up unsightly litter; we take pain medications. We wince at the bright-blue house in the otherwise earth-tones neighborhood. And our aesthetic palette ranges far beyond beauty; harsh or smooth, strident or placid, attractive or repulsive—each can get us where we live.

Of course, aesthetics work on us as well as for us, stirring us to believe and act, even to rationalize, but that's not the point. The point is that we matter, that

3. Dick Keyes, "The Theology of Imagination," cassette tape of his lecture at the L'Abri Conference given in Atlanta in June 1983, published and distributed by L'Abri Fellowship in Southborough, MA.

our responses matter, that we remain people, far more complex and significant than mere bundles of conditioned responses. The affections and aversions with which we respond to the pictures we see, the images we envision, the dramas we follow, the music we hear show our distinct, individual significance and the character of the culture we share.

Our age puts aesthetics first, partly in reaction to a preceding age which for good or ill put facts first, and partly because we like to feel good. We usually find stories more compelling than systems. Common idioms and sentiments speak clearly to this preference:

- "A picture is worth a thousand words" (early twentieth century, multiple sources).
- "Follow your heart. It rarely leads you astray. It's thinking that gets us into trouble" (Steve Berry).
- "A man should hear a little music, read a little poetry, and see a fine picture every day of his life, in order that worldly cares may not obliterate the sense of the beautiful which God has implanted in the human soul" (Wolfgang von Goethe).

Christians in the West have reacted broadly against the cognitive-dominant, doctrine-first culture of an earlier age[4] and have revised theologies, church structures, and mission strategies to reflect a "feelings first" model. The emerging church and followers of narrative theology prefer, as a starting point for dialogue, cultural and story forms to the content of historic doctrine. Systematic theology has slipped from the favor it enjoyed among Christians a hundred years ago. Literary approaches to the Bible have arisen, perhaps to take its place. Some evangelicals have begun exploring the long-neglected role of human affections.[5]

Christians throughout the centuries have sought to explain the arts and aesthetics consistently with faith. Some made and venerated icons; others destroyed them. Some patronized artists, while others dismissed art as worldly. Martin Luther wrote of music, "Music is a fair and lovely gift of God."[6] Christian churches have hunted for a consistent doctrine of feelings, following different

---

4. J. G. Machen wrote, "The chief obstacle to the Christian religion today lies in the sphere of the intellect." J. G. Machen, "Christianity and Culture" (originally published in *Princeton Theological Review* 11 [1913]), http://reformedaudio.org/audio/machen/Machen%20-%20Christianity%20and%20Culture.pdf.

5. Cf. James K. A. Smith, *Desiring the Kingdom* (Grand Rapids, MI: Baker, 2009); Hilary Brand and Adrienne Chaplin, *Art and Soul: Signposts for Christians in the Arts* (Downers Grove, IL: InterVarsity Press, 1999); Ned Bustard, ed., *It Was Good: Making Art to the Glory of God* (Baltimore: Square Halo, 2000).

6. Quoted in Roland Bainton, *Here I Stand* (Nashville: Abingdon, 1950, 1978), 266–67, www.christcentric.net/articles-n-teachings/luther-quote-on-music.

theologies into widely differing approaches to culture. Richard Niebuhr cataloged most of these traditional approaches in *Christ and Culture*, setting the terms of this discussion for a generation.[7] Most of these traditions arise from concerns for integrity between Christian doctrine, church practices, and artistic experience, but few derive from the Bible, and most remain incapable of gaining much agreement among Christians outside their own traditions.

Much has been written in the late twentieth and early twenty-first centuries to find light among these traditions. The strengths of such works lie chiefly in their descriptions of this complex, often contradictory, conjunction of art, beauty, feelings, and faith. Such strengths often dissipate in their prescriptions. And prescription—a clear and hopeful direction for our thinking and acting and feeling—we need.

To know who we are and what we must do, we need wisdom greater than our own. This effort to understand our affectional experiences (all experiences, really) and our responses to them (aesthetics) entails a conundrum and an opportunity. Can we feel our way into a reliable understanding of our feelings? Can we think and act wisely about our passions? We need to get to the roots of feelings, emotions, affections. Those roots are not in us.

We of this aesthetic age did not start this discussion, nor will we finish it. Furthermore, folly easily overtakes us; we trade wisdom for pleasure, and we slide into convenient compromises that support our fun habit. We need help to feel rightly what we think and to think wisely what we feel.

## A Reluctant Holstein

If we scan the Scriptures, looking for art and beauty as concepts, principles, or abstractions, the text behaves like a reluctant Holstein who won't let down at milking time. We won't starve, but we won't make much butter. Ask instead what the Bible wants to talk about. What does it say about affections and passions, beauty and revulsion, love and hate? How does God articulate his own passions and pleasures? What does that say to the broad category of our experience of affective responses? How do my aesthetic sensibilities relate to his? How does God describe these things, and how do they invite us to know him better? If we look for the aesthetics of God's glory in creation and redemption, we will need more buckets.

Can the Bible make even a foolish reader wise in the ways of arts, passions, and aesthetics? It makes enormous, puzzling claims:

---

7. Richard Niebuhr, *Christ and Culture* (San Francisco: HarperSanFrancisco, 2001).

> How sweet are your words to my taste,
> sweeter than honey to my mouth!
> I gain understanding from your precepts;
> therefore I hate every wrong path.
>
> —Psalm 119:103–4

The psalmist hangs his loves and hates on God's Word—hardly our instinct. If the Bible could really do for us what God's Word did for the psalmist, we might hope for far better than merely improving our fundraising strategies, solving disagreements over music in our churches, helping those caught in pornography or anorexia, stopping sex-trafficking, and reasserting Christian presence in the arts. We can hope to become whole, undivided people before God, to participate in God's joys and grow in them, and to share those joys with others. In this pursuit, we will find that we need not—must not—talk about integrating aesthetics with faith or integrating affections with knowledge, much less about balancing them, as if a gain in one area required a loss in the other. Wisdom and hope for aesthetically driven people come from God himself through the gospel. All this we discover as we seek him, including his aesthetics, through his Word.

## READ, REFLECT, DISCUSS, SING

1. Suggested reading: "The Crisis of Spirituality within American Evangelicalism," chapter 1 of *Spirituality in an Age of Change: Rediscovering the Spirit of the Reformers* by Alister E. McGrath.
2. Q1. Think of three experiences that gave you great pleasure. Think of three more that caused you great pain, or repelled you. What patterns and similarities do you see?
3. Q2. Remember a time God seemed sweet to you. Did you ever find him unpleasant? Tell or briefly write about those times. How has your taste for God changed?
4. Sing: "Fairest Lord Jesus," including the long-overlooked verse that begins, "All Fairest Beauty..."

## Chapter 2

# ART OR AESTHETICS?

*Kenaniah the head Levite was in charge of the singing; that was his responsibility because he was skillful at it.*

—1 CHRONICLES 15:22

Digging for the roots of our passions—beauty and ugliness, love and loathing, pleasure and pain—leads us to the roots of our humanity and so to the Scriptures. What question are we to ask the Bible to gain wisdom for our affections? What premise should guide our study? We need help to focus, to find passion in its essential form. With good questions, we can read through Scripture with hope that we can find real help for the daily experiences that delight us and trouble us.

## Creation and Beauty

What stirs up our feelings? We naturally consider creation—mountains, ocean, sunset. The Bible has a lot to say about creation, but often without comment on its beauty or people's delight in that beauty. Biblical references to human pleasure in any created beauty are rare, and scriptural allusions to natural beauty always illustrate larger religious themes in the text. Note just a few examples of the ways God uses natural beauty to draw our attention and underscore meaning.

- "From Zion, perfect in beauty, God shines forth" (Ps. 50:2).
- "Since the creation of the world God's invisible qualities—his eternal power and divine nature—have been clearly seen, being understood from what has been made, so that people are without excuse" (Rom. 1:20).

- "I will be like the dew to Israel; he will blossom like a lily. Like a cedar of Lebanon he will send down his roots; his young shoots will grow. His splendor will be like an olive tree, his fragrance like a cedar of Lebanon. People will dwell again in his shade; they will flourish like the grain, they will blossom like the vine—Israel's fame will be like the wine of Lebanon" (Hos. 14:5–7).
- "The rich should take pride in their humiliation—since they will pass away like a wild flower. For the sun rises with scorching heat and withers the plant; its blossom falls and its beauty is destroyed. In the same way, the rich will fade away even while they go about their business" (James 1:10–11).

Creational beauty in the Scriptures points somewhere; it is referential. It speaks to us of something else; it leads us somewhere but doesn't stop at the beautiful view.

## Art

We modern Westerners tend to conceive art as a discrete category of discourse, like science and politics. We consider that art stirs feelings, even when it may present as intellectual art. Art is evocative. When Christians search the Bible for examples of art like this, we turn often to God's creation, to the wilderness tabernacle and Solomon's temple, to the works of craft contributing to the ornaments, furnishings, and garments of worship. Some find art popping up in the Prophets and in Jesus' parables, though since these always have a rhetorical purpose, some do not see them as pure, essential art.[1]

Still, we see a clear correspondence between the work of our artist friends and certain Bible passages. By this correspondence we reason: God creates, and humankind, made in his image, also creates. We see that people create art, so we reason that God also must create art, taking *our* definitions to *his* creativity and calling him, by analogy, the Master Artist.[2] This formula further locates art as a human enterprise from which we reason something of God: art is what God makes, because art is what people make. The first reasoning can be a valid syllogism: God creates; people are made in his image; therefore people create. The second argument, however, is not valid: people create art; people are made

---

1. Cf. Madeleine Boucher, *The Mysterious Parable: A Literary Study* (Washington, DC: Catholic Biblical Association of America, 1977), 15–16. Boucher uses the term *poetic* to distinguish literary art, calling it "aesthetic" and "autotelic: having an end or purpose in and not apart from itself."

2. For example: "God . . . is the supreme Artist." Philip Graham Ryken, *Art for God's Sake: A Call to Recover the Arts* (Phillipsburg, NJ: Presbyterian and Reformed, 2006), 22.

in God's image; therefore God creates art. It would be valid only if God were made in the image of humankind, which he resoundingly is not. One might well wince, considering God's attributes as derivative of those of people rather than the reverse. Also potentially troubling, lumping God and people together in one group called "artists" risks blurring the vital distinction between the artist and the Artist, the creature and the Creator, the Artist and his work: he created us, and we did not create him.

Perhaps hoping to keep the Creator-creature distinction more clearly in view, some define art as our response to God.[3] This definition maintains the Creator-creature distinction, but it overlooks the correspondence between them. Whether this oversight is intentional or not, it gives us an opportunity to make of art what we will; no continuity between God's art and human art could be expected, so no lack of continuity should surprise us. This location for art offers us freedom to define art as we choose, usually by cultural convention.

## Art and Scripture

Defining art is notoriously tricky, but we need at least a working definition. Just to get started, let us define art as *all that people make or perform for chiefly or solely aesthetic purposes.* If art is defined this way, some person makes it or does it, giving it particular forms for the sake of their aesthetic properties, possibly to elicit pleasure or some other feeling in the viewer-receiver or even for the artist's experience of it alone. No innovation here; others have noted art's aesthetic focus, which I refine only a bit.[4] Students of literary approaches to the Scriptures will recognize the aesthetic emphasis in most efforts to define literature in order to identify this approach in terms of its distinctive, artistic approach to words.[5]

Asking the Bible to show examples of art defined this way runs certain risks. Art's various cultural definitions feature its intent, audience, and effect. The Bible has its own purpose, audience, and effect, and they do not quite line up with

---

3. For example: "Art is one way for men and women to respond to the Lord's command to cultivate the earth, to praise his Name. Art is neither more nor less than that." Calvin Seerveld, *Rainbows for the Fallen World: Aesthetic Life and Artistic Task* (Toronto: Tuppence, 1980), 25. "Music-making is human activity." Ibid., 24. "Our art is offered up to God in covenant response." William Edgar, *Taking Note of Music* (London: SPCK, 1986), 98.

4. For example: "A work of (fine) art is *an entity made or presented in order to serve as object of aesthetic contemplation.*" Nicholas Wolterstorff, *Art in Action* (Grand Rapids, MI: Eerdmans, 1980), 18 (emphasis in the original). "The sportsman's first object is not aesthetics, whereas the artist's is." Edgar, *Taking Note of Music*, 45.

5. For example: "artistic form . . . delight . . .", "structured to achieve its effects." Leland Ryken and Tremper Longman III, eds., *A Complete Literary Guide to the Bible* (Grand Rapids, MI: Zondervan, 1993), 18. Also, Robert Alter, *The Art of Biblical Narrative* (New York: Harper, 1981).

those of art, culturally defined. These differences may impede the discussion we hope for between art and the Bible.

We should here refine somewhat our definition of aesthetics as *a conversation between the maker's intention, the character and properties of the work, the impression made on the receiver's senses, and his affectional response.* This is broad enough to begin our discussion with artists and the Bible. Notice, as we define aesthetics, its close association with form. Others notice this connection too. "With a literary text, form is meaning," observe Ryken and Longman, scholars of literary approaches to the Bible. [6] In fact, form is meaning everywhere we look or listen; the same association of form with meaning applies in every medium of communication. A parent who instructs his pouty child to "now, say it nicely" knows that the form of a child's words can say more than the words alone. Form is meaning outside of literature as well.

We've been discussing art and aesthetics almost interchangeably. That's a good start, since art speaks chiefly in the conversation of aesthetics and aesthetic conventions. We seek the roots of our affections, to understand their power in us, good and bad; we hope in this way to become more human, freer to thrive and to enjoy shalom. We want to follow our Lord and to build his kingdom. To this end, we will search the Scriptures. For what shall we search, art or aesthetics? What questions shall we ask? What concepts and language form our questions?

## Art in the Bible

Art seems the category most likely to yield the fruit we want. Art is more than a field of cultural activity; it seems inherently as human as the image of God that defines humanity. God created and we, his image bearers, likewise create, including art. Our fine arts form the values, concepts, and skills that permeate our culture. A painter's or draftsman's eye informs illustration, graphic design, advertising. The dramatist's theatrical sensibility trickles down into movies, TV, advertisements, and YouTube clips. Consider the continuum between literature and journalism and even ad copy. A preacher's skill has striking similarities to that of the orator.

We can search the Bible for the word *art* first, then for art-the-concept. Most English translations of the Bible use the word *art* rarely and almost always in reference to craft.

- "the art of the apothecary" (Ex. 30:25 KJV)
- "the art of engraving" (2 Chron. 2:7 NIV)

---

6. Ryken and Longman, *Complete Literary Guide*, 17.

- "the perfumer's art" (2 Chron. 16:14 ESV)
- "an image formed by the art and thought of man" (Acts 17:29 NASB)

Even "artistic designs" (Ex. 31:4 ESV) suggests decoration more than art as it is commonly conceived today. To ask Scripture about art, we need a definition. We've provisionally defined art as all that is made or done with principally aesthetic purposes. What does Scripture say about things that are done and made with aesthetic purposes?

## Artists and the Bible

If we use art as we have defined it as a Bible search criterion, would our findings apply chiefly to artists and their patrons? Would our findings do more for the rest of us than to call us to make artists feel at home among us? We all know people who identify themselves as artists and wrestle to live honestly and faithfully in a suspicious or a fawning church. If art were to exclude all but a carefully defined swath of life, would it not also exclude all but a few carefully defined people? We may well wonder what help comes to Christian unity from the implication that some of us are nonartists. Or is everyone an artist? If so, how is the concept useful as a Bible search criterion?

## Audiences and Definitions

Taking this definition to the Bible raises other questions. Who is making or doing? Who is the intended audience? What sort of aesthetic response, what affectional experience, does the maker or doer intend? What does affectional experience have to do with the other themes of the Bible? Although we all think we distinguish intuitively art from nonart, our various intuitions can cross swords. You may have heard, even used, these or other proverbs and phrases that illustrate conflicting definitions of art.

- "I don't know much about art, but I know what I like."
- "Beauty is in the eye of the beholder."
- "There's no accounting for taste."
- "Pop culture" versus "folk art" and "high art"
- "Art for art's sake"

These proverbs and phrases illustrate the complexity and the potential for misunderstanding art and each other. And so we find it: definitions of art vary from culture to culture, even within cultures.

MGM Studios uses the Latin for "art for art's sake," *Ars gratia artis*, in their logo encircling their trademark lion. This is meant, we gather, to assure viewers that they can sit back and have a good time watching the movie, putting other considerations out of their minds. We can expect true art to mean only itself and to be free of purposes outside itself—to be autotelic. Still, movies carry ideas and require fees, hardly pure art by this definition. We viewers usually take this discontinuity in our stride.

Marcel Duchamp, an early twentieth-century French artist, played with art's definition by inclusion: he bought a manufactured urinal, named, signed, and dated it, and submitted it for an art exhibition.[7] Art defined as a way of seeing can include anything an artist sees as art. Although this caused an uproar at the time, Duchamp's joke may not be far astray. Masks made in tribal Africa for religious purposes have been displayed as art in Western museums. Similarly, many Bible readers see art in the tabernacle (Exodus 25–27), also made for religious purposes.[8]

Duchamp's urinal highlights art's great weakness: it can include anything, but it can exclude nothing. Art cannot be defined negatively. How can art be reliably distinguished from nonart? What can art justly exclude? Much, in theory. Think of the instruction manual for your new phone—clearly not art. But we have seen some surprisingly pedantic, apparently nonartistic objects woven into artistic creations or simply labeled art. Always something new and surprising cast as artistic. While art's distinctives seem clear to our intuitions, our intuitions behave unpredictably in conference with others'. In practice, art can reliably exclude nothing.

While our intuition balks at this conclusion, the history of art—some call it a slide—admits no other. Whatever one can name for exclusion from art, another can say, "No, I see that as art." Art-the-concept can only add, and go on adding, items for inclusion. Art is incapable of a negative definition. We rightly question the usefulness of a concept that can exclude nothing, that cannot be negatively defined. We must look beyond art in search of the original defining concept that will shape our questions and studies in this field in the light of Scripture.

## Aesthetics and Art

"Art for art's sake" reflects a nineteenth- and twentieth-century movement to identify art by excluding all purposes and intentions other than the aesthetic.

7.  Martin Gayford, "Duchamp's Fountain: The Practical Joke That Launched an Artistic Revolution," *Telegraph* (February 16, 2008), www.telegraph.co.uk/culture/art/3671180/Duchamps-Fountain-The -practical-joke-that-launched-an-artistic-revolution.html.

8.  For example: Ryken, *Art for God's Sake*, 29–38.

The movement strives to preserve the integrity and purity of art by freeing it from the need to be true or effective or religiously correct, thus freeing it from control by the church, from being used by the government as propaganda, or from being used by business as advertising. Art so defined is said to be autotelic, having no purpose outside itself, with the understanding that the purpose of authentic art lies in the feelings, the affections, or the aversions it evokes—its aesthetic effects.

We should sympathize with the "art for art's sake" movement. If art has had a rocky relationship with scientific and religious truth and with utility, power, politics, technology, and profit, it's been only for the last millennium or so. If beauty has been oppressed, subordinated to truth and power in a win-lose, zero-sum game, you can well imagine how a divorce might seem the only path to artistic freedom.[9] Divorce of art from truth and power has worked for several hundred years and still gets plenty of traction in modern culture.

Defining art by isolating it from all nonaesthetic criteria seems an obvious solution, but in application, "art for art's sake" becomes messy. People do not only have aesthetic needs that can be met with a cable subscription or season tickets to the symphony orchestra. A person does not live in a sequence of separate compartments. In real life, separating purely aesthetic media from other aspects of life devolves quickly into unworkability. The Bible alludes to exclusively aesthetic pursuits a few times and makes a similar observation.[10] We must look for a more whole, human theme to frame our questions of the Bible.

What about aesthetic excellence? Can't we distinguish art by its pursuit of objective aesthetic standards? Identifying art by its aesthetic excellence assumes some incontrovertible aesthetic absolute, an objective aesthetic value. This argument has many recommendations: it fits the observed growth and development of aesthetic tastes; it acknowledges wide agreement in tastes across time and place, preserving paintings and music that retain their appeal for centuries; and it provides a vocabulary for criticism and training in the arts, which has been going on successfully for a long time. It seems capable of devout pursuit in God's name.

Defining art as aesthetic excellence also has its weaknesses. It's weak on cross-cultural aesthetics; it's weak on divergent and changing tastes within a culture, individual or shared. It also squares poorly with our personal experience; I hope it may not reflect badly on my flexibility that I may not live long enough

---

9. Abraham Kuyper characterizes art's freedom with this image; cf. Jordan J. Ballor and Stephen J. Grabill, eds., *Wisdom and Wonder*, trans. Nelson D. Kloosterman (Grand Rapids, MI: Christian's Library Press, 2011), 117.

10. See, for example, Ezekiel 33:32 ESV: "Behold, you are to them like one who sings lustful songs with a beautiful voice and plays well on an instrument, for they hear what you say, but they will not do it."

to come to share my friends' delight in kimchi. Can objective aesthetics explain subjective tastes? Who can tell what is good or bad, what is excellent or inferior?

Art's use in marketing both supports and challenges the excellence definition. First, it can define excellence according to results. Results measured by sales volume or polls may not show true excellence, but it works for business and political purposes. As Paul Simon sang, he was just "trying to keep the customer satisfied."[11] Aesthetic objectivity is reserved, seemingly, for those who need no customers.

## Aesthetics: Objective or Subjective?

Wide swaths of agreement within and even between cultural groups about what people find pleasing and what they find displeasing lead us to conclude that aesthetic properties have a direct connection to personal taste. By this objective formula, we ascribe excellence to the good. Still, tastes differ, and the market (think of popular versus classical music) proves that our tastes lead us toward aesthetics that do not match the excellent. Such evidence of differing tastes we can use to bolster objective aesthetics by demeaning the subjective approach: "The aesthetic of immediate and constant entertainment does not prepare the human consciousness well for recognition of a holy, transcendent, omnipotent, and eternal God, or to responding to his demands of repentance and obedience."[12]

Music and popular culture tend to pioneer these opposed criteria for evaluating aesthetics. Church music has long divided Christians. Churches who draw the unchurched often use popular music, and often with powerful results. This subjective approach still observes objective standards, though in a distinct genre with its own vocabulary. Objective and subjective approaches usually lean on each other. Aesthetic excellence sounds likely to lead the way until applied to widely differing cultures. The slow slide of the sitar string toward its eventual resting note sounds excellent to some but can sound obscure and random to those who speak a different aesthetic language. Are we then to learn the language, training ourselves to recognize and enjoy excellence within a different tradition? Yes, but even this answer cannot account for the entire project of human aesthetics, since tastes differ widely within each tradition. The internet has formed a compromise: "Come customize media and products to your own tastes. As you do, our software and marketers will look for patterns and similarities, following market demand.

11. Paul Simon, "Keep the Customer Satisfied," *Bridge over Troubled Waters* (New York: Columbia Records, 1970).
12. Kenneth A. Myers, *All God's Children and Blue Suede Shoes: Christians and Popular Culture* (Wheaton, IL: Crossway, 1989), 132.

We will learn your preferences and provide them." Finally, neither objective nor subjective aesthetic standards can dominate, but neither is dispensable. We need God's wisdom for aesthetics.

## Aesthetics and Scripture

Scripture offers little that can be construed to define art by its aesthetic excellence. This lack arises not because Bezalel and Oholiab, the men appointed and gifted by God to build the tabernacle and its appurtenances, did poor work. Rather we find little in these passages that suggests objective standards for beauty or any other aesthetic property, and less articulating what those standards might be. The Bible's reluctance on aesthetic excellence should not surprise us: an objective aesthetic principle, even excellence, that God himself must follow in his creation would be a standard outside God. In short, the standard would rule God. We will explore the Bible's approach to objective and subjective aesthetics in chapter 4.

Still, many evangelicals who care about aesthetic excellence in art seek to connect it with the Scriptures. "The Bible says little directly about the arts or aesthetics," writes Frank E. Gaebelein, a well-known twentieth-century advocate for the arts in Christian education. He identifies the arts with aesthetics, an identification nearly unanimous in Western culture, including evangelicals; he defines art's aesthetic focus in terms of excellence in pursuit of objective criteria. These criteria do not appear in Scripture, but he looked to Scripture to correct them: "[The Bible's] basic insights must provide not only the foundation for an authentic Christian aesthetic but also the corrective for artistic theory derived from other sources, however excellent these may be."[13] Fair enough; the Bible should correct our aesthetic standards. Still, this arrangement needs details.

### *The Bible and the Aesthetics of Comparison*

We have noted that most contemporary discussions of art focus on its aesthetic intentions, properties, and effects.[14] Our working definition combines *aesthetics only* with *aesthetics mainly*. Aesthetic intention provides a workable definition, both intuitive and useful. This definition distinguishes art by what it does: it illumines something else, by comparing it, inciting a feeling, say, of satisfaction or comfort, dissatisfaction or discomfort. Begbie suggests "the heart

---

13. Frank E. Gaebelein, *The Christian, the Arts, and Truth: Regaining the Vision of Greatness* (Portland, OR: Multnomah, 1985), 56.

14. See, for example, Ned Bustard, ed., *It Was Good: Making Art to the Glory of God* (Baltimore: Square Halo, 2000), 71; Myers, *All God's Children*, 26–27; Seerveld, *Rainbows*, 14, 43; Wolterstorff, *Art in Action*, 17–18, 39.

of art [is] metaphor."[15] No less than Jeremiah suggests that comparisons touch our feelings: "What can I say for you, to what compare you, O daughter of Jerusalem? What can I liken to you, that I may comfort you, O virgin daughter of Zion? For your ruin is vast as the sea; who can heal you?" (Lam. 2:13 ESV).

The Weeping Prophet knows that metaphors can comfort. Metaphor, together with its friends and relations—allegory, symbolism, types, tropes—engage feelings, aesthetics. The Bible confirms this. Begbie distills art to metaphor; Jeremiah attributes to metaphor aesthetic power. Scripture is full of metaphor and of aesthetics; studying the Bible for aesthetics might yield fuller insights than studying it for art.

## The Bible: Root of Aesthetics?

Why not look to the Bible, not for art but for aesthetics itself? Art's deliberately aesthetic character serves as a working definition. Art, as we have seen, is best considered for what it leaves in—aesthetics—not for what it leaves out. So questioning Scripture about aesthetics will miss nothing that could be called art. Aesthetics is a far larger category than art, more suitable for our scriptural exploration of God, ourselves, our communities, achievements, disorders, and needs.

We can ask the Bible about aesthetics, acknowledging that

- we live, feel, respond, and act individually and together;
- our tastes differ and change;
- we feel, speak, and work by a dynamic that goes beyond the mechanical or the conditioned; and
- inner attitudes and affections show up in outward words, works, and passions.

Searching the Bible for aesthetics will take in much more than what might be called art. The beauty of nature, widely acknowledged and independent of art, leads us to expect this. The Bible is itself powerfully and intentionally crafted for aesthetic form and effect. Literary approaches to Scripture have in recent decades contributed enormous gains to biblical scholarship. Scripture resembles literature, giving warrant to this approach. What characteristics distinguish literature from other kinds of text? Many proponents of the literary approaches to Scripture cite literature's intentional aesthetic shaping. If we approach Scripture the same way we approach literature, we look for aesthetics.

---

15. Jeremy Begbie, *Voicing Creation's Praise: Towards a Theology of the Arts* (Edinburgh: T&T Clark, 1991), 158.

We should search Scripture also for the definitions and categories that suit its meaning. This is but justice to a revered ancient text. Further, the Bible's claim of authority calls us to even higher respect for these premises. Because the Bible goes beyond literature, being a sort of proto-literature, we examine it for its definitions of literature and aesthetics, lest we interpret the Bible by premises foreign to it. We want to see, after all, what the Bible has to say about aesthetics in context with its other major themes: systematic theology and redemptive history, sin and salvation, and the coming rule of God.

We have defined aesthetics, for now, as the conversation between a maker's affectional intentions for his work, the form of that work, the impression formed on the receiver, and the receiver's affectional responses. This conversation encompasses what academics call *discourse*—a word, work, or action, an outward expression that springs from inner belief, passion, and will. To keep from sounding stiff, let's simply define discourse as what people do and say. Jesus calls this *fruit* (Matt. 7:16; 21:43). Of course, this fruit has its divine ectype: God originates discourse by creating and by speaking with unique power, notably in his Word. This gives special incentive to search the Scriptures for aesthetics: we do so looking for God's aesthetic intentions.

## Nine Reasons to Ask Scripture about Aesthetics

1. Considering aesthetics avoids constrictive definitions of art and broadens the field to consider all discourse: everything we do, any deliberate action, word, or artifact. This breadth is an advantage, not a disadvantage. It accommodates the fuzzy lines in and around art, sidestepping the infighting over art's boundaries and between genres (high art versus low art, popular versus elite, culture versus marketing, fine art versus graphic arts), and defers the argument between the conflicting dynamics of "media corrupts the masses" (objectivist) and "market molds media" (subjectivist).

2. Taking aesthetics for our subject of inquiry broadens our field of view so we can consider other aesthetic qualities besides beauty. Thus we need not attack or defend beauty as the central feature of aesthetics.

3. *Aesthetics* is a more dynamic term than *art*, lending itself to a dynamic understanding of changing people and cultures. This shift of terms also helps us lean against the tendency to treat aesthetics negatively, to turn away from aesthetics to other aspects of discourse—logic, reason, knowledge—as more reliable.

4. While discussion of art tends to focus either on philosophical abstractions or on particular works, considering aesthetics brings theory and

practice together, dodging the pesky problem of distinguishing art from nonart, artists from nonartists. Asking the Bible about aesthetics can help us take God's perspective when considering real people, the maker and the viewer, their predispositions and intentions, their tastes and affections.

5. Changing our question to aesthetics considers the viewer—his active role as interpreter or meaning maker—more deliberately. It replaces questions like, "Is this Christian art?" "Is it good art from a Christian perspective?" and "Is this artist a Christian?" with questions like, "What does the maker mean?" "What do I make of it?"[16] "How can I respond?" and "What part does my response take in my discipleship and in building the kingdom of God?"

6. This change of terms makes it possible to consider the effects of sin and redemption on people's aesthetic sensibilities and responses.

7. Changing the term from art to aesthetics fosters recognition of aesthetic sin, opening the door to considering and practicing aesthetic redemption in all areas and disciplines, not just arts and media. We will explore these effects in chapters 8 and 11.

8. Considering aesthetics rather than art frees us from accepting uncritically the conventional cultural definitions of art and makes us more likely to examine the aesthetic aspects of cultural artifacts on either side of some indefinite line separating art from non-art.

9. This change in terms from *art* (whether as a concept or as an object) to *aesthetics* (a discussion) leans against our desire for mastery of an objective discipline, whether music or some other craft, even for good purposes, and leans toward our discipleship to a just, merciful, and loving Master.

The Bible is full of aesthetics. Beyond the shapes, colors, and smells of the tabernacle, more than the literary forms of its poetry and narrative, aesthetics permeate Scripture. This is where the milk starts to flow!

## The Church: Long Busy with Aesthetics

Desires, aversions, and affections play a larger role in motivation than does theology; churches have long addressed people's affections in singing, preaching,

---

16. Cf. Dorothy L. Sayers, *The Mind of the Maker* (New York: Harcourt, Brace, 1941; San Francisco: HarperSanFrancisco, 1987).

liturgy, icons, architecture, evangelism, and pastoral care. Churches have also subordinated, marginalized, even suppressed aesthetics and their attendant affections.

The various church approaches to aesthetics cluster around two poles: (1) *objective aesthetics*, wherein aesthetic properties inhere in objects, and most people respond with the same feelings to these properties because they are inherent and generally recognized; and (2) *subjective aesthetics*, wherein people's various tastes and perceptions determine their feelings in response to any artifact. Objective and subjective approaches to aesthetics depend on each other, though uncomfortably. Neither has dominated the church or the broader culture. Not bad, really, since each approach is partly right and partly wrong.

The church has taken not only various approaches to aesthetics but also various corresponding methods of aesthetic discipleship. Niebuhr treats several historic church approaches to culture, offering also a fair sampling of historic Christian approaches to aesthetics.[17] Many notable Christian treatments of aesthetics and culture discuss basic cultural categories—art, beauty, aesthetics, culture itself—as these are commonly assumed.[18] Most make little attempt at building a biblical case for these categories or locating them within systematic or pastoral theology.

Our present cultural moment in the West places aesthetics on center stage. Similarly, facts and practice (noetics and ethics, if you like rhymes) occupied center stage in previous centuries. In the present aesthetically driven culture, the church faces challenge and opportunity similar to those that occasioned the careful, rich developments in theology, apologetics, and pastoral practice of earlier ages. Much as we owe them, we can improve our aesthetic discipleship with a biblically developed theology of aesthetics. The need of our age seems especially urgent.

## Alternate Biblical and Theological Categories

But, some might wonder, what about the already-familiar categories and doctrines? Why not question Scripture about beauty or pleasure or creation or art or culture or common grace?

We define terms and concepts in order to understand and apply them. To find Scripture's wisdom for preferences and passions, we need the headwaters, the

---

17. Richard Niebuhr, *Christ and Culture* (San Francisco: HarperSanFrancisco, 2001).

18. For example: Abraham Kuyper, "Calvinism and Art," in *Lectures on Calvinism* (Peabody, MA: Hendrickson, 2008; originally Grand Rapids, MI: Eerdmans, 1931); Niebuhr, *Christ and Culture*; Wolterstorff, *Art in Action*; Myers, *All God's Children*.

original as God created. Scripture teaches concepts and can help us find words to match the concepts it addresses. Scripture balks at ill-conceived questions and pressures readers to change our questions before it will answer us generously. In defining terms, we look to the root, the source, the foundation, without which each of these categories appears either penultimate or incomplete in some way.

- *Beauty*, as a premise, overlooks the ugly, the degraded, the repugnant— which cannot be defined merely as beauty's absence. *Pleasure*, likewise, tends to overlook disquiet, revulsion, and pain. A more comprehensive category would serve better to help us frame our questions of the Scriptures.
- *Creation*, beautiful as it is, can also be dark, hard, brutal, frightening. Our response to creation needs to be in view here, not creation itself; it cannot serve as our premise of this Bible study. Our pursuit of the ontological foundation of preference cannot stop at creation.
- *Art*, as we have already discussed, is not big enough. By its aesthetic focus, art is a subset of aesthetics.[19] We need the bigger category, for which much groundwork is already laid in literary approaches to the Scriptures.[20]
- *Culture* is often discussed without definition; sometimes it's described as what people believe and do together or as a human response to God's creation, to God's mandate to "cultivate."[21] While such definitions have value, they omit exploration of the image-like correspondence between human cultures and God. Is there a way in which human culture-making reflects something of bearing God's image? Is there something in God to which human culture-making corresponds? Most culture studies rely little on a scriptural or doctrinal foundation.
- *Common grace*, considered as a foundation for the independence of art's aesthetic values from other considerations, has been widely explored by Abraham Kuyper and his heirs.[22] In expressions applying to art, we find lacking certain key features that might otherwise locate it within the doctrines and confessions of the church. As with beauty, art, and culture, common grace, together with its meaning and value, remains fixed,

19. For example: "I have suggested that at the very center of the institution [of high art] is a passionate commitment to the importance of perceptual contemplation of works of art, and more particularly, to *aesthetic* contemplation. And I have argued that the delight attained in aesthetic contemplation is good." Wolterstorff, *Art in Action*, 193 (emphasis in the original); Ryken, *Art for God's Sake*, 14.

20. Cf. Alter, *Art of Biblical Narrative*, 3; Ryken and Longman, *Complete Literary Guide*, 18.

21. Cf. James A. Gustafson, preface to Niebuhr, *Christ and Culture*, xxii; D. A. Carson, *Christ and Culture Revisited* (Grand Rapids, MI: Eerdmans, 2008), 2; Andy Crouch, *Culture Making* (Downers Grove, IL: InterVarsity, 2008), 23; Henry R. Van Til, *The Calvinistic Concept of Culture* (Grand Rapids, MI: Baker Academic, 1952, 1979), xvii.

22. Cf. Kuyper, *Lectures on Calvinism,* 135, 145.

static. Common grace, when used to reify the arts, takes little account of redemptive history, even to the minds of many proponents, sitting rather uneasily with the antithesis between the mind set on the flesh and the mind set on the Spirit.[23] Common grace, when invoked to justify art's distinction from other fields of human endeavor,[24] becomes static. When divorced from redemptive history, common grace begins to look a lot like brute grace, having exactly the same value and power for the rebellious heart as for the penitent one. We will explore a redemptive perspective on common grace in chapter 13.

Aesthetics, in contrast, precedes art and culture; it includes ugliness and aversion; it need exclude nothing but can show an aspect rather than a part of anything. Scripture is shot through with aesthetics. We can search Scripture for aesthetics—not the word but aesthetic realities—with hope for answers. We can hope our "hermeneutical circle" will yield more suitable words and concepts, but this gives a better starting point for biblical study of human affections than the others we have noted.

Our impulse toward brute aesthetics arises from our conviction that our aesthetic sense is basically reliable and thus perhaps a proper restraint or corrective to our overly cognitive focus on doctrine. We recoil from especially rigid doctrine that subordinates pleasure and other forms of meaning to hard-edged theological categories, either superior to or preceding the affections. This dichotomy is unnecessary, even harmful.

God's holiness, says David, has splendor (Ps. 29:2). Though unfathomable, God's glory demands a faithful exploration of aesthetics, of his splendor. Pastoral care for his people's feelings would find support and clarity in a biblical and systematic theology of aesthetics, especially in this aesthetically driven era. Scripture will help us connect God's glory, human aesthetic experience, pastoral practice, and creedal confessions.

---

23. For example: Richard J. Mouw, *He Shines in All That's Fair* (Grand Rapids, MI: Eerdmans, 2001), esp. 100–101.

24. For example: Kuyper, *Lectures on Calvinism*; Seerveld, *Rainbows*; Wolterstorff, *Art in Action*; Joe Rigney, *The Things of Earth* (Wheaton, IL: Crossway, 2015).

## READ, REFLECT, DISCUSS, SING————————————

1. Suggested reading: "Problem Picture," chapter 11 of *The Mind of the Maker* by Dorothy L. Sayers; "Cultural Analysis," chapter 1 of *Creative and Creating: A Biblical Theology of Culture* by William Edgar.
2. Q1. When have you experienced an artistic work or performance that deeply stirred you? What about popular and social media that stirred you? How were these experiences alike? How did they differ?
3. Q2. What role did art play for the faithful people in Old Testament times? In New Testament times? How are we like them in this? How are we different?
4. Sing: "O Worship the King."

# Chapter 3

# THIS AESTHETIC BIBLE

*His delight is in the law of the LORD.*
—PSALM 1:2 ESV

The Bible is beautiful. We might not skip movie night for an extra Bible study, we might not relax to streamed Bible reading like we might to our favorite music, but the Bible is on the same page with everything we call fun, with all our pleasure practices. Elegant poetry, gripping stories, well-crafted sayings, thematic coherence, and accessibility in mystery combine to make it so. Not only lovely in itself, Scripture also describes the incomparably lovely—creation before the Serpent; certain women such as Sarah, Abigail, Tamar; Solomon's beloved; the day of the Lord the prophets describe; the New Jerusalem. The Bible excites readers' love by beautiful forms—poetic and narrative—and beautiful content.

The Bible also excels in the grotesque. Nobody will read certain passages without cringing first, asking questions later. Later bits of Judges and parts of Ezekiel never find their way into most Sunday school curricula. Such repulsive passages got that way on purpose; the writers meant them to jolt their intended audience, to get them going in a certain direction. They still jolt us years later. The Bible stirs many affections, and readers even respond with different feelings to a single passage.

Motivation starts with pleasure and pain, with attraction and revulsion. Aesthetics appeal to our passions, our feelings of love and hatred, in all their variety. Our attraction or revulsion leaps up, almost of itself, from a scent, a familiar face, a memory, a gesture, a logo or brand, the first few notes of a song, a turn of a phrase. So it is with the Bible.

## Beauty and Other Aesthetics

The ugly in the Bible builds tension and expectation, like a white paper coffee cup dropped on a trim green lawn or a picture hung crookedly on a wall, only stronger. The Bible excites love and other passions. Some of its stories start like epics, then turn disappointing, then brutal, even revolting. We get frustrated! Great stories come almost to the point, then leave out important details, leaving us unsatisfied. Ugliness and depravity sour our stomachs. This too is our aesthetic Bible.

Following aesthetic themes can lead us through the whole of Scripture. Let's stroll through the vineyard and sample some low-hanging aesthetic clusters, some tastier than others.

- "God saw everything that he had made, and behold, it was very good" (Gen. 1:31 ESV).
- "The LORD God made all kinds of trees grow out of the ground—trees that were pleasing to the eye and good for food. In the middle of the garden were the tree of life and the tree of the knowledge of good and evil" (Gen. 2:9).
- "When the woman saw that the fruit of the tree was good for food and pleasing to the eye, and also desirable for gaining wisdom, she took some and ate it. She also gave some to her husband, who was with her, and he ate it" (Gen. 3:6).

God made people for his own pleasure first, then for their pleasure as they shared his enjoyment. Even after the ugly fall, God gave his people a place to share his delights, in the intense, wide-ranging richness of the tabernacle and the temple.

The Bible also shows aesthetics in human culture gone horribly astray: God's own people turn away from the excellent and love the loathsome.

- "Stolen water is sweet; food eaten in secret is delicious!" (Prov. 9:17).
- "Why spend money on what is not bread, and your labor on what does not satisfy? Listen, listen to me, and eat what is good, and you will delight in the richest of fare" (Isa. 55:2).
- "Get her for me. She's the right one for me" (Judg. 14:3). Samson, the "last hero standing" in decadent Israel, *will* have the woman he finds attractive even though she's a Philistine.
- Then Jehu went to Jezreel. When Jezebel heard about it, she put on eye makeup, arranged her hair, and looked out of a window (2 Kings 9:30). Israel's evil foreign queen uses her beauty to manipulate for the last time.

- "They shall eat, but not be satisfied; they shall play the whore, but not multiply, because they have forsaken the LORD to cherish whoredom, wine, and new wine, which take away the understanding" (Hos. 4:10–11 ESV).

Scripture wraps its chief aesthetic statement in mystery; the repulsive crucifixion stands as the centerpiece.[1]

The Bible is crafted using all kinds of beauty and ugliness meant to move readers to many passions. These passions, though familiar, always have a change in mind—action. God made us for aesthetic pleasure, to delight in good and recoil from evil, yet these affections the Bible evokes are not an end in themselves, nor a mere means to an end. The Bible introduces and develops this major thread of the mystery of aesthetics' purpose. Our intent is not to prove that the aesthetic values of the text are more or less important than the truth it conveys but rather to show that this less studied aspect of the Bible pervades each part and the whole of Scripture, with divine purpose. That purpose is not just to provoke the reader's passions but to change them and to draw the reader to share God's passions. Aesthetics in the Bible speak profoundly, even radically, to readers' feelings and always with change in mind.

## Aesthetics in What the Bible Shows

The Bible depicts objects and practices that display aesthetic qualities which the narrator invites the reader to see and appreciate in the mind's eye. First, the formless emptiness of the creation was not good yet (Gen. 1:2). Then the whole completed creation looked good to God, with a goodness that encompassed the aesthetic (Gen. 1:4, 10, 12, 18, 21, 25, 31). The trees planted in the center of the garden in the center of creation were "pleasant to the sight" (Gen. 2:9 ESV); Aaron's priestly robes were made "for glory and for beauty" (Ex. 28:2 ESV); Sarah and other women are described as beautiful (Sarah in Gen. 12:11; Abigail in 1 Sam. 25:3; Bathsheba in 2 Sam. 11:2). The youthful David is beautiful (1 Sam. 16:12), as are land (Ps. 16:6) and a figurative crown of wisdom (Prov. 4:9). In each case, the pleasantness or beauty described is meant to explain someone's motivation through his passions or to invite the reader's passion and action.

Ugliness too plays its part in God's Word, motivating characters and readers away from the repulsive object. Just as God saw that all he had made was very

---

1. Acts 2:22–36; 4:10–12; 1 Cor. 1:18, 23–24; 2:2; Gal. 6:14; Phil. 2:8–11.

good, so he later saw the ugly and pervasive effects of sin: Genesis 6:3–12 mentions three times that God saw the corrupting effect of evil in the earth. What he saw made him sorry and grieved, and he was stirred to action: the judgment of the flood.

Yet even after the flood of God's wrath, moral ugliness persisted, even among—especially among—God's chosen people. God's revulsion is aroused, and he takes action again, this time to purify. Isaiah describes judgments to come on Israel's beautiful, corrupt women: "Instead of fragrance there will be a stench; instead of a sash, a rope; instead of well-dressed hair, baldness; instead of fine clothing, sackcloth; instead of beauty, branding" (Isa. 3:24).

The Bible describes some objects for their aesthetic properties, such as the tabernacle and the temple, with their furniture, sacrifices, anointing oil, incense, and priestly clothing, all of which the text describes in language of aesthetic properties—sights, shapes, colors, textures, smells, tastes—and in God's aesthetic response: "pleasing . . . to the LORD" (Ex. 29:18).

## Aesthetics in the Bible's Literary Forms

Here especially form is meaning, and the Bible crafts the shape of its words as carefully as their content. These forms are intended to stir readers' affections while informing them. Bible readers also find aesthetics woven into Scripture's larger structures and genres. History and poetry, prophecy and apocalyptic literature, law and wisdom—Scripture's several genres are full of carefully crafted literary forms, and those forms are meant to arouse readers' affections.

Narrative draws readers to wonder what happens next, by building tension. The book of Judges builds tension, then ends without resolution, leaving readers hanging. Yet that very absence makes the book's main point: something must be done now to fix the tension. The book of Ruth resolves its tensions pleasingly, redemptively, and points to a larger redemption still to come, drawing the reader to look for it beyond the text of that book.

The Bible depicts characters that attract or repel, and sometimes do both. Personalities appearing in the Scriptures can be beautiful like Boaz or ugly like Lamech, who sang a song about his vengeance (Gen. 4:23–24), or ambiguous like Lot (Gen. 12–14, 18–19) and King David.

The Bible also uses relational forms, which are often overlooked. God's covenant is based on a shape, that of bilateral symmetry, in which one side of the form mirrors the other side, as the human face does: covenant parties make promises, then match their actions to those promises. Consider also the

Bible's law promising that the punishment for sin will correspond to the sin[2]—another mirror image, a shape whose aesthetic qualities include the satisfaction of justice. Scripture describes the relational form of marriage with rich aesthetic connotations.

## Aesthetics Integrated throughout the Bible

The Bible speaks aesthetically, but not for static entertainment or even for catharsis or ennoblement. Biblical aesthetic forms, language, descriptions, stories, and characters never stand alone but always stand in conjunction with other meanings and purposes in the text; these don't violate the aesthetic meaning but complement it. As in all biblical forms, these relational forms locate affections in context, together with truth, in a united, God-centered purpose. They stir readers, inform them, and push them to do something.

Biblical aesthetics serve the gospel, focusing the whole Scripture on its mysterious central theme: Jesus Christ's birth, death, resurrection, and ascension. Combining the pleasures of literary forms with the truth about God and his redemptive plan might seem unfamiliar or appear to subjugate art to theology. As we will see, the combination reflects perfectly God's glory and his redemptive plan for his world and his people. The redemptive-historical approach to Scripture informs this perspective on Scripture's narrative unity.[3]

The Bible uses forms, individually and together, to grip readers' vitals, stir up our intellects, and turn our wills to God. Hatred of sin and love of God stir us to turn, to repent. They stir us also to love, believe, and act like God's people. We see this purposeful use of multiple modes of engagement in the objects and events the Bible describes and in the way the writers describe them—the text itself. What does this look like? Let's glance at a few examples.

- The garden in Eden was the site of God's meeting place, the temple where he lived with his people. The tree of life, so tantalizingly close yet in the end untouchable as God drove his people, our parents, away from the meeting place and into exile. Yet God gives its echo and promise in the tabernacle, the new place of intimacy with God to which access was restricted, a place lit by its specially designed lampstand, the treelike menorah. This too God's people spurned, so he drove them once more into exile. Yet even

---

2. For example: Ex. 21:24; Ps. 57:6; Luke 12:47–48.

3. Cf. Geerhardus Vos, *Biblical Theology* (Edinburgh: Banner of Truth, 1948); Edmund P. Clowney, "Preaching Christ from All the Scriptures," in *The Preacher and Preaching*, ed. Samuel T. Logan Jr. (Phillipsburg, NJ: Presbyterian and Reformed, 1986), 163–91.

there God sends a promise in a vision, embodied in the mysterious words of Ezekiel, of the glorious tree that God's beloved will one day approach, touch, and eat from to be filled and healed. The temple of their coming intimacy with God will be furnished, as Jesus reveals in a later vision to his beloved John, with the tree of life—Eden's and Ezekiel's trees fulfilled and consummated. God and all God's people will see the blessing of life together. God, by giving these unfolding biblical accounts to his people, covenants with them, assuring them that they live in his story and will reach its true and satisfying conclusion in him.

- The wilderness tabernacle, built to God's design and specifications, focused on aesthetics: architectural shapes, images, smells, textures, colors, incense, and blood, all presented to the audience of one, to God. The priestly garments, which God intended "for glory and for beauty" (Ex. 28:2 ESV), were carefully woven, cut, stitched, and embroidered. The beauty of these must have been staggering. Then God surprised everyone with horrible distortion. He required the priests to deliberately stain these glorious clothes with blood and oil. He gave Moses no instructions to clean these impossible stains out of these previously spotless clothes! Instead successive generations of priests wore them, stains and all. God's people see from this that God's aesthetic eye differs from theirs. God is the intended audience for all this aesthetic richness; he delights in things that delight his people—gold, incense, glorious clothes—and also in things that jar them.

- Moses' story ends unsatisfyingly. He never reaches the land of promise. Instead he dies in Moab, where God disciplines him with death for his disobedience. God assured through means now hidden that a reliable account of Moses' last surreal vision of the promised land, of God's final words to him, of Moses' death and what God meant by it, reached the remaining Israelites and later generations of God's people through the text. God stirs all his people, by these events and by the true and crafted record of them, to love holiness, to believe that law keeping is necessary for holiness, to fear that since not even Moses could enter God's promises through law keeping, none of us can either. Another means must be found. Great fear and great expectations, as if God were to say, "Watch what happens next!"

- The Levite near the end of Judges cut into twelve pieces the body of his raped, murdered concubine and sent them to the twelve tribes. This horrible dismemberment was less horrid than the atrocity done to her in life. The Levite sent her body parts to horrify and unite in shock twelve assemblies of tribal elders and so stir them to discipline by deadly force those who had brought their repulsive guilt on the whole nation. The account mentions no cover letter; each mutilated member was enough. So the account of these events is enough for the reader to likewise say, "This is horrible, and something has to be done." So says the Levite about those events, and so says the narrator about this day through this story, even though by his time the Levite's days are long past. God's presence is unclear; even the relatively good guys look bad. Seeing something this horrid demands action. So does reading about it.

- The Israelite army that used to win was losing, unable to keep the Philistines from recapturing the land God promised to his people. "Why not bring the ark of the covenant," someone must have said. "I remember hearing that it's got some sort of magic about it; maybe it will help us win this fight, and then we can go back to our regular idol worship." But God, working symbolically through the ark, will not serve them; he will rule, and he will teach through easy-to-read signs. When the Israelites bring the ark to the battlefield, he humiliates them. The Philistines slaughter all who stand and fight; most leg it. The Philistines grab the ark of God's presence, carry it home, and set it down right beside their pet god Dagon, boasting symbolically that they beat Israel's God, so now he will work for them, like Dagon does. Only, God puts Dagon in his place: facedown in front of the ark. When they put him back, the Philistines find next day's religious theater episode even clearer, even worse: their idol prostrate again in front of the ark, but with head and hands cut off—not broken, this was no earthquake—and laid on the threshold, the Philistines' access to their temple. The signs are clear; God's enemies saw him simply, powerfully humiliate them and honor himself. And he made sure his people heard all about it (1 Samuel 5).

- Isaiah's Suffering Servant "had no beauty or majesty to attract us to him, nothing in his appearance that we should desire him" (Isa. 53:2). He looked plain. Nothing noteworthy here—no website features his profile shot; no one wants a selfie with him. More on this aesthetic mystery in chapter 9.

- The temple curtain was torn in two, from top—no human could reach it there to start the tear—to bottom, where everyone could see it. The loud ripping must have been heard all over the temple grounds. Again the signs are clear: the Father has inaugurated a new temple, cutting the ribbon on the place of intimacy, finally opening access to this space so long under construction. His message comes through a beautiful symbol whose destruction was widely seen and heard, the meaning of which is clear to all—no need to ask the priests to explain it.

- God himself is the aesthetic ultimate. Notice with what affectional language David describes God and God's deeds.

### A Miktam of David

Keep me safe, my God,
    for in you I take refuge.

I say to the LORD, "You are my Lord;
    apart from you I have no *good* thing."
I say of the holy people who are in the land,
    "They are the noble ones in whom is all my *delight*."
Those who run after other gods will *suffer* more and more.
    I will not pour out libations of blood to such gods
    or take up their names on my lips.

LORD, you alone are my portion and my cup;
    you make my lot *secure*.
The boundary lines have fallen for me in *pleasant* places;
    surely I have a *delightful* inheritance.
I will praise the LORD, who counsels me;
    even at night my heart instructs me.
I keep my *eyes* always on the LORD.
    With him at *my right hand*, I will not be shaken.

Therefore my *heart is glad* and my *tongue rejoices*;
    my body also will rest secure,
because you will not abandon me to the *realm of the dead*,
    nor will you let your faithful one *see decay*.
You make known to me the *path of life*;
    you will fill me with *joy in your presence*,
    with *eternal pleasures at your right hand*.
                —Psalm 16 (emphasis added)

Our feelings delight us, terrify us, mystify us. We have many questions about passion and aesthetics. The Bible knows passion; it locates aesthetics. We can reasonably bring our questions about beauty and ugliness, attraction and revulsion, here.

## READ, REFLECT, DISCUSS, SING————————————

1. Suggested reading: *Creation Regained: Biblical Basics for a Reformational Worldview* by Albert M. Wolters.
2. Q1. Describe a time when a passage of Scripture stirred your imagination. Don't leave out the unpleasant images.
3. Q2. Did you tell someone about what you saw in the Scriptures and what you felt about it? If so, how well did you and your friend agree? If not, briefly tell about it now.
4. Sing: "How Firm a Foundation." Notice the pictures.

# Chapter 4

# AESTHETIC GENESIS
## The Eye of God

*God saw that the light was good.*
—GENESIS 1:4

We intend to ask Scripture about aesthetics, so we need a suitable definition, preferably a scriptural definition. For the present, let us work with this definition: aesthetics consist in forms and other formal properties of objects, sounds, and immaterial ideas, as perceived by the senses and by the mind, together with affectional responses to these forms. We use *affections* in its old-fashioned sense of emotions and feelings. We include in our definition responses together with intrinsic properties for reasons that will emerge from Scripture, but for now let us include both, acknowledging that neither the objective approach to aesthetics (the pursuit of excellence) nor the subjective approach ("if it feels good, do it") has been able alone to offer a coherent system of thought, though they often go hand in hand.

We need also something like an ontology of aesthetics. Where lies its being, source, origin, and essence? Scripture can help us here too. Pursuing aesthetic origins in Scripture leads us beyond the aesthetic qualities we expect.

When I began to search Scripture for how to write better songs, I scanned Bible passages for aesthetic qualities in objects and in stories—the beautiful, the ugly, anything vivid, visceral, attractive, or repellant; I hoped that God, through the text, would explain those properties and connect them to faith in Christ. I expected to find riches beyond songwriting, qualities which could also guide a painter, dancer, or novelist. I found plenty of these aesthetic properties: the beauty of creation, the rich tabernacle, the glorious temple, the pathos of Israel's story, the gripping imagery of the Psalms, the simple beauty of Jesus' parables, all the passages we reviewed in the previous chapter, and more.

I kept running into complications, though, when looking for aesthetics' origins, sources, foundation—its pure essence and its derivation. Jubal, the musician of Genesis 4:21, seemed at first a good candidate for proto-artist, but a closer look at his bad ancestors, worse father, and miserable end made him an awkward founder of a cultural movement one wants to join. The tabernacle and its furnishings (Exodus 25–31, 38–40) were beautiful in many ways, but the author focuses on their beauty less than on other themes. Besides, the most excellent artifact, the Ark of the Covenant, was also the least accessible. The "beauty of holiness" (Ps. 96:9 KJV) seemed well and good, but the next words, "fear before him, all the earth," seemed a counterintuitive response to beauty. I wondered, as many others have, why God, through Isaiah, describes his Servant as having "no beauty or majesty to attract us to him" (Isa. 53:2)? Was Jesus ugly? Or was something wrong with the way we see him? Many such darkened corners tangled my pursuit of aesthetics in Scripture, until the first few chapters of Genesis guided me away from considering aesthetic properties alone and prodded me to look harder at aesthetic perceptions, especially God's aesthetic perception.

## The Source of Aesthetics

Genesis 1–3 seems especially suited to speak to the origin of aesthetics, on three counts. First, the creation gives an early glimpse at human life the way it was supposed to be before sin shouldered its way in and messed things up. Second, this passage speaks of aesthetics. Those early mentions of "pleasing" (2:9; 3:6) connect pleasure to creation, suggesting we are on the right scent here. Third, the passage explains human life in a dynamic that might explain the dark corners of aesthetics; the account of Adam and Eve's disobedience, its results, and God's punishment promises some help in seeing what went wrong with our pleasure, our whole aesthetic perception.

When God sees that his creation is good, we read the summary of the properties of created objects. This appears seven times, an emphasis as strong as printing letters in bold plus capital letters plus italics: ***GOOD***. So we listen. The word *good* (Hebrew *tov*) signifies here "excellent of its kind,"[1] encompassing all kinds of goodness and appropriate to all kinds of created things. This goodness includes the aesthetic.

---

1. *The New Brown-Driver-Briggs-Gesenius Hebrew and English Lexicon* (Peabody, MA: Hendrickson, 1979), 374.

While those seven *good*s emphasize creation's enduring qualities, they point also to the goodness God saw in time; the sequence of the first day's work, followed by the second day's work, and so forth, was also good in God's eyes. We find it hard to think about the beginning of time, but God began time, and he tells us about it in Genesis 1:1: "In the beginning God created the heavens and the earth." Time is good; God saw it so.

## Creation's Timely Goodness

God reveals his glory in time. In time he makes promises and he keeps them. God commands in time, directing in the present decisions that will be made in the future. Obedience happens in time. Hope consists in time, since we do not have now what we will have. In time creation can grow. In time people learn, grow, and gain skill and wisdom. In time a story unfolds, a plan develops and comes to fulfillment. In time things get better. Or worse. For now. For worse and for better, we think, believe, love, and act only in time.

Stories consist of time, and we love stories! They have special power to stir us and hold our attention. We get to know people by their stories. We know ourselves by our own story. We know God by his grand story. God formed his creation in time and saw that the time too was good. And he told us the story in time.

Poetry and all literature depend on time. Music consists in time; each note vibrates at its own frequency, each vibration occurring in time. Music goes somewhere and develops, reaching a conclusion of some sort. This it could not do without sequence, without time. This time has aesthetic quality; God saw that the six-day period of creation, creation's timing, was good!

In time we see one aspect of the form God worked into his formless creation. God recognizes aesthetic qualities in forms. The formless creation of Genesis 1:2 was not good, but goodness came into it through God's shaping. He shaped it into time. This chronological form adds this divine dimension to all the created goodness—the pleasingness, truth, and power—that God shaped into his creation. The forms God gave his creation, including time, are indispensably part of creation's goodness. In this goodness consist all aesthetics. Those forms can be distorted and perverted, but form is created good and not inferior to content, which can also be corrupt.

God gave his creation chronological form to reflect his complete freedom. In seeing creation's time as good, God recognizes in it the reflection of his freedom. He is always the same, yet his sameness never binds him. God loves his glorious consistency and his perfect freedom. God made creation to reflect his consistency (he is always the same) and his perfect freedom (he does whatever he pleases). Creation shows God's consistency in its steady features, in its orderliness and its steadiness in truth, beauty, power; creation shows God's freedom in its time, in its unfolding sequence of earlier and later, promise and fulfillment, change and development. God saw in creation the reflection of his own goodness in these two essential categories: consistency and freedom.

## Creation's Consistent Goodness

God made trees grow out of the ground that were "pleasing to the eye," clearly an aesthetic quality, and one that is grouped with "good for food" (Gen. 2:9). The goodness God saw in his creation, seven times recorded, consists at least in these two qualities, further confirming that we are right to look for aesthetics in this account and in the creation itself. A third quality emerges from the immediate context.

Genesis 2:9 describes the trees in the garden using aesthetic language: "The LORD God made all kinds of trees grow out of the ground—trees that were *pleasing to the eye* and good for food. In the middle of the garden were the tree of life and the tree of the knowledge of good and evil" (emphasis added).

This description looks backward and forward. Looking backward, "good for food" uses the same word *(tov)* used seven times in Genesis 1 for the goodness God saw in his creation. Looking forward, the tree of the knowledge of good *(tov)* and evil returns to this word. Contrasting good with evil in the tree gives this goodness an ethical tone, suggesting a similar ethical goodness in creation as God saw it. These two special trees, the tree of life and the tree of the knowledge of good and evil, have each its special, proper purpose. The proximity of these two special trees to those in the rest of the garden, mentioned a sentence earlier, suggests that these special trees share the qualities of all the trees—"pleasing to the eye and good for food." The two special trees, then, are described as having three qualities: pleasingness to the eye, goodness for food, and purpose or special power.

The three aspects of the goodness of these special trees, by their centrality "in the middle of the garden," represent all of creation. The Lord, in making these trees, gave them *form* with aesthetic character, *content* with intrinsic value, and *purpose* with power. These features articulate the consistent goodness God saw in his whole creation.

These three aspects of the two special trees in Genesis 2:9 look forward to a corresponding triad of aspects in Eve's temptation (3:6). When tempted, she saw that the tree of the knowledge of good and evil was "good for food and pleasing to the eye," nearly echoing the earlier passage, although here the order is reversed. The tree's purposive aspect, "desirable for gaining wisdom," appears third again. Why the order reversal? Perhaps to suggest that these two elements consist in a group of three, a formal relationship in which superiority cannot be inferred from their order in the text. Similar triads appear later in Scripture, with similar alternations of the first two aspects. Some of these we will notice later, in their places, as we consider the significance of forms.

## Creation's Goodness in Three Aspects

These three aspects articulate the goodness of creation as God saw it, seven times in Genesis 1. Even the earth's pre-good state exhibits a similar triad of aspects: "formless," "empty" (lacking content), "darkness was over the surface of the deep" (Gen. 1:2).

God sees the beauty of his creation because he is beautiful; he sees truth because he is true; he sees power because he is powerful. Each quality describes God and the other qualities. These are perspectives, aspects, not parts. So we may speak of God's beautiful glory, of God's powerful glory, and of God's true glory; we may also speak, since each qualifies the others, of God's true beauty, of his strong truth, of his true power. You get the idea. Each aspect refers to God and to the other two aspects.

Evangelical writers on the arts remark often on Genesis 1, for good reason. Much has been made of the goodness of creation here.[2] Most assume that creation's goodness appears clearly to God because the goodness is objective and inherent, but not more. This assumption means that any ordinarily objective human viewer should be able to see and recognize this goodness, and for the same reason: goodness is objective. Yet the text gives clues that question these assumptions.

## Creation's Goodness and God's Seeing

Let us not miss who is looking. This text draws readers' attention beyond creation's goodness to God himself as creation's first and proper audience. Creation's goodness is indeed intrinsic, but it becomes intrinsic goodness not only through God's creation but also through God's seeing. God looks for creation's goodness to correspond to his own. When we overlook God's audience here, we objectify

---

2. For example: Ned Bustard, ed., *It Was Good: Making Art to the Glory of God* (Baltimore: Square Halo, 2000).

creation's goodness, imagining an objective aesthetic standard outside of God's character. In this we blur the Creator-creature distinction and minimize sin's incalculable effects on our seeing, including our aesthetic sensibilities.

Commentators often note that God here declares his creation good, as if by a legal pronouncement God were drawing the hearers to acknowledge creation's adherence to the highest objective standards.[3] While excellence can have value, it cannot be an objective standard by which we evaluate God and to which God must conform. A standard that would rule God, whether objective truth or aesthetic beauty or effectiveness, would bind God to follow, in creating, a standard rooted not in himself but outside himself. Beauty, truth, and power would outrank God.

In Genesis 1's account of creation's sevenfold goodness, though, God pronounces nothing; he *sees*. In seeing, he completes creation's goodness. Genesis signals the end of this creation narrative—"Thus the heavens and the earth were completed in all their vast array" (2:1)—only following God's seventh, climactic seeing on the seventh day. His creation found its completion not in being good, as if its aesthetic and other qualities were only inherent, nor in God's declaration, but rather in God's seeing its goodness. Let us hear this text, and see this goodness, on its own terms.

## "God Saw ..."

This phrase appears seven times in the creation account of Genesis 1. Creation's threefold goodness—its form, rich in aesthetic beauty; its true content; and its powerful purpose—finds fulfillment in God's seeing. This is creation's purpose: he made it so he could see it and appreciate it, for his glory's sake. The same eye with which God appreciated himself in his Trinitarian glory before creation he now turns to creation, to see that the created glory corresponds to the uncreated. And it does! Creation's glory reflects God's glory not only because of its intrinsic character, its inherent goodness, but by God's very seeing itself. Who else could be qualified to fully appreciate it?

God sees actively, not only passively as we expect. God's creation is good because he sees it so; he interprets it according to his own character. God can be said to see goodness *into* his creation. God's goodness shines in creation because he made it to reflect his glory and because he sees it so, excelling it in its every

---

3. For example: Bustard, *It Was Good*, 14; Philip Graham Ryken, *Art for God's Sake: A Call to Recover the Arts* (Phillipsburg, NJ: Presbyterian and Reformed, 2006), 38; Abraham Kuyper, *Lectures on Calvinism* (Peabody, MA: Hendrickson, 2008; originally Grand Rapids, MI: Eerdmans, 1931), 129; Albert M. Wolters, *Creation Regained: Biblical Basics for a Reformational Worldview* (Grand Rapids, MI: Eerdmans, 1985), 48.

perfection. Creation's goodness is intrinsic because it is derived from the good God and because he alone fully appreciates it. Creation's beauty, together with all its truth and power, consists first in the eye of God, its first and eternal Beholder.

God also rules with his eye. In seeing that his creation is good in all its breadth and richness, he thus ratifies it. He made it to see it, and in his seeing, it finds its initial fulfillment. God's seeing goodness into his creation confirms and consummates its truth, beauty and goodness to correspond suitably to his own.

God's active, ruling eye appears in Genesis soon again, the next time the text uses the word for seeing: "He brought them to the man to see what he would name them; and whatever the man called each living creature, that was its name" (2:19). Just as God, by seeing that his creation was good, ratified and established that goodness, God here, as Adam's witness and king overseeing his coregent, similarly witnesses and ratifies Adam's authoritative naming of the animals.

God's active eye affects what it touches. His active eye appears elsewhere in Scripture, powerful to judge, evaluate, interpret, divide good from bad.

- "His eyelids test the children of man" (Ps. 11:4 ESV).
- "When you hide your face, they [creatures] are terrified; when you take away their breath, they die and return to the dust" (Ps. 104:29).
- "He who looks at the earth, and it trembles" (Ps. 104:32).
- "The eyes of the LORD range throughout the earth to strengthen those whose hearts are fully committed to him" (2 Chron. 16:9).
- "Nevertheless, my eye spared them" (Ezek. 20:17 ESV).
- "His eyes like flaming torches" (Dan. 10:6).
- "The Lamb had seven horns and seven eyes, which are the seven spirits of God sent out into all the earth" (Rev. 5:6).

Scripture depicts people's vision too in active terms, fitting for those who bear God's image.

- "When a king sits on his throne to judge, he winnows out all evil with his eyes" (Prov. 20:8).
- "The eye is the lamp of the body. If your eyes are healthy, your whole body will be full of light. But if your eyes are unhealthy, your whole body will be full of darkness. If then the light within you is darkness, how great is that darkness!" (Matt. 6:22–23).

The Old Testament frequently uses the phrase "in your eyes" or "in his eyes" to show the constructive, interpretive act of forming judgments, discernments, evaluations. Every eye sees actively, not merely passively, since our conscience shapes our vision, as the Old Testament so often describes. This ancient biblical understanding connects our seeing to God's seeing, as interpretive, and exposes our presumed objectivity.

God's active eye sees the finite creation with infinite clarity and thoroughness. He sees creation's goodness richly—true, pleasing, and strong. He sees its goodness widely—all the manifold perceptions and judgments of God to which human senses are analogs. In God's seeing, creation reaches its initial fulfillment in truth, beauty, and power because God's eye recognizes his own infinite perfections in its finite reflection.

## Human Co-Seeing: "Behold . . ."

God made Adam to participate in his seeing and drew Adam into his exquisite appreciation of his own glory in creation. This appears in a key word from the Hebrew text, sometimes overlooked: *hinneh*, frequently used throughout the Old Testament and usually translated "behold." This word makes its first and arguably most dynamic appearance in Genesis 1.

*Hinneh*, "behold," invites the hearer to see together with the speaker,[4] a shared appreciation. "Behold," used twice in Genesis 1, continues this text's theme of seeing and develops it. These uses, while they differ slightly, both invite shared seeing.

- First, God addresses *hinneh* to Adam and Eve—"Behold, I have given you every plant . . ." (1:29 ESV)—to declare to them and to draw their acknowledgment of his gift of food.
- Second, the author addresses *hinneh* to the reader, perhaps on God's behalf—"God saw everything that he had made, and behold, it was very good" (1:31 ESV)—inviting the reader to participate with him in God's appreciation of creation's goodness.

"Behold" has imperative force in English, but the Hebrew *hinneh* commands nothing.[5] First, God uses it to formally point to his gift of food to Adam and Eve (v. 29); then the author uses it, "enabling the reader to enter into the surprise and

---

4. *New Brown-Driver-Briggs-Gesenius*, 243–44 (2009 b, c).

5. *Hinneh* is a demonstrative particle (BDB, 243) of exclamation. Willem A. VanGemeren, gen. ed., *New International Dictionary of Old Testament Theology and Exegesis*, vol. 4 (Grand Rapids, MI: Zondervan, 1997), 1032.

satisfaction of the speaker or actor concerned" (v. 31).[6] This word declares, invites, enables, but does not command. It is not law. We see God's generosity in this!

To no other earthly creature does God say "behold."[7] The six preceding times God made and then saw his creation, "God saw" has no "behold" following. The first two uses of *hinneh* in Scripture immediately follow God's creation of people and are addressed to people. Both invite and enable our first parents' shared seeing with God. The second use especially invites and enables the reader, corporately through Adam and Eve and also individually, to see and appreciate creation's goodness *with God*. Adam and Eve responded and shared in God's seeing. They saw creation's goodness together with its Maker and theirs.

Adam and Eve responded, co-seeing with God. They saw, with God, creation's goodness in all its various forms. When Eve saw the tree of the knowledge of good and evil in Genesis 3:6, the text uses the same Hebrew verb for seeing attributed eight times to God (1:4, 10, 12, 18, 21, 25, 31; 2:19), now in its ninth appearance. Like God's earlier seeing, Eve's seeing includes visual perception ("pleasing to the eye") together with perceptions that go beyond the visual ("good for food . . . desirable for gaining wisdom"). Before the temptation, Adam and Eve's seeing included the full creaturely range of perceptions, judgments, discernments, appreciations, *in co-participation with God*. Autonomous, independent seeing changed that; we now cannot imagine the richness, the heights and depths, of this shared divine-human experience but can only guess at it from our great distance.

## God Sees His Goodness in Creation's Story

The goodness that God saw in his creation and shared with Adam and Eve included an additional feature—sequence, the flow of time. "In the beginning God created the heavens and the earth" (Gen. 1:1). With God's sovereign pleasure, "most free,"[8] he began creation, also beginning time, together with all sequence; he began redemptive history through creational history. He shows us here that he begins sequence, and history with it. He tells us later about history's end: "It is done. I am the Alpha and the Omega, the Beginning and the End" (Rev. 21:6).

God begins and ends; he fills everything between the beginning and the end. He shows this to us in this account of his sequential creation over seven

---

6. BDB, 244.

7. God says this word to Satan, his nonhuman, personal creature, in Job 1:12; 2:6.

8. Cf. Westminster Confession of Faith II, I, from *The Trinity Hymnal*, rev. ed. (Suwanee, GA: Great Commission, 1990), 849.

days. He shows his human creatures that he fills all history, by locating them in a place, Eden, and in a time. He locates them by talking to them, telling them about time to come. They are to respond by believing, loving, and obeying him and so discovering and loving and ruling this place and this story. God gives them, as he talks, four interwoven features of their story: a *future*, in future food and office (1:28–30); a *setting*, Eden and its surroundings, filled with material for the mission (2:8–14); a *mission*, keep, tend, and obey (2:15–17); and a *cast* of characters, Adam and Eve and their children (2:18–25).

He calls Adam and Eve to believe him, to love him, and obey him, by living the story he describes, eating the food he provides and leaving alone the food he forbids. God may have planned another step in the story, a probation period, so that after Adam and Eve showed that they believed, loved, and obeyed him by refraining from eating the fruit he prohibited, they would receive eternal life through eating from the tree of life.[9] Such a period would show that God planned for some time to pass as they worshiped and waited for an even better outcome. Either way, God meant them to enjoy and love him by loving and following his story from beginning to end.

Our love for stories like theirs shows our worship. Every gripping narrative, every stirring come-from-behind underdog victory, every dystopian drama, every work of poetry or music,[10] every hope fulfilled or disappointed—"that's not the way it's supposed to go!"—together with our attraction or revulsion to them, finds its genesis in God's utterly free and sovereign story of creation and redemption. God delights in his freedom, in the story he plans and accomplishes: "Our God is in heaven; he does whatever pleases him" (Ps. 115:3). Redemptive history is that story. Adam and Eve, and we their children, worship by loving a story we write about our own heroism or by loving his: this one.

## Creation Aesthetics

Our search for aesthetics in the Bible, focused on the creation account in Genesis, reveals the root of aesthetics in the glory of God. God also sees what he shows. He sees creation's pleasingness, its aesthetic aspect, in company with content—"good for food"—and with power to accomplish a purpose. These three aspects of creation's goodness, created and seen by God, come into sharp focus in the two trees in the middle of the garden. Like the other trees all through the garden,

---

9. Cf. John Murray, "The Adamic Administration," *Selected Lectures in Systematic Theology*, vol. 2 of *The Collected Writings of John Murray* (Edinburgh: Banner of Truth, 1977), 48.

10. Including Schoenberg's twelve-tone row that seeks the meaning of musical sequence separated from narrative.

the Tree of Life and the Tree of the Knowledge of Good and Evil were "pleasing to the eye and good for food." They also had particular power to give the eater either knowledge of good and evil or life. These three aspects in God's creation first suggest God himself in his Trinitarian fullness; second, they elaborate his glory in its three major aspects: truth content, form and shape (including time), and powerful purpose. These aspects of God's glory cannot be justly separated, and though they remain distinct, they are not *parts* of his glory but aspects of it, each informing and qualifying the other. This theme of God's glory appears, in various language, throughout the Scriptures and redemptive history.

Genesis shows the origin of aesthetics in God and in his seeing. Genesis shows aesthetics in context; it always appears in concert with other excellences. God created to reveal his glory in three dimensions. Creation's many forms, together with their affectional, aesthetic character, constitute one dimension. Aesthetics appear here together with truth and with power, as the three principal aspects of God's glory.

God who makes also sees; the aesthetics of God's glory is for God's pleasure. He is the audience. He sees and appreciates creation's aesthetic aspects together with other aspects of his glory. The author draws readers' attention to each subsequent moment of God's appreciation, including aesthetic appreciation. He signals a similar event of aesthetic appreciation: "When the woman saw that the tree was . . . a delight to the eyes . . ." (Gen. 3:6 ESV). While similar, Eve's independent aesthetic seeing of the Tree of the Knowledge of Good and Evil changed aesthetics for her and for us all.

We have seen that God's creation includes aesthetic excellence and that his appreciation includes his own aesthetic pleasure. The first human pleasure comes through God's pleasure. We conclude that all human experience of pleasure derives, originally and properly, from God's own aesthetic experience. God is the primary author and audience for aesthetics. Aesthetics appear first not alone but in parallel with content and purpose in proclaiming God's glory. Human perception of aesthetics and its allies consists rightly in co-seeing with God. What riches! What loss!

Objective aesthetic standards and diverse, changing, subjective aesthetic tastes each catch a piece of the truth about aesthetics, but both divest God of his primacy. The God-centered approach to aesthetics gives the baseline by which all human experiences of pleasure and pain, all human preferences, are to be compared. The correspondence between what people see and how people see it remains too clear to be plausibly denied; only, it is not a direct correspondence but an interpretive one, and that interpretation has been corrupted. The first two corruptions attack the two points we have established here: first, that God's eye is primary; and second, that aesthetics belong together with truth and power, pointing to God's truth, his beauty, and his power—the main themes of his glory. The corruption of these two points stands out in the Genesis account, as it does in our experience.

## READ, REFLECT, DISCUSS, SING————————————

1. Suggested reading: "God Is Good Like No Other" by Ned Bustard, from *It Was Good: Making Art to the Glory of God,* edited by Ned Bustard.
2. Q1. How did your family have fun when you were young? What simple pleasure satisfies you nowadays?
3. Q2. What does God have to do with your pleasures? How do you share pleasure with God?
4. Sing: "All Creatures of Our God and King."

*Chapter 5*

# THE GLORY TRIAD
*Aesthetics in Context*

> *The LORD God made all kinds of trees grow out of the ground—*
> *trees that were pleasing to the eye.*
> —GENESIS 2:9

S eeking scriptural wisdom for aesthetics, we have found in Genesis' first two chapters that aesthetics appears in a three-aspect triad of God's glory, that aesthetics is linked to forms, and that God himself rightly occupies the first place in aesthetic considerations: he is supremely pleasant and satisfying, and he is fully satisfied and pleased with his glory. He sees his creation and is pleased because it reflects his glory. He made people to share his satisfaction with his creation and with himself, in richness that includes its beauty and all other aesthetic properties.

Similar triads throughout Scripture reveal God's glory, always with a form aspect, replete with aesthetics. We can discover, through a few examples, that God consistently reveals himself in such triads and that his glorious attributes always include aesthetics, together with content and with power.

## An Organizing Framework:
## The Good, the True, the Beautiful

Triadic thinking is not new. Philosophy, religion, science, psychology, and marketing have routinely dealt with triads and triadic approaches to a topic. Variations on the triple ideals of truth, beauty, and goodness, often associated with Plato's writing, appear almost ubiquitous in ancient and modern thought.

From Aquinas to Emerson to Einstein to Gandhi, in every sort of religious or philosophical system, this triad draws comment and organizes perspectives. A cursory internet search finds "truth, beauty, goodness" on sites for business, marketing, cognitive behavioral therapy, and dozens of framed quotes for your wall.

The good, the true, and the beautiful populate the historical writings of Christianity and of other systems as well. A smattering:

- Augustine notes three aspects of creation—beauty, goodness, and existence—that correspond to God's characteristics.[1]
- The *Catechism of the Catholic Church* places this triad within the discussion of "I believe in God the Father Almighty, Creator of Heaven and Earth": "God created the world to show forth and communicate his glory. That his creatures should share in his truth, goodness and beauty—this is the glory for which God created them."[2]
- Francis Schaeffer cites a triad of actions—thinking, feeling, and doing—to argue that since God does all these, he is necessarily personal.[3]

More contemporary and particular to Scripture, Harry Lee Poe notes these triads in Genesis 3:

"When the woman saw that the fruit of the tree was good for food (the good), and pleasing to the eye (the beautiful), and was also desirable for gaining wisdom (the true), she took some and ate it." The little phrase "the Good, the True, and the Beautiful" is an ancient, three-legged stool for the highest virtues from the perspective of the Greek philosopher Plato. His philosophical system revolved around his concern for the good, the true, and the beautiful. Within his system, "the good" was the ultimate reality. As such, "the good" represents the ideal from which all other ideals emerge. "The Good" would be Plato's concept of "God"; but only in the sense that he conceived of no higher reality. The Good was not a personal being who could relate in any way to personal beings, nor was the Good the intentional Creator of the heavens and the earth.[4]

1. Augustine, *Confessions* XI, 5, trans. Rex Warner (New York: Penguin, 2009), 255.
2. *Catechism of the Catholic Church with Modifications from the Editio Typica*, 2nd ed. (New York: Doubleday, 1995), 94.
3. Francis A. Schaeffer, *Basic Bible Studies* (Wheaton, IL: Crossway, 1972), 11, 13.
4. Harry Lee Poe, *See No Evil: The Existence of Sin in an Age of Relativism* (Grand Rapids, MI: Kregel, 2004), 55–56.

Dorothy L. Sayers, early twentieth-century British scholar, connects a similar, tantalizing triadic approach to art, which she then commends to all of daily life. Quoting her own play, *The Zeal of Thy House*:

> For every work [*or act*] of creation is threefold, an earthly trinity to match the heavenly. First [*not in time, but in order of enumeration*] there is the creative Idea, passionless, timeless, beholding the whole work complete at once, the end in the beginning: and this is the image of the Father.
>
> Second, there is the creative Energy [*or Activity*] begotten of that idea, working in time from the beginning to the end, with sweat and passion, being incarnate in the bonds of matter: and this is the image of the Word.
>
> Third, there is the Creative Power, the meaning of the work and its response in the lively soul: and this is the indwelling Spirit.
>
> And these three are one, each equally in itself the whole work, whereas none can exist without the other: and this is the image of the Trinity.[5]

Sayers's triadic, even Trinitarian, approach to art in *The Mind of the Maker* is scripturally informed, suggesting a triadic character to the Scriptures themselves.

Each of these broader, historical triads includes one element that is uniquely aesthetic, affectional, feeling-related.

## Street-Level Biblical Interpretation

Whenever we discuss the Bible with others, we expect diverse interpretations. These different understandings fall into two basic types: contradictory (mutually exclusive, at least one of which is mistaken) or complementary (both can be true, focusing on different aspects of a text or enriching each other within a single aspect).

We need patient discernment and careful attention to keys the author gives to his own interpretation. Often ignorant at the outset, we grasp meaning better and recognize more plausible interpretations by listening closely to the author and understanding his context. A passage that puzzled or troubled us at first can take on sudden depth and value when we notice the author's signals.

We may prefer one interpretation to another, sometimes feeling confident and sometimes simply trying it out as a hypothesis. We develop a pattern of Scripture interpretations and improve our interpretive approach in private study,

---

5. Dorothy L. Sayers, *The Mind of the Maker* (New York: Harcourt, Brace, 1941; San Francisco: HarperSanFrancisco, 1987), 37–38 (brackets and italics in the original).

in meditation and prayer, and in reading and conversation with other Bible believers.

Respect for the text and for the authors improves our interpretation of Scripture as we read it. In the process, Scripture also interprets us, changing how we read as well as what we read. We have noticed that the Bible pushes the respectful reader to stop asking certain questions and to start asking others. The best questions and interpretive methods arise from within the text itself, its clarity and tensions, its silences and puzzles. When we accept its invitation, these features enrich us and our respect for the text. The study of Bible interpretation—hermeneutics—ranges widely across the centuries and the theological spectrum.

## A Triadic Hermeneutic

In the chapters that follow we will consider many Bible passages especially familiar to those who study culture and the arts. We hope to interpret these passages consistently with their own internal logic and clues, and we will use an approach that highlights the Scriptures' frequent use of triads to describe, especially, the glory of God. As this approach may be unfamiliar to the reader, we will introduce triadic approaches briefly here, first as an academic discipline, second as an experienced intuition.

John Frame and Vern Poythress have pioneered a triadic approach to Scripture and theology that they call multiperspectivalism.[6] They seek by this approach to make sense of the rich diversity of different human perspectives, human limitations, the wide variety in Scripture and the simplicity it urges. In multiperspectivalism, three associated themes consist harmoniously, each as a perspective on the whole and on each other.

Frame and Poythress have introduced two principal triads in their writings: "the triad for Lordship (authority, control, and presence), and the triad for ethics (normative, situational, and existential)."[7] In both triads, each perspective

6. See particularly John M. Frame, *Doctrine of the Knowledge of God* (Phillipsburg, NJ: Presbyterian and Reformed, 1987); *Perspectives on the Word of God: An Introduction to Christian Ethics* (Phillipsburg, NJ: Presbyterian and Reformed, 1990); *Theology in Three Dimensions: A Guide to Triperspectivalism and Its Significance* (Phillipsburg, NJ: Presbyterian and Reformed, 2017). Also Vern S. Poythress, *Symphonic Theology: The Validity of Multiple Perspectives in Theology* (Grand Rapids, MI: Zondervan, 1987); *God-Centered Biblical Interpretation* (Phillipsburg, NJ: Presbyterian and Reformed, 1999). Dr. Poythress has a new book in press on triadic perspectives, its working title *Knowing and the Trinity: How Threefold Perspectives in Human Knowledge Imitate the Trinity* (Phillipsburg, NJ: Presbyterian and Reformed, forthcoming).

7. Vern Sheridan Poythress, "Multiperspectivalism and the Reformed Faith," published in John J. Hughes, ed., *Speaking the Truth in Love: The Theology of John M. Frame* (Phillipsburg, NJ: Presbyterian and Reformed, 2009), 3.

informs the others, functioning at once independently and in close cooperation to qualify and enrich the others.

The triad of aspects to God's glory articulated first in Genesis 1–3 seems worth testing elsewhere in Scripture, a triadic interpretive method consisting in these three interconnected aspects: content, form, and purpose. In applying this model, we will use several different names for these aspects, as appropriate to the passage in view: noetic, aesthetic, and ethical; telling, showing, and doing; morals, models, and making; and others. The three aspects always connect like those in the triads described by Frame and Poythress: independent, complementary, harmonious, each qualifying the others.

The study of select passages in Genesis takes its triadic shape from triads in the text itself, which I glimpsed the more clearly through my reading the work of Frame and Poythress. The triad for glory that emerged from these texts articulates three perspectives for glory, rather than for Lordship or for ethics as developed by Frame and Poythress. I acknowledge my debt to them in preparing me to recognize similar triads in Scripture.

Even before we meet the scholarly evidence for triadic approaches, we already have intuitive inklings of the mysterious connection between basic specialized fields. The role of aesthetics in Galileo's scientific theory is widely attested.[8] Artists and art lovers have long found that truth and beauty, though they often stand alone, cooperate at their best to make a powerful statement, for good or ill. Hymns that coordinate sound doctrine, good poetry, and fitting music, each qualified to stand alone, can make a synergistic statement that endures for centuries. Popular music appears almost always with lyrics. Paintings that tell stories or depict recognizable images have a much longer history than do abstract paintings. Even financial management, considered an art in some circles, develops a category for socially conscious ethical investing. In all these fields, the ethics ("goodness") of the scientist, the artist, the performer, the investor qualifies the work.

These and many other intuitions show that although we wrestle to reconcile different perspectives, we appreciate the superiority of their occasional synergy, often viscerally. The well-attested triad of truth, beauty, and goodness (alternatively, power) suffuses our regular experience, despite our counterstruggle to keep them as freestanding ideals.

The Bible has rich wisdom for our interpretive struggles, and we meet that wisdom first in the early chapters of Genesis. The triad of glory that we

---

8. Richard Tarnas, *The Passion of the Western Mind: Understanding the Ideas That Have Shaped Our World View* (New York: Ballantine, 1991), 255.

find there, the same triad we find elsewhere throughout Scripture, warrants special consideration for two reasons: first, it locates aesthetics in its context; and second, it appears in the forms of many Scriptures as well as their content, in the Bible's details as well as in the broad sweep of its unity. That Scripture's forms convey this triad suggests that the original authors intended this approach and that we can interpret their work better by approaching their writings using this same triad.

## Biblical Aesthetics: Forms and Showing

For those who have reflected on the beauty perceived in the shapes and forms of creation, the aesthetic qualities of forms may need little corroboration. In the shapes visible on photo paper, on canvas, or in three-dimensional sculptures, in the shapes audible in music, and in the shapes envisioned in the literary forms such as stories or poetry, forms elicit responses. Scripture guides us and helps us understand this association of forms and aesthetics, as a brief sampling will show.

The Genesis creation account associates form and aesthetics by reporting, "God saw that it was very good," then explaining that this good *(tov)* includes "pleasing to the eye" (2:9). The triadic properties of the trees in the garden, repeated in Eve's temptation, suggest that God, revealing his glory triadically in creation, links creation's form with pleasure, making it "pleasing to the eye" (2:9; 3:6). Although the Hebrew differs in these two accounts, the NIV translators render them the same, emphasizing the similarity of their contexts.

God's elaborate design for the tabernacle and its furnishings has aesthetics in mind, including in their scope both the seen beauty of the priestly garments designed and worn "for glory and for beauty" (Ex. 28:2 ESV) and the smelled beauty of the "pleasing aroma," the sacrifice of burnt offering (Ex. 29:18). All this design connects aesthetics with forms, again with God himself as the chief audience.

Isaiah responded in almost delirious terror to his vision of the Lord "high and exalted" on a throne in the temple (Isa. 6:1). He cried, "Woe to me! ... I am ruined! For I am a man of unclean lips, and I live among a people of unclean lips, and my eyes have seen the King, the LORD Almighty" (v. 5). Not the customary aesthetic impact but a visceral response to God's terrifying appearance in visible form!

Jeremiah asks how to comfort his countrymen in exile. He would like to ease their sorrow with a comparison but can find no metaphor adequate to their grief: "With what can I compare you, Daughter Jerusalem? To what can I liken you, that I may comfort you, Virgin Daughter Zion?" (Lam. 2:13). He assumes that a form of speech should have power to comfort, clearly an aesthetic effect, though not in their extreme case.

Scripture overflows with many similar associations of form with aesthetics. So do its commentators; Calvin mentions God's gift of form to the creation as an "adornment" that adds "beauty,"[9] probably echoing Augustine, who writes much the same in his *Confessions*.[10] A contemporary commentator describes the aesthetic experience as "typically one of detached contemplation with a view to the apprehension of form."[11] We can accept the connection of forms with aesthetics as a reasonable premise for continued exploration. So wherever we see forms, shapes shown or alluded to in Scripture, let us also look for something intended to arouse affections, to attract or to repel—their aesthetic properties.

## Triads of God's Glory in Scripture

The Bible often shows God's glory in groups of three aspects. Each of these triadic appearances features these aspects' unity. Of many biblical examples, we here briefly suggest three corresponding triads from the Old Testament and three from the New Testament.

### *Old Testament*
*Exodus 33–34*

Moses asked God in Exodus 33:18, "Show me your glory." God answered Moses beyond what he asked, promising to reveal his glory to Moses in three coordinated ways: by showing, by telling, and by doing.

> I will cause all my goodness to pass in front of you [showing], and I will proclaim my name, the LORD, in your presence [telling]. I will have mercy on whom I will have mercy, and I will have compassion on whom I will have compassion [doing].
>
> —Exodus 33:19

God's answer, promised and fulfilled, takes place in sequence, displaying his glory in time.

Having promised triadically, God also fulfilled triadically.

---

9. John Calvin, *Institutes of the Christian Religion*, ed. John T. McNeill, trans. Ford Lewis Battles, Library of Christian Classics (Philadelphia: Westminster, 1960).

10.  Augustine, *Confessions* XII, 4, trans. Rex Warner (New York: Penguin, 2009), 282–83.

11.  Jeremy Begbie, *Voicing Creation's Praise: Towards a Theology of the Arts* (Edinburgh: T&T Clark, 1991), xviii.

Then the LORD came down in the cloud and stood there with him and proclaimed his name, the LORD [telling]. And he passed in front of Moses [showing], proclaiming, "The LORD, the LORD, the compassionate and gracious God, slow to anger, abounding in love and faithfulness, maintaining love to thousands, and forgiving wickedness, rebellion and sin. Yet he does not leave the guilty unpunished; he punishes the children and their children for the sin of the parents to the third and fourth generation [doing]."

—Exodus 34:5–7

This passage helps us, but we need a few connections to see how. First, nowhere else in the Old Testament do we read the record of anyone asking God to show him his glory, much less God answering. This passage thus has a certain prominence, giving special weight to these details.

First, we read two expressions of God's glory, the promise and the fulfillment; both consist in triads. Second, Moses seems to have understood the triadic promise to be itself a telling, the triadic fulfillment to be itself a showing. These first two tokens suggest to Moses a third, and he immediately asks for it. Moses responds so quickly with a pointed question that he seems to expect that a doing must follow. Moses asks, as it were, "So where is the third aspect of your revelation of your glory that fulfills the first two? What are you going to do? Will you go with us?" The Lord again answers Moses with more than he has asked: yes, God will go with them; how can it be otherwise, since he is making a covenant with them? Such triadic richness of perception need not surprise us, coming as it does to Moses, whom many hold to have penned the creation account, strewn as we have seen with similar triads.

By this triad of triads, God reveals his glory and confirms the glory pattern of creation. The three glorious aspects, though they differ somewhat, maintain the same relationship: three equal aspects, not parts. God's telling in Exodus 33–34 corresponds to the truth content of the Genesis triads, his doing to the purposive aspect there. The showing aspect of God's glory here corresponds to creation's forms and pleasingness. We notice too that showing appears first in the triadic promise, but in the triadic fulfillment it appears second. This echoes the reversed order of form and content we observed in the character of the trees twice depicted in the Genesis account. As we noted, God saw the trees as pleasing (form), good for food (content), and able to impart life or knowledge (purpose); whereas Eve saw them as good for food (content), pleasing to the eye (form), and desirable for wisdom (purpose). Again, the careful reader may infer that this difference in order connotes the complete equality of the aspects, a formal relation we have seen before and will see again.

## 1 Samuel

Samuel's public ministry first appears in a similar triad.

> The LORD continued to appear at Shiloh [showing], and there he revealed himself to Samuel through his word [telling]. And Samuel's word came to all Israel [doing].
>
> —1 Samuel 3:21–4:1

The pattern in which God speaks to his people finds its echo here, and the aesthetic, form aspect finds first mention. We may see the author foreshadowing his parenthetical explanation, "Formerly in Israel, if someone went to inquire of God, they would say, 'Come, let us go to the seer,' because the prophet of today used to be called a seer" (1 Sam. 9:9). Earlier, the seer published what God had shown him and he had seen; the man of God, now called a prophet, publishes what he heard of what God had told him. The comparison suggests that seeing and hearing are as parallel and equal as the Seer and the Prophet. This association we see anticipated in the earlier summary of Samuel's ministry, which also further corroborates the triadic expressions we have explored.

### Theocratic Offices in Ancient Israel

We see a final example of God's triadic glory in the whole biblical sweep of God's dealing with Israel. God gave his chosen people three offices: priesthood, prophethood, and kingship. Priests were representatives; Prophets proclaimed the word of the Lord; the king wielded power to act for God. The priestly office found its setting in the tabernacle, carefully designed by God, in all its construction, its furnishings, and its practices, to focus on forms and their aesthetic qualities, presented first to God's eye. The prophets declared God's truth content, and the kings got the job done, fighting battles and building justice. This triad of offices reflects and further corroborates the triad of God's glory declared in creation.

# New Testament
## Temptation Accounts

The New Testament includes many examples of the glory triad we saw in the Old Testament. Jesus' temptation in the wilderness, with its three venues of Satan's appeal, echoes the three aspects of Eve's temptation. All three of the Synoptic Gospels mention Christ's temptation, and Matthew and Luke recount its three satanic trials. In each of these trials, the Enemy offers our Lord the attractions of one familiar aspect of God's glory, but isolated from the others, to master as his own. In each account, the three temptations center on three themes: truth content; form, with its aesthetic value; and purpose. Each aspect in the two triadic accounts of Jesus' wilderness temptation corresponds to an aspect of Eve's temptation.

The bread that Satan challenged Jesus to make from stones corresponds to "good for food" with which that same Tempter deceived Eve (Gen. 3:6). This "good for food" echoes the earlier description of the trees in the garden (Gen. 2:9). In both luminous events, food value signifies truth content, often the first aspect of the glory triad.

Satan enticed Jesus with the nations' glory, a temptation that appears third in Matthew's account and second in Luke's. The glory Satan offered Jesus was beauty, a little like the beauty of Jesus' own bride-to-be, the church; this corresponded to aesthetic temptation. John uses the same Greek word in describing the New Jerusalem: "The kings of the earth will bring their glory into it," and again, "They will bring into it the glory and the honor of the nations" (Rev. 21:24, 26 ESV). Jesus resisted Satan's temptation, more challenging than Eve's "pleasing to the eye," the aesthetic aspect of a corresponding triad.

At the pinnacle of the temple, the Tempter offers Jesus autonomous power: power to compel belief, and power over the Father by forcing him to keep his promise. This corresponds to the power Eve saw in the fruit for gaining wisdom, the third aspect in the Genesis glory triad that we have seen elsewhere in the Old Testament. Satan poses the temptation to Christ that he posed to Eve, to "become as God" instead of participating with God.

## Other New Testament Examples

John's gospel records Jesus' seamless weaving of showing, telling, and doing in contrasting his life with that of his spurious believers.

> I speak [telling] of what I have seen [showing] with my Father, and you do [doing] what you have heard [telling] from your father.
>
> —John 8:38 ESV

In 2 Corinthians, Paul describes triadically the false ministry he and his associates reject.

> We have renounced secret and shameful *ways* [doing]; we do not use deception [showing], nor do we distort the word of God [telling]. On the contrary, by setting forth the truth plainly [telling] we commend ourselves to everyone's conscience [doing] in the sight of God [showing].
>
> —2 Corinthians 4:2

Paul, closing as he does with "in the sight of God," restores God's audience as primary, and human seeing as derivative.

## Old and New Testaments Together
### Three Offices: Prophethood, Priesthood, Kingship

The unity of the Old and New Testaments testifies to the triadic character of God's glory. Supremely, Jesus Christ himself finally and fully personifies the Father's triadic glory in his three offices. He is the Prophet who speaks with authority, personifying as the Word his Father's truth content. He is the Priest who shows God by his presence as the Father's image, "the image of the invisible God" (Col. 1:15). He is the King of whom the Father says, "I have installed my king on Zion, my holy mountain" (Ps. 2:6), the King of Kings who accomplishes all the Father's will. King Jesus wins his bride by triumphing over his enemy in single combat, like King David his father. Israel's three offices reach their fulfillment in Christ, and their pinnacle in Christ's crucifixion, resurrection, and ascension, which he presented to the Father's view, reuniting in his person the aspects of the Father's triadic glory that we have presumed to isolate.

### Christ Himself: The Word of God, the Image of God, the Power of God

## Word

- The first chapter of John's gospel establishes Christ as the Word of God personified (John 1:1–14).
- John again names Jesus as the Word in Revelation: "His name is the Word of God" (Rev. 19:13).
- Jesus, the Word of God, is also truth: "Sanctify them by the truth; your word is truth" (John 17:17).
- Jesus identifies himself as the truth: "I am the way and the truth and the life. No one comes to the Father except through me" (John 14:6).

## Image

- Jesus is the image of God: "The Son is the image of the invisible God" (Col. 1:15).
- Of himself he said, "Anyone who has seen me has seen the Father" (John 14:9).
- The writer of Hebrews says of Jesus, "The Son is the radiance of God's glory and the exact representation of his being, sustaining all things by his powerful word" (Heb. 1:3).

## Power

- Jesus the power of God can be identified throughout the Scriptures in the contexts of prophecy and of stories about his identity and his acts, but also in overt claims to his being God's power and authority.
- "Jesus came to them and said, 'All authority in heaven and on earth has been given to me'" (Matt. 28:18).
- "To those whom God has called, both Jews and Greeks, Christ [is] the power of God and the wisdom of God" (1 Cor. 1:24).
- "We did not follow cleverly devised stories when we told you about the coming of our Lord Jesus Christ in power, but we were eyewitnesses of his majesty" (2 Peter 1:16).
- "I heard a loud voice in heaven say: 'Now have come the salvation and the power and the kingdom of our God, and the authority of his Messiah'" (Rev. 12:10).
- Highlighting that Jesus is both the image and the power of God: "In Christ all the fullness of the Deity lives in bodily form, and in Christ you have been brought to fullness. He is the head over every power and authority" (Col. 2:9–10).

## Triads of God's Glory in Creation

Just as God's glory appears throughout the Scriptures in triads like those we have noticed previously, these same three themes appear everywhere we look, in creation and in human lives. These themes we have called *content, form,* and *purpose*; also *telling, showing,* and *doing*. We have noticed that these themes point to Christ as Prophet, Priest, and King, and through him to the Trinity—Father, Son, and Holy Spirit—the object and fountain of all glory. Jesus reveals his glory in these three aspects: *truth, beauty,* and *power,* now our old friends, but now rescued from our abstractions, no longer ideals or principles but essentially personal.

### Ask a Rock

Creation's three aspects come clear in an illustration. Think of a stone you might hold in your hand. Like every other stone, it has its own special shape—pointed or rounded, rough or smooth, featured or plain. The rock's form may please or displease, but either way the shape has aesthetic properties, and we respond with feelings of some sort. This is true even of the stone in our shoe. Your stone also has content, usually identified by its minerals. This little rock also has a purpose. God has been using it to make soil, grinding off bits to get it down to the size you hold in your hand, and all the other bits are busy as beach sand or topsoil.

Your rock's three aspects—content, form, and purpose—cannot be separated but go always together. We might change one without changing the others, though. We might shape a piece of wood exactly like your rock, but it would have a different content—wood, not mineral. Or we might pound the stone into small pieces, changing its form but leaving its content unaffected. We might put this rock to different purposes. We might throw it, skipping it over a still pond; we could lay it with many others to form a roadbed, or we could set it on a shelf to be admired.

We could use the stone for any of these purposes without changing either its form or its content. Your rock's three aspects remain inseparable, though they consist separately. As with your rock, God created all that he made with these three aspects. All the glory of these aspects points to him, to his triadic glory. Likewise, everything people do and say has these same basic aspects, meant to point to God. These outward acts spring out of our worshiping hearts, which consist in similar inseparable aspects: mind, affections, and will.

## Aesthetics' Place

We have made some sweeping observations about aesthetics' proper location in God's glory; now let us refocus on the aesthetic perspective itself. We have seen in Scripture and corroborated from experience that aesthetic properties attach to creation's forms, noting that God's creation in time gives its form another dimension. Creation was formless at first, and the subsequent form God gave it consisted in time. Thus all human speech, which consists in time, gets its shape from God. All performing arts consist in time, and even music, musical tones, and sound itself take place in time. Form, together with its aesthetic qualities, comes from God. Sin can pervert, twist, and distort the forms of creation, but it cannot take away its "form-ness." Nor can we take away the content and purpose of creation, nor its "about-ness," its giving glory to God in its triadic fullness. Creation is always about God. Form and its aesthetic character always accompany content and purpose, or truth and power if you prefer, and are always about God. Aesthetics has a place and a Person.

We began our exploration looking for aesthetics; with God's help we have found it, and much more, we have found its root in God himself, and its context in the other aspects of God's glory. In summary, then, God revealed his glory in creation and explained it in his Word; that glory is triadic, exhibiting content, form—including aesthetic properties—and purpose, to varying degrees and with varying emphases. God himself saw and ratified creation as the triadic expression of his glory in Trinity; his eye alone is capable of fully and accurately recognizing in his creation the stamp of his glory. To consider aesthetics especially, we observe that because God delights in his own beauty, he also enjoys the beauty of his creation. He takes special notice of the creation's subjection to futility; he hears its groans![12]

## Aesthetics in Human Communication

Guided by God's Word, we have in your rock—creation—a pattern for interpreting all communication, including what people say and do. Scholars call this *communication* and *discourse*. All communication—indeed, everything people do—ascribes some kind of glory or aspect of glory to some object. Although the objects vary, that glory is always triadic, like your rock, and with various differing emphases. For example, an instruction manual emphasizes content and power, but it has form even so. Decorations in hotels emphasize forms, but they retain content and purpose. Whatever we select to consider, we must consider in all three aspects, interpreting it carefully to discern the object to which it ascribes glory. We might consider works of art or culture or literature, but those concepts highlight aesthetics primarily, or aesthetics alone, and Scripture pushes us to consider more broadly—triadically.

Because God reveals his glory triadically, many scripturally based triadic formulae can cooperate to express that glory. We have considered a few: content, form, and purpose; telling, showing, doing; truth, beauty, and goodness. Contemporary theologian John Frame has identified another, naming the *normative*, *situational*, and *existential* aspects of Bible texts in his *Perspectives on the Word of God*.[13] Vern Poythress identifies a similar triad of perspectives on God's speaking: *meaning*, *control*, and *presence*.[14] All these triads, far from competing, can shine their individual lights on the infinite richness of God's glory.

Bible education and pastoral training often divide theology proper into a similar triad: systematic theology (corresponding to truth content, noetics), biblical theology (corresponding to aesthetics of form, especially the narrative form of the unfolding of the canon), and practical theology (corresponding to ethics and will). No one of these can properly be pursued in isolation from the others or be allowed to dominate the others. Each has its function, and each serves the others.[15]

---

12. Cf. Romans 8:20–22.

13. John M. Frame, *Perspectives on the Word of God: An Introduction to Christian Ethics* (Phillipsburg, NJ: Presbyterian and Reformed, 1990), 52–3.

14. Vern Sheridan Poythress, *In the Beginning Was the Word: Language—A God-Centered Approach* (Wheaton, IL: Crossway, 2009), 24–5.

15. Cf. Richard B. Gaffin Jr., "Systematic Theology and Biblical Theology" in *The New Testament*

## Further Systematic Observations

We saw in Genesis 1 and 2 the importance of God's seeing for human interpretation. Other Old Testament authors frequently use seeing in the same way, notably in the frequent use of the expression "in his eyes," by which they draw our attention to individual perception and evaluation. Words and phrases connoting vision appear throughout the Old Testament as a metaphor for individual interpretive perception.

The New Testament echoes the Old Testament theme of seeing as discernment with the word conscience.[16] Paul equates conscience and seeing in 2 Corinthians 4:1–4. First, he articulates what is seen and presented to the conscience in three aspects. Paul denounces bad ministry triadically, using the same showing/telling/doing we saw in God's revelation of his glory to Moses in Exodus 33 and 34: "we have renounced secret and shameful ways; we do not use deception, nor do we distort the word of God" (2 Cor. 4:2). Paul uses this triad to negate the full scope of the bad ministry for which this church has developed a taste. Again, the order of the three aspects has changed, and again their correspondence and coequality are unmistakable: bad doing ("shameful ways"), bad showing ("deception"), and bad telling ("distort the word of God").

Second, he characterizes his ministry as personal ("we commend ourselves"), as presented to listeners' individual discernment ("to everyone's conscience"), and as presented simultaneously for God to see (in the sight of God). Those who hear Paul preach are to exercise their own judgment, in the hope that their consciences may even agree with God's sight.

As we have seen, God reveals and sees his glory in a triad, and this triad includes forms and their aesthetic responses together with truth content and purposive power; we have seen this corroborated throughout the Scriptures. This pattern gives us a baseline from which to explore the aesthetic effects of sin, to which we must now turn, starting in Genesis 3 and 4.

---

*Student and Theology*, ed. John H. Skilton (Nutley, NJ: Presbyterian and Reformed, 1976), 32–50.

16. I am indebted to Dr. David Powlison for this connection.

## READ, REFLECT, DISCUSS, SING————————————

1. Suggested reading: "Pentecost," chapter 8 of *The Mind of the Maker* by Dorothy L. Sayers; *Theology in Three Dimensions: A Guide to Triperspectivalism and Its Significance* by John M. Frame (Phillipsburg, NJ: Presbyterian and Reformed, 2017); "Multiperspectivalism and the Reformed Faith" by Vern Sheridan Poythress, in John J. Hughes, ed., *Speaking the Truth in Love: The Theology of John M. Frame* (Phillipsburg, NJ: Presbyterian and Reformed, 2009), 173–200.

2. Q1. What cluster of three things in the Bible do you remember noticing? What did you make of it then? What do you think about that triad now?

3. Q2. What group of three things in the Bible still puzzles you? Why? Consider praying with your study partners for understanding of these tougher bits of Scripture.

4. Sing: "Holy, Holy, Holy!"

## *Chapter 6*

# DISTORTED VISION

*When the woman saw . . .*
—GENESIS 3:6

W*hen* the woman saw" marks a moment, an event, a first. What event does the author mean? He rules out one possibility: "when" cannot signal Eve's first glimpse of the tree. She had to know about it, since she almost quotes God's prohibition of it. No, Eve, together with Adam, had previously seen everything—the tree and the rest of creation—with God, co-participants in God's seeing creation's goodness, including its aesthetic goodness. That seeing included a command, a projection into the future, along the line of a story God laid out. But something changed all that.

First, the Serpent pitched Eve a new story: "You will not certainly die. . . . For God knows that when you eat from it your eyes will be opened, and you will be like God, knowing good and evil" (Gen. 3:4–5). Notice this new story's key plot elements: a new beginning (suffering under God's stinginess), a new ending (becoming God's equals), a new hero (Eve and Adam), and a new story author to be believed, loved, and obeyed (the Serpent—in effect, a new god).

Second, Eve listened to the Serpent; his new story appealed to her. The Genesis account connects Eve's twisted vision in verse 6 to the Serpent's new story in verse 5, using a Hebrew word whose meaning—usually "and"—can vary widely with the context. Some English versions, like the ESV, translate it "so," making the Serpent's new story the cause of Eve's new seeing. Whatever its meaning, this word connects Eve's new seeing to the Serpent's new story with narrative intention; it's more than just something that happened next.

## Vision Hijacked

Adam and Eve despised their co-seeing with God "when the woman saw" (3:6). "When" signals her innovation: she saw the tree *alone*, no longer in participation with God, but without him. In Eve's disobedience, human seeing was cut off from God's seeing.

What did Eve see? She saw the very tree God had made. The language that describes what Eve saw in 3:6—"good for food and pleasing to the eye, and also desirable for gaining wisdom"—so closely resembles "pleasing to the eye and good for food" that describes all the trees including this one (2:8) suggests that Eve saw what God first saw as very good.

Eve saw the tree she had seen with God, the tree about which she heard God's command, "You must not eat." Only now she saw it differently in two ways. Her seeing it as "good for food and pleasing to the eye" seems hardly to differ at all, only reversing the order of 2:8. Even in these two features, though, the interpretation differs; she saw it interpreted no longer by God but through the eyes of the Serpent. Second, although Eve, in her temptation, saw in the tree what an objective viewer might mistake for the identical content (good for food) and the identical form (pleasing to the eye) to what she had seen before with God, this tree's special purpose—"the tree of the knowledge of good and evil"—now becomes, as interpreted by the Serpent, no longer a test but an opportunity to rival God.

Creation's three features—content, form, and purpose—looked familiar to Eve; she had been seeing them every day since she first opened her eyes, sharing her Maker's vision. Now her glance itself was different, now that she believed the lie that she would "be like God, knowing good and evil" (Gen. 3:5). She was evaluating the fruit's content ("good for food") as if she were a god, without God; she enjoyed its pleasures ("a delight to the eyes") alone, a solitary indulgence; she assessed the tree's power ("to be desired to make one wise") with a personal agenda.

Eve now saw in pretended, God-defying independence. Eve commandeered shared truth into self-rule, subsumed shared pleasure into an auto-aesthetic, and wrenched derived, subordinate power into a splinter kingdom. She believed, loved, and willed autonomously. And she had not yet touched the fruit.

As always, the heart pours out in action. Having seen rebelliously, Eve acts out the rebellion now in her heart, taking the fruit and giving it to her husband.

The results are immediate and unmistakable, as the narrator elaborates. "Then the eyes of both of them were opened" (Gen. 3:7). Their newly opened autonomous eyes saw themselves as no longer good but shameful in their naked-ness. Unthinkably, they hid from the God who sees, whose seeing they had shared.

Their descendants have been seeing with the same pretended independence, while hiding from God's sight, ever since. We too deny that God is the first audience and that our own seeing subsists rightly in his. Sin's first effect was to make people autonomous knowers-believers, auto-aesthetic enjoyers, and self-driving cars. This was bad enough, but a second and third perversion soon followed. All three have had horrible, lasting, and progressive impacts.

The impact that Eve and Adam's disobedience had on our pleasures, on the whole aesthetic aspect of human life, has become second nature to us. This is why our feelings thrill us and betray us, why they shake us up. The help we need starts with looking carefully at the monuments that mark this continental shift.

## Vision Fragmented

Genesis' next chapter shapes a list of Cain's descendants to show the reader Lamech's three sons, whose specialties form a triad like the one we saw in 2:9 and 3:6. Christian musician-scholars have long looked to Jubal (Gen. 4:21), the second son, as the founder of music, even of all the arts.[1] Some see in the three brothers the founders of human culture.[2]

The author seems to have something more in mind in mentioning these three brothers and their sister than tracing the roots of human culture. Some suggest that the author contrasts their culture with the worship of God, founded earlier by Seth's descendants and mentioned a few verses later: "At that time people began to call on the name of the LORD" (Gen. 4:26).[3] These two genealogies alone link the creation story to the flood story. They speak of two cultures, both dynamic, whose continuities and changes over time had purpose for the original audience and for us.

The text of Genesis 4–5 contrasts two families, Cain's and Seth's, with several literary signals. Still, the differences between them are minimal. Both are among those later described when God looks at his creation and sees it *not* good: "The LORD saw how great the wickedness of the human race had become on the earth, and that every inclination of the thoughts of the human heart was only evil all the time" (Gen. 6:5).

---

1. For example: William Edgar, *Taking Note of Music* (London: SPCK, 1986), 24; Donald P. Hustad, *Jubilate II: Church Music in Worship and Renewal* (Carol Stream, IL: Hope, 1993), 6.

2. For example: Kenneth A. Myers, *All God's Children and Blue Suede Shoes: Christians and Popular Culture* (Wheaton, IL: Crossway, 1989), 46; Brian J. Walsh and J. Richard Middleton, *The Transforming Vision: Shaping a Christian World View* (Downers Grove, IL: InterVarsity, 1984), 57.

3. Edgar, *Taking Note of Music*, 24.

We gather that Cain's family died in the flood, together with all Seth's descendants except Noah and his family. No implication that Shem, Ham, and Japheth were better than their cousins; rather God spared them for their father's sake and for the sake of his promise.

Every name in the line of Seth has children other than the named firstborn, with the text focusing on Noah and his three sons. Cain's line ends with the three sons of Lamech, who apparently died in the flood along with most of Seth's descendants. The text takes special notice of the fathering of children. Cain's line ends; Seth's line continues. We learn, though, that the first two of Lamech's sons, Jabal and Jubal, became fathers to people who practiced their respective specializations, shepherding and music. These specializations were readily recognized by the original readers, although neither they nor the shepherds and musicians they knew could have descended from the Lamech brothers. We may infer that these sons of Lamech fathered not children but disciplines, ideas that persist in human culture, a cultural approach: specialization.

Academics know as well as anyone how readily we seek our own specialty niche where we can make a contribution and gain recognition. We focus our attention on a narrow field, often hoping to master it. If the field we pick is small enough, we can become an expert, a specialist, earn a doctorate. Our pursuit of specialization often has mastery in the background.

Specialization has a golden place in the Scriptures, from Bezalel (Ex. 31:1–3), the God-appointed and Spirit-filled craftsman of the tabernacle; through Huram (1 Kings 7:13–14; Huram-Abi in 2 Chron. 2:13–14), who was filled with "wisdom, understanding, and skill" (1 Kings 7:14 ESV); to the members of the Corinthian church, endowed with the several gifts of the Spirit listed in 1 Corinthians 12. Spirit-filled specialists know their place in the community and their place before God as recipients of their skills. But the first specialists had mastery in mind. With that mastery came the same fragmenting impulse that still plagues us.

Lamech's three sons adopt cultural pursuits in a triad resembling that of the fruit in the garden. Jabal's livestock suggests food, even before God gave Noah animals for food; the content of the trees was likewise good for food. Jubal's music suggests the aesthetic character of the fruit's form, pleasing to the eye. Tubal-Cain's tools accomplish purposes, just as the fruit from the trees accomplished purposes. While no shame should come to them or anyone for simply specializing, the text nudges the reader. If there were two or four or five specializations among Lamech's sons, we would have a different conversation. If there were no correspondence between food value of the fruit and food value of livestock, if there were no correspondence between the pleasing sight of the fruit and the pleasing sound of instrumental music, if there were no correspondence between the powers of each tree to accomplish its purposes and the power of tools to accomplish their user's purposes, then our take on this text must move in a different direction. As it is, we see correspondences in all three areas.

These three brothers look like makers, and so they are; but notice what they had to break to do it: they broke God's glory in creation, the way he saw it in goodness of three principal aspects—form, content, and purpose. Like their first parents, they saw these aspects alone, then separated them. From each fragment, each formed a separate and independent field, a specialty to master.

## Vision Darkened

Sin's third effect on seeing is far more intuitive, yet worth considering. It depends on the other two effects: on hijacked vision and fragmented vision. The sons of Lamech darkened their vision by taking their special fields of cultivation separately. In this, they lost a vision of creation as referential, derivative, subordinate. As their first mother Eve had done with the fruit, they did to the whole creation. They saw creation's content, its aesthetic form, and its purpose not as being about God's glory but as abstractions, qualities in themselves, to be adapted and used. Their vision, darkened by being cut off from God's eye, is reduced to mere objectivity; thus, they cannot see the glory of God in created things.

Paul may have had this darkening effect in mind when he wrote, "We fix our eyes not on what is seen, but on what is unseen, since what is seen is temporary, but what is unseen is eternal" (2 Cor. 4:18).

He wrote here not of two parallel universes but of two ways of seeing one reality—one radiant in glorifying one invisible God in many visible aspects, the other objective, fragmented, opaque.

## As If . . .

Imagine the rose window at Notre Dame Cathedral in all its color, its coherent and detailed composition, its architectural and structural integrity, and its vivid narrative. Sunlight shines through this window, radiating through the colored glass fragments, illuminating the story of Christ in his last judgment, and lighting the inner spaces. Let this stand for creation's original translucency.

Now for opacity: Responding to this window like caricatures of Lamech's three sons, we might say, "Now, how can we use this window? Here's an idea! Let's nail plywood over the outside of the window opening. Now let us build a scaffold inside, so we can climb up close. We'll mount floodlights on those columns to get a really good look at it. Set the generator behind that screen over there. Say, this bit of blue glass would look great as a pendant! I've heard that red glass has gold in it; how could we extract that gold?" No more translucency; no more light coming in from a mysterious star at an incalculable distance, bringing its radiance close through every colored fragment to the enormous design and to the interior. No more story, no more "about." This is opacity. Jabal, Jubal, and Tubal-Cain teach us how to put up the plywood as they did. This opacity the Teacher explores in Ecclesiastes. Without referential transparency "under the sun," allowing us to see God, every created pleasure goes flat.

We have not been entirely clear about this opacity that results from our rejection of creation's God-glorifying translucency. Do we lose the transparency of creation or replace the sun with a different light source? Both. We imagine that we see truth objectively, that we appreciate beauty for its intrinsic qualities alone and that we recognize power and purpose when we see them. Instead, we see them "according to our lights," in an attempt to master these qualities, so that their glory reflects toward us. The sun's radiance through the rich, intricate glass window is lost to the scaffolding crew. We have despised it, so we can pretend to be its designer, builder, and illuminator. These show our power to seize, comprehend, appreciate, get results. We commandeer God's glory, hiding behind a layer of four-by-eight-foot objectivity.

Only the Holy Spirit pulls off the plywood, revealing our sin and God's glory in creation and in our redemption. Until then, we remain in our blindness, imagining our vision is more or less objective and right, or subjective and right. We resist any suggestion that our vision has been warped. Let us set aside for now this work of the Holy Spirit in regeneration and sanctification, promising to take it up again in its later place.

Meanwhile we may look to these three culture leaders not for legitimate cultural leadership but as pioneers of our own distortion. We are their sons and daughters. They do not overtly argue against the primacy of God; rather he is not noticed, has a certain invisibility in the story. The text refers to the first two as the fathers of those who followed their specialty; they themselves follow their first parents. Eve and Adam spurned God's eye, his beliefs, his pleasures, and his power for their own. Here the heirs of their disobedience further degrade the cultural mandate: they usurp God's mastery over his discourse and theirs, together with its goal in his supreme glory; they objectify God's glory and fragment its three aspects into three parts of their own. As their influence has persisted, so God's Word persists to expose it.

## Distorted Vision in Later Scriptures

Sin distorts vision in three ways: it hijacks, it fragments, and it darkens.

God targets sin's first effect, a person supplanting God as first Beholder, when he gives instructions to prevent it in the use of the tabernacle. God restricts the use of the special anointing oil and the incense to his audience alone (Ex. 30:32, 37). God reserved to himself the pleasure of these special symbols; he forbade his people to use them for private, personal pleasure, though other formulations of oil and of incense were expected and not forbidden. By this restriction, God reminded the Israelites that he alone is the first viewer, the one whose pleasure has primacy.

The fat of sacrificial animals was considered the best cut of meat, and all of it—all the fat from the shared meal of the fellowship offering and even from ordinary meat for daily use—God kept for himself (Lev. 7:23–25). Eli's sons, ignoring this marker of God's primary aesthetic pleasure, grabbed this best of the best from the offerings of pious worshipers, savoring as a private indulgence this symbol that God is the primary audience (1 Sam. 2:15–17, 25), the one whose delight has primacy. Their notorious sin earned them a notorious end.

David, in his adultery with Bathsheba, had imagined that his own eye was primary. He saw her, he desired her, and he sent for her. In his song of repentance, Psalm 51, David compares God's hiding his face from David's sin—ceasing to see it—to blotting out David's guilt, making it cease to exist, as if he were to say, "When you stop looking at my sin, it will disappear." God's eye is first and strong! Many more such examples may come to the reader's mind.

Sin's second effect on seeing, the rebellious wrenching of beauty from truth and from power, appears throughout Scripture. Consider a few examples.

In God's name Isaiah warns his countrymen who separate private aesthetic indulgence from the Lord's power: "Woe to those who rise early in the morning to run after their drinks, who stay up late at night till they are inflamed with wine. They have harps and lyres at their banquets, pipes and timbrels and wine, but they have no regard for the deeds of the LORD, no respect for the work of his hands" (Isa. 5:11–12). No word here condemns the use of musical instruments or of wine; the only thing condemned is private pleasure with disregard for God, his work, and his preferences.

King David describes God's rules as "sweeter than honey" (Ps. 19:10). This sounds pious but outside our experience. David knows something we do not. We can imagine aesthetic beauty in God's law only with difficulty, but David grasps what we lost years ago: the unity of beauty with truth and power. And it tastes good to him.

God condemns, through Amos, Israel's isolation of aesthetic beauties in their worship, and ignoring the truth and righteous power that should accompany them: "I hate, I despise your religious festivals; your assemblies are a stench to me. Even though you bring me burnt offerings and grain offerings, I will not accept them. Though you bring choice fellowship offerings, I will have no regard for them. Away with the noise of your songs! I will not listen to the music of your harps. But let justice roll on like a river, righteousness like a never-failing stream!" (Amos 5:21–24).

King Jehoiakim burned the scroll containing God's Word given through the prophet Jeremiah, using his God-given power to attack God's truth. "Whenever Jehudi had read three or four columns of the scroll, the king cut them off with a scribe's knife and threw them into the firepot, until the entire scroll was burned in the fire. The king and all his attendants who heard all these words showed no fear, nor did they tear their clothes" (Jer. 36:23–24). Much good did it do him (Jer. 36:29–31).

Sin's third effect—that we see no light through created objects, no reference to God and his glory—shouts to us through Isaiah: "Half of the wood he burns in the fire; over it he prepares his meal, he roasts his meat and eats his fill. He also warms himself and says, 'Ah! I am warm; I see the fire.' From the rest he makes a god, his idol; he bows down to it and worships. He prays to it and says, 'Save me! You are my god!' (Isa. 44:16–17). Isaiah's carpenter (v. 13) doesn't see what is there and also sees it wrong. Blind to the glory of the one true God in this hand-clapping tree of the field, he crafts from its fallen substance artifacts to serve his own purposes, the idol no less than the barbecue.

Jesus, master of the parable, described ordinary objects pointing to luminous truth, knowing well that some eyes could not see his meaning beneath the objects. He used these rhetorical puzzles to distinguish those with ears to hear from those who lacked them.

John the apostle, when he directs his "dear children" (1 John 2:1), "Do not love the world or anything in the world" (2:15), surely has in mind an eye that sees and loves opaque objects but does not see through them the light of God who made the world, "the true light that gives light to everyone [that] was coming into the world" (John 1:9).

The apostle Paul recaps sin's effects on our vision in its three now-familiar aspects (Rom. 1:18–32).[4] He explains why we deserve God's anger, calling out our guilty misinterpretation in three exchanges. Ignoring the revelation of God's glory, we instead give our full attention to substitutes: we have exchanged God's

---

4. I am indebted for this insight to Dr. Peter Wallace.

glory for images (1:23), "the truth about God for a lie" (1:25), and "natural sexual relations for unnatural ones" (1:26). Paul notes our perversion of the same three aspects we found in Genesis: forms with their attendant aesthetics, truth with its utter "about-God-ness," and practices signaling our inclinations, will, and purpose.

## A Personal Example

We heirs of Jabal, Jubal, and Tubal-Cain have longed ever since to extract purer and purer principles so that we can grasp and master their essence. Often our first move toward mastery is, like theirs, decontextualization. We rule out of court God's larger context, the about-God-ness of created things—not by direct attack but by presumed irrelevancy—and imagine ourselves the champions of meaning. We defend an object or ideal or principle as if we alone can save it from perversions. Never mind that the meaning we preserve is our own without regard for God.

And we have done this for years. My wife and I discovered, during a mid-1990s visit to the Barnes Foundation collection of paintings in Philadelphia, that no placards, labels, or explanatory notes were posted with the paintings displayed there. At that time, they offered no tours (though they are now allowed) and prohibited even informal, private guidance. The object of these strictures, we were told, was to maintain the freedom of each work to speak for itself according to recognized and self-evident aesthetic standards, liberated from imposed meaning. They fenced the paintings against imposed context to preserve viewers' experience of the work.

I too decontextualize. After years as a working singer-songwriter, I set about to study the Bible to learn how to write better songs. I intended to do this using the aesthetic and rhetorical principles I knew must be there. I wanted to master songwriting, so I spent what turned into five years in full-time theological studies at Westminster Theological Seminary. All for honing my art to use with a better biblical and theological foundation. Instead God restrained me and drew me to himself. He mastered me kindly and showed me what a child, and probably the reader, could see: that beauty is personal and always found in context, in God, and that Christ alone can restore the context I have broken.

Jabal, Jubal, and Tubal-Cain may have been headed full-tilt on this decontextualizing trajectory, until the flood cut off their line. Still, the text suggests they became cultural fathers to many others. Not even the flood could break the chain of sin in the hearts of Shem, Ham, and Japheth, the redeemed survivors, grandsons of the other Lamech (Gen. 5:28–32). We, their successors, show that we keep their road in our three fields of human endeavor—pure science (for knowledge's sake alone), technology (that puts accomplishment first), and the arts (kept free from the demands of power and ideology, for pure aesthetic expression).

A little-discussed effect of sin on our vision is our hijacking, fragmenting, and darkening of the shared vision we were given, and we add flat denial. We assume we see all things well. Christians assume we see objects and evaluate them according to the same abstract principles God uses. As if we were to say, "Is it true? If so, this is because God sees it that way too. Is it beautiful? Of course; God, in giving us beauty, followed objective aesthetic standards. Does it work? Naturally; God uses and endorses our criteria for effectiveness, our standards for objective right and wrong." By denying sin's effects on our seeing, we presume to subject God to the principles of truth, beauty, and power that we have imagined, rather than locating truth, beauty, and power in him.

We will discuss later the restoration of vision in Christ; for now, it is enough to notice that these three effects of sin on the vision of Lamech's sons, lightly described in Genesis, persist in us and find confirmation throughout the Scriptures.

## READ, REFLECT, DISCUSS, SING——————————

1. Suggested reading: "The Dynamic Heart Corrupted," chapter 3 of *The Dynamic Heart in Daily Life: Connecting Christ to Human Experience* by Jeremy Pierre.
2. Q1. When did you dislike a book or a movie that your family or friends liked, or liked what they disliked? When did something impress you with its truth, excellence, or beauty when your friends didn't appreciate it? How did you resolve the difference, even in your own mind?
3. Q2. When have you had a simple pleasure, just plain fun? When did you feel guilty for having fun? What do you think now about pleasure's connection to truth, based on your own experience?
4. Sing: "Amazing Grace," verses 1 and 2.

# Chapter 7

# MY DISTORTED VISION

*If your eyes are unhealthy, your whole body will be full of darkness.*
*If then the light within you is darkness, how great is that darkness!*
—MATTHEW 6:23

Scripture introduces us, in Genesis and later texts, to the three principal effects of sin on interpretation. Like our ancestors and their trusted serpentine counselor, we steal God's role as first seer, we break up the unity of his glory into separate fields of endeavor, and we kill those fields' witness to the Creator. This is not just a tempest in a pot of herbal Bible tea; these beliefs work in each of us, scholars and all. We like principles; they're easier to master than God. We recognize our autonomy only with great difficulty, yet we know it intimately.

## My Vision Hijacked: I See First

Consider the impact of sin's first effect on our aesthetics, the human pretension to be the viewer. I, the number one aesthetic audience, stand by my inalienable right to my private personal preferences. I might even stand for yours too, so nobody can challenge mine. The proverb "There's no accounting for taste" means more than that one cannot explain differences in private tastes and preferences; it means no one needs to explain himself. "I'll eat anything but Brussels sprouts." "Whatever turns you on." "It doesn't matter what you believe, as long as you're sincere." "Everyone's entitled to an opinion." Private preference trumps all.

We cling just as tightly, though, to the universality of our private tastes. "What could she possibly see in *him*?" "Don't they know how tacky that poster looks there?" "If it ain't country, it ain't music!" We take charge of our own tastes and order a burger today and pasta tomorrow, just as we like. Whether we take the low road of personal private preference or the high road of objective aesthetic standards, God disappears. He is either out of sight or demoted to be, like us, one who recognizes and follows objective aesthetic standards. God's loss is our gain; we take his primacy in aesthetics without even noticing.

True children of our age, we expect private aesthetic delight. What could be more appealing, more obvious? Whether we count beauty as objective, reasoning that God gives us a sense of it just like his own because it is obvious in creation, or as subjective, reasoning that our preferences are simply our own and are valid as such. In the beauty envisioned here, though, we might not acknowledge God's view, nor do we see him referentially through the beauty of his creation. We may assume a sort of aesthetic deism: God, having given us a sense of beauty, stands back to let us practice it on our own. We are the first seer, the primary one. This compelling story line puts us in charge; it seems natural and fitting.

"It's on my bucket list." Most activities on people's bucket lists—the things they dream of doing before they die—focus on collecting memories of pleasant or otherwise satisfying personal experiences. They focus on collecting aesthetics. Even the good we want to do, the public services and benevolences, seem to find their place on our lists chiefly by appealing to our self-image as a doer of good; the subtext goal is private, personal satisfaction. With a genteel jerk of the thumb, we direct God again to the back seat.

## My Vision Fragmented: Siloing

Sin's second effect on seeing infuses us like bad breath. We separate aesthetic experiences from truth and from doing, expecting that each function independently. Many compelling reasons argue this move; we want to protect each area of discourse from enslavement to another. We've seen art as political and social propaganda, art pulling the plow of evangelism, art constrained and needing liberation. A corrective insists that aesthetics operates in its own special area, away from other aspects of discourse, such as truth or practicality.

The romantic movement of the eighteenth and nineteenth centuries declared art's independence with the slogan *L'art pour l'art*, "Art for art's sake." "Art itself—music, literature, drama, painting—took on a virtually religious status for the Romantic sensibility. In a world made mechanical and soulless by science, the pursuit of beauty for its own sake assumed extraordinary psychological importance."[1]

---

1. Richard Tarnas, *The Passion of the Western Mind: Understanding the Ideas That Have Shaped Our World View* (New York: Ballantine, 1991), 373.

"Art for art's sake" argues the freedom of art from constraint by goals outside itself—political, ideological, or commercial goals. Art and graphic design, in service to rhetoric, polemic, propaganda, marketing, evangelism, and church-growth efforts, exercise power in proportion to the affections they stir in us. Even when they do good, this good does not qualify as pure art. Pure art has been called autotelic, meaning much the same as the slogan. The slogan and the academic moniker assume that the proper reader-viewer response to "art for art's sake" is restricted to affections— enjoyment or perhaps pathos, independent of logos or ethos. Indeed, this seems the whole point.

> I have suggested that at the very center of the institution [of high art] is a passionate commitment to the importance of perceptual contemplation of works of art, and more particularly, to aesthetic contemplation. And I have argued that the delight attained in aesthetic contemplation is good. It constitutes, so far forth, a facet in the attainment of our human destiny. The attainment of that delight typically requires, I suggested, certain modes of separation of art from ordinary life.[2]

While art's independence originally intended to preserve our essential humanity, isolated aesthetics could just as easily serve commercial purposes. MGM wrapped the Latin version of this slogan around its trademark roaring lion in its early films. Used in this way, the slogan argues that art exists for experience's sake and no other, as if to say, "Leave our artists alone so they can give us catharsis or pleasure. Require of them no service to church, to science, to commerce, or to government." Art, whether it serves idealistic or commercial purposes, relies on singling out aesthetic considerations from all other aspects of discourse, of what people say and do.

We silo aesthetics to save us from being mastered by desire, sometimes so we can master unruly desires with truth. Christians, who trust God's Word, his eternal Logos, often look to our reason to rule our affections. We seldom *say* that our reason is just a touch less fallen than our fallen emotions; we believe it, though, and rely on reason to tame and sanctify our unruly emotions.

> Whether we like it or not, the abundance of images, ceremonial beauty, the visual triumph of liturgy, and purely visual symbolism—all these things were the main source of all the medieval and later errors in the Roman and Orthodox Churches. . . . images also teach: they give a resume' of the

---

2. Nicholas Wolterstorff, *Art in Action* (Grand Rapids, MI: Eerdmans, 1980), 193.

Bible and Christian doctrine in altarpieces, stained-glass windows, and bas-reliefs: "These are like stories written for the simple and ignorant." However, even so these images produce a feeling of adoration that goes far beyond mere teaching.[3]

All images include within themselves the same danger [utter falsehood]. Thus, theologians, priests and pastors are contaminated by the relentless triumph of images. . . . By allying itself with images, Christianity gains (perhaps!) efficacy, but destroys itself, its foundation, and its content.[4]

Ordinary passions, if they are not to run away with us, must serve common sense; it stands to reason! Dorothy L. Sayers says as much, explaining about *Gaudy Night*, one of her best detective novels, "In the meantime, the detective-plot situation was concerned with a woman [the villain] in whom the emotions had gained control of the reason."[5] A familiar formula in her age, and widespread even today. We have seen how emotions can get people into trouble. Reason's cool voice can help keep people safe. Our reason, though, is sometimes hard pressed to stay in the driver's seat.

Human emotions are fallen and can be unruly. Our feelings, and the pictures and stories that stir them, must wait their turn, move to the back of the bus. A movie, a song, a picture can stir tears or deep darkness or uncontrolled giggles; only rarely does our intellect put us in such a vulnerable position. Aesthetics is the flamboyant uncle who always shows up at inconvenient times and embarrasses us. We cannot quite disown him, but we can distance ourselves from him, smiling and rolling our eyes. We hope, if not think, that our reason can protect us; it is at least more reliable at a party.

Aesthetics also have a proper, helpful place in life. Strong emotions can stir noble words and actions—faithfulness in marriage, heroic deeds, compassion, mercy. These and other emotions draw us in, enrich us. Still, emotions' power to stir us to good easily gets leveraged by systems intent on influencing us.

To keep our good emotions safe from manipulation, people have built walls of ideas around aesthetics to protect beauty from abuse by church, government, or academy. They reason, in effect, "If church people, politicians, scientists, and scholars would just stop trying to control our feelings to get what they want, these

3. Jacques Ellul, *The Humiliation of the Word*, trans. Joyce Main Hanks (Grand Rapids, MI: Eerdmans, 1985), 184.

4. Ellul, *Humiliation of the Word*, 202–3.

5. Dorothy L. Sayers, *The Mind of the Maker* (New York: Harcourt, Brace, 1941; San Francisco: HarperSanFrancisco, 1987), 76.

distortions of aesthetics would stop, and our feelings would be free to do good." Some imagine establishing a safety zone for aesthetics, subject to no authority but its own internal consistency. Some philosophers call it art. Abraham Kuyper invokes Calvin in arguing for art as an independent cultural category, free of everything, even of Christian doctrine.

> The logic of the mind may not scorn the feelings of the heart, nor should the love of the beautiful silence the voice of conscience. However holy religion may be, it must keep within its own bounds, lest, in crossing its lines, it degenerates into superstition, insanity, or fanaticism.
>
> When Scripture mentions the first appearance of art, in the tents of Jubal, who invented the harp and the organ, Calvin emphatically reminds us that this passage treats of "excellent gifts of the Holy Spirit." He declares that in the artistic instinct God had enriched Jubal and his posterity with rare endowments. And he frankly states that these inventive powers of art prove most evident testimonies of the divine bounty. More emphatically still, he declares, in his commentaries on Exodus, that "all the arts come from God and are to be respected as divine inventions."[6]

Wolterstorff, likewise, argues for art's independence from other ideals.

> Down through the ages, pietists and radical social reformers alike have characteristically dealt with the arts by failing or refusing to acknowledge the aesthetic as a dimension independent of the moral and religious. Either they take no note of the aesthetic whatsoever; or they assume that aesthetic value is decisively determined by moral or religious value. Books are burned, statues decapitated, paintings ripped with never so much as a glance at their aesthetic quality. If we are to attain clarity on the interaction of the aesthetic dimension with the moral and religious dimensions, we shall first off have to acknowledge the independence of the aesthetic. Not only is beauty neither truth nor goodness. Truth and goodness do not determine beauty.[7]

Some Christians envision aesthetics as the best way to lead people to God and to draw them closer to him. Ironically, one feels the weakness in the "reason first, practice and feelings later" approach to Christian discipleship. Having grown dissatisfied with the doctrine-first approach that many evangelicals take

---

6. Abraham Kuyper, *Lectures on Calvinism* (Peabody, MA: Hendrickson, 2008; originally Grand Rapids, MI: Eerdmans, 1931), 137.
7. Wolterstorff, *Art in Action*, 172–73.

to evangelism, some wonder if an appeal to good emotions, holy loves and desires, might help us toward better beliefs and better living. James K. A. Smith has proposed a more human path, an aesthetic and practical path, to whole discipleship, including right beliefs.

> Liturgies—whether "sacred" or "secular"—shape and constitute our identities by forming our most fundamental desires and our most basic attunement to the world. In short, liturgies make us certain kinds of people, and what defines us is what we love. They do this because we are the sorts of animals whose orientation to the world is shaped from the body up more than from the head down. Liturgies aim our love to different ends precisely by training our hearts through our bodies.[8]

Our loves and our desires, Smith says, are "pre-cognitive," and "our ultimate love/desire is shaped by practices, not ideas."[9] Maybe the cool voice of reason should step back.

In *The Beauty of the Infinite*, Hart argues that the only proper Christian apologetic is noncoercive, and that such an appeal can be made first and only through beauty. While not divorcing beauty from truth, an aesthetic appeal must launch a unified Christian apologetic; beauty leads the way. "Making its appeal first to the eye and heart, as the only way it may 'command' assent, the church cannot separate truth from rhetoric or from beauty."[10] By this argument, the beauty of the Christian faith should be presented first, if the reasons for faith are ever to appeal.

Begbie hints that faith and theology can serve aesthetics, that Christ can lead us to beauty, by which to better understand and practice art: "The most fruitful model for beauty for the artist will be found not by attempting to distill some formal principle from the contingent processes of the created world, but by directing our attention first of all to the redeeming economy of God which culminates in Jesus Christ."[11]

We carve off aesthetics to protect our feelings from manipulation, to use feelings for discipleship, to improve our persuasion, or to support our feelings by our faith. Art, the concept used to protect us or help us live more humanly through aesthetics, rarely takes account of God's eye. By it we often effectively exclude

8. James K. A. Smith, *Desiring the Kingdom* (Grand Rapids, MI: Baker Academic, 2009), 25.
9. Ibid, 27.
10. David Bentley Hart, *The Beauty of the Infinite: The Aesthetics of Christian Truth* (Grand Rapids, MI: Eerdmans, 2003), 4.
11. Jeremy Begbie, *Voicing Creation's Praise: Towards a Theology of the Arts* (Edinburgh: T&T Clark, 1991), 225.

God from our experiences; Eve and Adam did something like this. By it we often isolate aesthetic values from the other aspects of God's glory, like Lamech's three sons did. Art-the-concept is defined by our sinful fragmentation of God's glory. The works themselves can do us good, more good perhaps than the concept can.

The separation these scholars argue gets my ear because it seems to justify what I already feel: my pleasures are central; I may enjoy private delights or master them for good use; I may consider aesthetics in a category separate—either higher or lower—than Christian doctrines.

"Aw, Dad . . ." I have tried, foolishly perhaps, to springboard discussions from a family movie night. I asked questions of our children about a movie we were watching at home. Their reply has become a family proverb: "Aw, Dad, can't we just watch the movie?" Same impulse at work here: aesthetics is about pleasure, and it does its best work when it works alone, independent of truth and power. No glory arrows here; this is all just for fun, right? Siloing pleasure wasn't good for the kiddos, and it isn't good for me.

We face now crowd-sourced aesthetics. Who needs to distinguish between objective aesthetics and subjective? The internet can show us aesthetics that "work." We can count YouTube hits and track what most people like, what they think is pleasant, what attracts, what repels. We can predict results fairly reliably, so we know how to present a product, a candidate, a ministry with greatest success. We can craft our photos, paintings, books, songs, advertisements, brochures, websites, Facebook pages, blogsites for maximum effectiveness. We achieve this by singling out power from truth and beauty, giving it a special prominence that signals its chief importance. Power—influence over people's decisions—holds prominence over truth and beauty and so receives their service. God, bless him, need raise no objection but may stand back to notice and acknowledge our effectiveness. He might even thank us. Lamech's three sons can thank us too for preserving their legacy.

## My Vision Darkened: Opacity

Sin's third effect on seeing, the loss of transparency of everything seen by the infected eye, touches us everywhere, but most obviously in the popular conflict between science and faith. Truth is said to be objective, a last referee for all disagreements. We assume that we can recognize truth when we see it, that our interpretation is basically reliable, even if a correction or two could be in order.

We hear of this from our friend C. S. Lewis, who describes a conversation between a dead painter, having come from hell to heaven for a visit, and a painter friend. They discuss painting's goal:

"When you painted on earth—at least in your earlier days—it was because you caught glimpses of Heaven in the earthly landscape. . . . Why, if you are interested in the country only for the sake of painting it, you'll never learn to see the country."

"But that's just how a real artist *is* interested in the country."

"No. You're forgetting," said the Spirit. "That was not how you began. Light itself was your first love: you loved paint only as means of telling about light."

"Oh, that's ages ago," said the Ghost. "One grows out of that."[12]

Cornelius Van Til pulls off the final mask. He writes about philosophy and science—we can associate this field with the truth content of our earlier triad—but we can apply his remarks by analogy to forms with their aesthetic properties. Writing about the effects of sin on interpretation, he goes a bit farther; he suggests that the eye that sees objects without reference to God sees them as referring not to themselves only but to persons *without* God.

> [W]e shall have to concern ourselves first and primarily with the two oppos-
> ing *principles* of interpretation. The Christian principle of interpretation is
> based upon the assumption of God as the final and self-contained reference
> point. The non-Christian principle of interpretation is that man as self-
> contained is the final reference point. . . . In fact, it is in spite of appearances
> that the distinction between the two principles must be maintained. The
> point is that the "facts of experience" must actually be interpreted in terms
> of Scripture if they are to be intelligible at all. In the last analysis the "facts
> of experience" must be interpreted either in terms of man taken as auton-
> omous, or they must be interpreted in terms of God.[13]

Van Til writes about the impact of sin on knowledge for the apologetic discussions of Christianity with modern science in his time. We recognize the distortion he describes from our studies among Lamech's sons. When we see things with reference to ourselves alone, the light goes out of everything. When we assume that truth, beauty, or power are self-evident, we presume that we see just fine and that sin's blinding and distorting effects on our interpretation, on our seeing, simply don't exist.

---

12. C. S. Lewis, *The Great Divorce* (New York: Macmillan/Collier, 1946), 80–81 (emphasis in the original).

13. Cornelius Van Til, *A Christian Theory of Knowledge* (Phillipsburg, NJ: Presbyterian and Reformed, 1969), 44–45 (emphasis in the original).

# Works of Craft

We have seen paintings, songs, sculptures, all sorts of works misused and abused—wrongly condemned or wrongly approved. We have watched lavish Super Bowl advertisements for their entertainment value, or we have avoided them, not wanting to be exposed to their compelling influence. We have heard pop music in its sickeningly sweet spot, or we have declined to listen, avoiding contamination; we have seen popular media used to market vacation resorts and ministries with equal effectiveness. We have heard of the thoughtless condemnation of carefully, sometimes devoutly crafted objects, for fear of their misuse. Aesthetic works needed and still need protecting from the abuses: worshipful adulation manipulated by the church (medieval and modern), condemnation or destruction by pietists, and abusive harnessing to commerce.

Philosophers of the nineteenth and twentieth centuries saved aesthetic works by protecting the independence of art. Aesthetic abuses of many kinds were well established, and protecting the good of artistic works was a mighty task. The separation of aesthetics from other human capabilities through the concept of art makes sense. Still, we see abuses commandeering aesthetics. We know that pornography and morally objectionable movies, video games, and music sell very well because they appeal to aesthetic senses.

Many artistic works may have been worth saving from misuse, but the cost of protecting art was high. Isolating aesthetics from ethics and doctrine altogether kept out their bad influence but also ruled out their good influence. The alternative, redemptive use has gone largely overlooked. God calls his people to see artistic works with him in Christ, considering how they handle all three aspects of his glory—the noetic, the aesthetic, and the ethical. In practice, most of us are accustomed to this process already. We evaluate movies and novels, noting their main point, their affective impact, their compelling effect. Working artists and viewers are accustomed to fitting the various aspects together. This integration had a lot to do with the popularity of folk music, protest music, and sixties' popular music; it spoke insightfully to the passions and concerns of a generation that had grown weary of Tin Pan Alley, which produced the pleasure-first, narrow band of moon-June-spoon songs of the forties and fifties. Only a redemptive approach can restore our feelings to God's eternal purposes in Jesus Christ.

For wholeness and redemption, we need Jesus, our Prophet, Priest, and King. We need his redemptive eye. God sees his own creation, delighted that it reflects his glory in three aspects: true, strong, and unutterably lovely. We were made to share that vision with him, but in losing that vision, we've been downgrading it—stealing it for our own, destroying its unity by breaking its aspects into parts, and killing ourselves by extinguishing creation's translucent referentiality. Christ is doing far more than giving us pleasure, convincing non-Christians, or supporting the arts; he is restoring all glory, and all aspects of glory, to God.

In God no conflict exists between aesthetics and truth, or aesthetics and power, yet our hearts so readily and persistently see the values we love only for their own sake and not for what they show about God. For God's people, this warped seeing is forgiven and diminishing, while a new vision—personal, unified, and transparent—grows so that we see and hear more and more with the psalmist: "The heavens declare the glory of God; the skies proclaim the work of his hands. Day after day they pour forth speech; night after night they reveal knowledge. They have no speech, they use no words; no sound is heard from them. Yet their voice goes out into all the earth, their words to the ends of the world" (Ps. 19:1–4).

## READ, REFLECT, DISCUSS, SING————————

1. Suggested reading: book 5 of *The Confessions of Saint Augustine*.
2. Q1. What entertainment do you prefer? Which entertainment do you like, but you have to stay on your guard? Why? How's that working?
3. Q2. Where have you heard that heart knowledge is better than head knowledge? Did you believe it? What do you think about it now?
4. Sing: "When I Survey the Wondrous Cross," verses 1 and 2.

# Chapter 8

# THE AESTHETIC EFFECTS OF SIN

*Stolen water is sweet; food eaten in secret is delicious!*
—PROVERBS 9:17

Evil makes us ugly. We turn our eyes away so as not to look at what it does in us. But we can look at the hard things with hope, remembering that our redemption in Jesus Christ is more powerful, and very beautiful to the Father. We can look in hope.

## What Happened to Seeing with God?

Like our forebears, we just know our feelings are our own. This affectionate presumption clings with special closeness to our age and forms one of the aesthetic effects of sin.

Jeremiah spoke God's Word to people who felt like we do: "Do not run until your feet are bare and your throat is dry. But you said, 'It's no use! I love foreign gods, and I must go after them'" (Jer. 2:25).

Notice here that the Israelites know their attractions are bad, but they think they cannot change them. They think their feelings just *are*, even if they are misguided. As a result, their feelings wind up driving the boat, or blowing it off course.

Does Jeremiah describe someone you know? But God commands them to change their feelings and their actions. He even appeals to other feelings they have right now—bare feet on hot, rough ground, and dry throats.

Like the Israelites of Jeremiah's day, we love what we love. We trust our feelings. If they are basically reliable, there is no need to change them. We can't change what we love, we say. After all, we know beauty and ugliness when we see them. We look at things, crafted or imagined, and assess them for their values, good or bad or neutral. We do not consider the way we see.

Adam and Eve abandoned co-participation in God's seeing for the autonomous seeing of rebellion. They wanted to be like God, "knowing good and evil" (Gen. 3:5), evaluating whatever they saw as if God were not already evaluating it, as if they had never shared God's eye. Their voluntary abandonment of God's sight did not blind them, but it twisted their seeing and ours.

We see with Adam's eyes. We assume the first audience role. We weigh everything we see, hear, taste, sniff, or touch according to its properties and its effect. When we assume that our own standards are correct, they become invisible. When we meet people who disagree, we may try to persuade them or just shrug and withdraw.

Critics review art, painting, sculpture, music, books, and movies for what they say and how they say it; we often critique movies and other popular media, including high art, for their content and impact. Family values? Sex, drugs, violence, bad language? Christians may ask how well the content suits a Christian worldview. We rarely question our evaluative vision, rarely ask about *how* we *see* it.

Think for a moment about *Gilligan's Island*, a TV show produced in the mid-1960s and still being aired. How do viewers get to this island, far from civilization? How do we manage to see these fascinating castaways in their adventures? We can see because the producers put a camera "there." We see without being seen. We cannot speak to the characters or give them anything, but they have no need for us. We have a passive, distant view, a bit like God, who can see everywhere, but without his love and care. They serve us; we cannot serve them, nor are we expected to. The show's delivery system implies that the characters are not our neighbors. Yes, they remind us of ourselves in their weaknesses and small selfishness, but we excuse them and ourselves. With no sex, drugs, violence, or bad language, this series passes our content test easily.

How does God see *Gilligan's Island*? Is he merely screening for sex, drugs, violence, language? Questions about content can serve a good purpose, but what they leave out shows how far we have fallen from our parents' first shared vision with God. The media give much more than content. They give a look at the world, infused with values, premises, assumptions. The media eye usually assumes that the viewer, reader, or listener has the right and ability to assess form, content, and purpose entirely alone; God is not in the picture. This assumption falls far short of our need. All of us, Christians and non-Christians, have assumed that people are the audience and that we should be. This is not to suggest we should ask, "What would Jesus watch?" assuming that his "entertainment needs" are like ours, only better. Rather we are called to ask, "How does God see this?" We ask him, "How do you see this?"

What became of our shared seeing with God? We lost it. Having begun to recognize this in broad terms, let us examine it in more detail, especially as it pertains to our aesthetic perception. We have as much right—even duty—to search out and organize the Bible's reflections on forms and aesthetics as we have to gather and organize the Bible's teachings about God's character and attributes, calling it theology. We might even call the study of the Bible's forms and aesthetics "theo-analogy."

## General Aesthetic Effects of Sin

Sin has permeated every aspect of our seeing: our minds, our wills, and our passions. Bible scholars refer to sin's warping of our understanding (Rom. 1:18–32; Eph. 4:18–21; 2 Cor. 4:4) as the noetic effects of sin, from the Greek word *nous*, meaning "mind."[1] The impact of sin on our wills, our ethics, seems obvious even to a child, and Christian thinkers have considered it at length. The ethical effects of sin bite us experientially and fill the pages of Scripture; from Genesis to Revelation the corrupting of man's will shouts. Every promise of redemption God gives in the context of sin's perversion of our ethics (Genesis 3–6, Judges, Isaiah, Ezekiel, Jeremiah, Hosea, Amos [notably 3:10], Malachi, Romans, Revelation—everywhere). The aesthetic effects of sin (and redemption!) cry out for deeper analysis and remedy. Here we examine sin's effects on our loves, our feelings, our affections—sin's impact on our aesthetic judgments.

Scripture rings with sin's distortions to our sense of beauty, our attractions and aversions. We have already reflected on Genesis' account of the aesthetic sensibilities that Adam and Eve shared with God in their innocence, and the perversion of these sensibilities. We noted three chief effects, and now we go on to trace these through other Scriptures and to organize some systematic observations.

Ever since our parents' disobedience, our normal approach to pleasure goes wrong in multiple ways. Let me suggest six main areas.

1.  We define pleasure and pain in terms of the autonomous—or more accurately, auto-aesthetic—human experience: private indulgence. "I need

---

1. William Edgar, introduction to *Christian Apologetics*, 2nd ed., by Cornelius Van Til (Phillipsburg, NJ: Presbyterian and Reformed, 2003), 4.

a little comfort." "I just love this!" "That makes me sick!" We cultivate and even defend our own private tastes. I make aesthetic meaning, my private interpretation, alone.

2. We compartmentalize the three aspects of God's glory into three separate areas of human culture—content, form, and purpose—each to serve human mastery. We don't do this self-consciously. We instinctively prefer one over others and can play each against the other. Think of our universities, with their schools of "pure" sciences, their art schools and conservatories, and their schools of engineering, computer science, and graphic design. Think too of our churches, where worship wars pit doctrinal truth in words against delights of poetry, music, and drama. We try to "integrate" theology with art and culture, as if they were intrinsically distinct and equal disciplines.

3. We focus on aesthetic properties and ignore our fallen aesthetic senses by which we recognize and evaluate those properties; we suppress the distortions to these senses (Rom. 1:18). We consider aesthetic properties as objects to be manipulated and mastered. We seek to master creation's forms, interpreting their glory as merely intrinsic to the forms themselves. Subtly, though, we commandeer God's glory in them for ourselves; we assume that we are rightly qualified to recognize, evaluate, and use the aesthetic properties of creation's forms without regard to God. God saw his creation's forms as "very good" because they corresponded to his own glory. He sees them still, so we can still see these forms, despite sin's twisted blurring of our aesthetic vision.

These first three we have considered broadly in the preceding chapters; here we consider chiefly their aesthetic ramifications, and add others.

4. We feel pain and shame; we feel bad in situations where we were made to feel good.

5. We delight in the evil and the ugly; we feel good in situations where we were made to feel bad.

6. We interpret our pleasures and pains in terms of our own capacities, either as lack, deficit, and need or as enough. Our satisfaction and gratitude diminish and disappear.

Let us explore these basic effects in greater detail, with Scriptures and examples. We begin with a baseline and a puzzle from Psalm 19:9–10:

The fear of the LORD is pure,
    enduring forever.
The decrees of the LORD are firm
    and all of them are righteous.
They are more precious than gold,
    than much pure gold;
they are sweeter than honey,
    than honey from the honeycomb.

—Psalm 19:9–10

Who finds God's rules sweeter than honey? Even leaving aside our difficulty with loving the firmness, righteousness, and power of God's decrees, we are left to wonder that somewhere there is someone who savors God's decrees like honey and that we got left out of this delight—that something may be wrong with our tasters. The idea of sweet rules makes us shake our heads. The psalmist finds God's rules sweet. Everyone should. We do not. Could our taster be out of whack?

## Specific Aesthetic Effects of Sin

People are passionate by design. We feel and express ourselves feelingly because a passionate God made us like himself, to share and reflect his feelings. Something is wrong with our aesthetic senses. Our passions, real as ever, have jumped the track, have reversed field. Our loves and revulsions still work, but they work wrong. In fact, they're coming to pieces. We don't love and enjoy what we should. We love and enjoy what we shouldn't. Our impulse to follow our affections—what feels intuitively good, pleasing, attractive, wholesome, and worthwhile—is unreliable, sometimes dangerous.

   We know our pleasures are not on the square, even when we do not know God. Popular media too numerous to mention here give poignant voice to our conflicted feelings about our pleasures. The ancient authors of Scripture knew this too. Their reflections corroborate what we've already suspected, and have something to tell us that can do us good. We'll examine a few passages. Some texts have aesthetics in the foreground, others in the background. I have emphasized aesthetic clues.

- "How long [asks Lady Wisdom] will you who are simple *love* your simple ways? How long will mockers *delight* in mockery and fools *hate* knowledge?" (Prov. 1:22).
- "Wisdom will enter your heart, and knowledge will be *pleasant* to your soul" (Prov. 2:10).

- "Their [the arrogant's] hearts are *callous* and *unfeeling*, but I *delight* in your law" (Ps. 119:70).
- "Wisdom will save you from the ways of wicked men, from men whose words are perverse, who have left the straight paths to walk in dark ways, who *delight* in doing wrong and *rejoice* in the perverseness of evil" (Prov. 2:12–14).

Notice here our old friends, the triad of God's glory, perverted by wicked men: their words as content, the paths they walk as purpose, and especially for our notice here, their delights as aesthetics. The book of Proverbs reverberates with aesthetic evaluations, promises, and warnings like these, but we press on to other Bible passages.

- "They have harps and lyres at their banquets, pipes and timbrels and wine, but they have no regard for the deeds of the LORD, no respect for the work of his hands" (Isa. 5:12).
- "He had no beauty or majesty to *attract us* to him, nothing in his appearance that we should *desire* him" (Isa. 53:2).
- "A horrible and shocking thing has happened in the land: the prophets prophesy lies, the priests rule by their own authority, and my people *love* it this way. But what will you do in the end?" (Jer. 5:30–31).

God's people love lying prophecy and bad worship, and more: they love a distorted story, a never-ending now. They ignore God's story, a story with an ending that would terrify them, if they reread Moses and these other prophets.

- "You engaged in prostitution with the Assyrians too, because you were *insatiable*; and even after that, you still were not *satisfied*. Then you increased your promiscuity to include Babylonia, a land of merchants, but even with this you were not *satisfied*" (Ezek. 16:28–29).
- "You lie on beds adorned with ivory and lounge on your couches. You dine on choice lambs and fattened calves. You strum away on your harps like David and improvise on musical instruments. You drink wine by the bowlful and use the finest lotions, but you do not *grieve* over the ruin of Joseph" (Amos 6:4–6).

God sees how messed up our passions are, and he tells us about it. Let us try to assemble and organize these themes of aesthetic perversion. This is only a beginning, but we need it.

**We neither see God nor delight in him.** We do not delight in his Word, which is close to the same thing: "Their ears are closed so they cannot hear. The word of the LORD is offensive to them; they find no pleasure in it" (Jer. 6:10).

**We do not fear God.** We should fear him for his power in creation, by which he sustains our lives and blesses us. We should fear his judgment; our sin deserves his anger and horrible punishment, and we turn away, with a blind eye and deaf ear to our present peril and the misery that awaits us.

> "Hear this, you foolish and senseless people, who have eyes but do not see, who have ears but do not hear: Should you not fear me?" declares the LORD. "Should you not tremble in my presence? I made the sand a boundary for the sea, an everlasting barrier it cannot cross. The waves may roll, but they cannot prevail; they may roar, but they cannot cross it. But these people have stubborn and rebellious hearts; they have turned aside and gone away. They do not say to themselves, 'Let us fear the LORD our God, who gives autumn and spring rains in season, who assures us of the regular weeks of harvest.'"
> —Jeremiah 5:21–24

**We take pleasure in God's gifts without God.** Satan had in mind this effect of the fall when he made the accusation that Job was incapable of enjoying God, thereby indirectly accusing God of being incapable of regenerating people, of restoring to them the ability to love him for his own sake.

**We take created things out of context,** delighting in created things for their own goodness alone, without gratitude and without delighting in God's goodness, which he made them to reflect.

> Be careful that you do not forget the LORD your God. . . . Otherwise, when you eat and are satisfied, when you build fine houses and settle down, and when your herds and flocks grow large and your silver and gold increase and all you have is multiplied, then your heart will become proud and you will forget the LORD your God, who brought you out of Egypt, out of the land of slavery. . . . You may say to yourself, "My power and the strength of my hands have produced this wealth for me." But remember the LORD your God, for it is he who gives you the ability to produce wealth, and so confirms his covenant, which he swore to your ancestors, as it is today.
> —Deuteronomy 8:11–14, 17–18

**We love ideals, principles, excellence** instead of God and neighbor. Beauty, truth, goodness lose their about-ness, their godward referentiality, and become in our eyes objective, impersonal principles. We love these abstractions instead of loving and knowing God and neighbor. We were made to see God through every good thing. "I say to the LORD, 'You are my Lord; I have no good apart from you.' As for the saints in the land, they are the excellent ones, in whom is all my delight. The sorrows of those who run after another god shall multiply" (Ps. 16:2–4 ESV). We extract from God his personal qualities and characteristics, his glory in any aspect, call them "principles," other gods who will serve us.

**We delight in evil.** The urge to break a rule, or something more solid, just for the fun of it, seems to awaken in us from earliest memory. Those who live and work with children, even very young ones, can have their own early memories refreshed by a young rebel in a defiant instant. My frequenting of high-traffic men's restrooms reminds me that some of my fellows apparently like to destroy things. The temptation can reach me too; I am no better. Scripture knows us this way.

- "The wicked crave evil" (Prov. 21:10).
- "They cannot rest until they do evil; they are robbed of sleep till they make someone stumble" (Prov. 4:16).
- "Stolen water is sweet; food eaten in secret is delicious!" (Prov. 9:17).

**We are deprived of pleasures.** The harder we chase pleasure, the more it withdraws from us. Our simple pleasures, simple delights, get overwhelmed by our anxieties, our ingratitude, our craving, just as the seven years of plenty were eaten up by the seven years of famine in Pharaoh's dream.

- "Open wide your mouth and I will fill it. But my people would not listen to me" (Ps. 81:10–11).
- "A sluggard's appetite is never filled, but the desires of the diligent are fully satisfied" (Prov. 13:4).
- "She has not acknowledged that I was the one who gave her the grain, the new wine and oil, who lavished on her the silver and gold—which they used for Baal. Therefore I will take away my grain when it ripens, and my new wine when it is ready. I will take back my wool and my linen, intended to cover her naked body" (Hos. 2:8–9).

**We experience an entirely new set of feelings in our souls.** Fear, misery, sorrow, and shame come close to us. We were not made for mental suffering, though we have trouble imagining life without it. What a shock the first guilt feelings must have been to our first parents!

- "I was afraid because I was naked" (Gen. 3:10).
- "enmity" (Gen. 3:15)
- unmet "desire" and domineering "rule" (Gen. 3:16)
- "When I kept silent, my bones wasted away through my groaning all day long" (Ps. 32:3).

**We feel pain in our bodies.** Pain comes to all of us because of God's judgment for sin, though our present experience of pain can result from others' sins and from creation's subjection to futility, not always our own sin.

- "When you eat from it you will certainly die" (Gen. 2:17).
- "pains ... very severe" (Gen. 3:16)
- "painful toil," "thorns and thistles," "sweat of your brow," "return to the ground" (Gen. 3:17–19)
- "Oh, my anguish, my anguish! I writhe in pain. Oh, the agony of my heart! My heart pounds within me" (Jer. 4:19).

**Our senses are blunted, dull, numbed, and failing.** We become unfeeling, inured, sensibilities seared. We get bored. We want a little more than before. Like a drug addict, we want a bigger and bigger dose to get the high we seek.

- "Their hearts are callous and unfeeling" (Ps. 119:70).
- "Having lost all sensitivity, they have given themselves over to sensuality so as to indulge in every kind of impurity, and they are full of greed" (Eph. 4:19).
- "You struck them, but they felt no pain; you crushed them, but they refused correction" (Jer. 5:3).
- "They hit me," you will say, "but I'm not hurt! They beat me, but I don't feel it! When will I wake up so I can find another drink?" (Prov. 23:35).
- "[Their idols] have ears, but cannot hear, noses, but cannot smell. They have hands, but cannot feel, feet, but cannot walk, nor can they utter a sound with their throats. Those who make them will be like them, and so will all who trust in them" (Ps. 115:6–8).

**The fears and delights we have go out of joint.** Things that ought to please us do not. Things that ought to horrify us do not. Things terrify us that should not. We can blame media, but we should remember that what inures us also sells.

- "I said to myself, 'Come now, I will test you with pleasure to find out what is good.' But that also proved to be meaningless" (Eccl. 2:1).
- "People loved darkness instead of light because their deeds were evil (John 3:19b).
- "Do not call conspiracy everything this people calls a conspiracy; do not fear what they fear, and do not dread it. The LORD Almighty is the one you are to regard as holy, he is the one you are to fear, he is the one you are to dread" (Isa. 8:12–13).
- "Whenever Jehudi had read three or four columns of the scroll, the king cut them off with a scribe's knife and threw them into the firepot, until the entire scroll was burned in the fire. The king and all his attendants who heard all these words showed no fear, nor did they tear their clothes" (Jer. 36:23–24).
- "The sound of a windblown leaf will put them to flight. They will run as though fleeing from the sword, and they will fall, even though no one is pursuing them. They will stumble over one another as though fleeing from the sword, even though no one is pursuing them" (Lev. 26:36–37).

**We desire less than we should.** C. S. Lewis mentions this effect in his well-known passage about a child satisfied with playing in the mud when he's invited to a day at the shore. Lewis observes, "It would seem that Our Lord finds our desires not too strong, but too weak. . . . We are far too easily pleased." [2] Lewis highlights here sin's limiting effect on our sense of pleasure but overlooks its perverting effect, that we crave what God finds disgusting and find his delights repellant. The effects of sin are far more radical than merely making us too easily satisfied, a difference of degree. The nature of our desires and our satisfactions is twisted. We look for satisfaction in things that should send us rushing away.

**We crave and can't get enough.** Our perverted appetites always outstrip our satisfactions. This effect grows on us, like the well-known effect of street drugs: the user, through habituation, needs higher doses to achieve the earlier effects. We all need more and more of whatever it is to get less and less satisfaction—"an ever increasing craving for an ever diminishing pleasure," as C. S. Lewis puts it. [3]

**Our desires bloat,** becoming inordinate, exceeding their proper order. "[The wicked man] boasts about the cravings of his heart; he blesses the greedy and reviles the LORD" (Ps. 10:3).

2. C. S. Lewis, *The Weight of Glory and Other Addresses* (San Francisco: HarperOne, 2001), 26.
3. C. S. Lewis, *The Screwtape Letters* (San Francisco: HarperOne, 2001), 44.

**We recast our desires as unmet needs.** Trusting our own independent judgment, our taste buds, enables us to speak in deficit language. To conceal or justify our swollen cravings, we rename them needs, and thus entitled expectations. We call "never satisfied" admirable, heroic.

**We abandon gratitude.**

- "Although they knew God, they neither glorified him as God nor gave thanks to him" (Rom. 1:21).
- "What do you have that you did not receive? And if you did receive it, why do you boast as though you did not?" (1 Cor. 4:7).

**Sin does not repel us.** This is a form of blunting, but worth noting separately. We neither hate our sin nor loathe ourselves as we should.

- "Then you will remember your evil ways and wicked deeds, and you will loathe yourselves for your sins and detestable practices" (Ezek. 36:31).
- "You love evil rather than good, falsehood rather than speaking the truth. You love every harmful word" (Ps. 52:3–4).

## Solitary Pleasure

We substitute our solo passions for God's passions. Satan tempted Eve to imitate God's delight instead of sharing it. She became autonomous enjoyer and autonomous sufferer. C. S. Lewis explores this by analogy in his novel *Perelandra,* as he recasts Eve's temptation in a new unfallen world, tantalizing its solitary Lady with proffered delicious disobedience.[4] Ever since the fall, we have enjoyed whatever we thought we wanted, or suffered deprivation or pain, alone. Further, we imagine that only other people see us with pleasure or disgust, so we play to their audience alone.

The Lamech of Genesis 4, Cain's descendant, sings a song to his wives, a strictly human audience. Lamech models arrogant discourse for his sons. Seth's descendants, by contrast, call on the name of the Lord (Gen. 4:25–26).

Consider some familiar cultural avenues for a similar autonomy in our own day.

In a novel, an often-invisible author sees all and offers the reader a godlike view. Movies and television offer the viewer an autonomous, passive seeing, to which he is to respond with his affections but usually not with action.

---

4. C. S. Lewis, *Perelandra* (New York: Macmillan, 1944), 128–39.

Pornography promises auto-aesthetic experience, free from the complications of context. Gaming can provide a private alternate reality of power, competition, cooperation, extreme feats of bravado and skill: adrenaline high without risk, social engagement without responsibility or love.

The internet caters in eye-trapping detail to our individual, private preferences. "Cookies" and a digitally long memory develop our personal profile of interests and tastes, offering to fulfill these in complete privacy.

But privacy isolates. In C. S. Lewis's *The Great Divorce*, those who occupied "the gray town," representing hell, kept moving farther and farther away from each other for greater and greater autonomy, resulting in ever-greater isolation.[5] One of the most compelling auto-aesthetic practices, prescription or illicit drug abuse, can also be one of the most isolating from man and God.

Songs, movies, novels, and videos lure us daily with just the message we want: that the good life consists in collecting good feelings in our memory. Since songs stick in my head, let me share some old examples; Frank Sinatra's "It Was a Very Good Year," Ronnie Milsap's "I Wouldn't Have Missed It for the World," Kenny Chesney's "Never Gonna Feel That Way Again" all suggest that personal pleasures and our memories of them comprise the good life.

The prodigal son in Jesus' parable thought so. The younger brother believed pleasure was solitary, saying in so many words, "Dad, I need you to sell everything you have so I can take my part away from you. I can't enjoy anything here with you!" The elder brother had the same idea of enjoyment; he complained that his dad never gave him the pleasures he thought he had earned: "Look! All these years I've been slaving for you and never disobeyed your orders. Yet you never gave me even a young goat so I could celebrate with my friends" (Luke 15:29). His idea of fun excludes the father but invites his friends. The father, like God, envisions his sons' delight as shared with himself. He tells his older son, "My son, . . . you are always *with me*" and then includes all good things he has, enjoyed together: "Everything I have is yours." He even casts shared enjoyment as their shared duty: "*We* had to celebrate" (vv. 31–32, emphasis added).

"Get in touch with your feelings." Our age treasures personal, private feelings, even unpleasant ones like anxiety, fear, inordinate craving, greed, envy, vengeful spite, wrath, pride, sensuality. Parts of the psychological movement, with a thousand popular spin-offs, focus on helping people turn inward to discover passions of all kinds—some with a healing perspective, some not. These inner worlds we readily define as private and personal; we turn inward on ourselves in a shrinking, downward spiral of introspection, with no goal but self-knowing and no exit.

5. C. S. Lewis, *The Great Divorce* (New York: Macmillan/Collier, 1946), 18–21.

# We Love a Sinful Story

We reject God's take on time, first given in his command forbidding the tree, in which he said, in effect, "I command you today; you obey me tomorrow, and our fellowship will continue; disobey tomorrow, and you will die." God's take on time may include a probationary period in Eden.[6] Obey me now, I reward you later with myself. Eve would not wait. These days we insist on reward now; let later look to itself. *Carpe diem.* Delayed gratification? We drink our coffee from a mug inscribed, "Life is uncertain. Eat dessert first."

We love a story we have written, a narrative of pleasure: we hope for pleasure, success, and honor now; we postpone or avoid painful duty and suffering and deny or ignore God's story, with its consequences.

- "Tomorrow will be like today, or even far better" (Isa. 56:12).
- "All the [false] other prophets were prophesying the same thing. 'Attack Ramoth Gilead and be victorious,' they said, 'for the LORD will give it into the king's hand'" (1 Kings 22:12).

We make up and love a story that differs from God's story in three key ways.

1. *We play lead:* "You will be like God" (Gen. 3:5).

    We love a story of our own heroism, in which even our disobedience gets counted to our credit. We love a story of victory and glory without suffering, humiliation, or death. If our story does involve personal sacrifice, the temptation may be like that of the Green Lady in *Perelandra,*[7] to make ourselves the tragic heroine, taking the place of Christ for the "good." If we must suffer, it is for our own glory, placing ourselves as the lead character. Our love of story is complicated by the many stories available to us in movies, books, news sources, fundraising materials, sermons, songs, conversations. All of these we find more or less appealing according to our complex loves and aversions, our beliefs and our goals.

2. *Happy ending without God:* "You will not certainly die" (Gen. 3:4).

    We love happy endings, even if achieved by a so-so hero. We can accept a tragic ending if the hero is good. We like short stories, tales that reach their satisfying conclusion without reference to God's final

---

6. John Murray, "The Adamic Administration," *Selected Lectures in Systematic Theology,* vol. 2 of *The Collected Writings of John Murray* (Edinburgh: Banner of Truth, 1977), 48.

7. Lewis, *Perelandra,* 112–19.

judgment or his glory. We recoil from stories that appear to end badly, even from God's story where it includes eternal judgment.

3. *God is not trustworthy; he is the problem, not my sin:* "God knows that . . . your eyes will be opened, and you will be like God" (Gen. 3:5).

  Our love of story often revolves around great threat or trouble, evil of a human or extra-human sort. Think of horror stories, war stories, spy stories, even noble outlaw stories. Think too of partisan political stories loved by fundraisers and news media. They work because we love the premise: that the main problem, the real threat, lies outside ourselves. Defeat the bad guys (or diseases or natural threats), and all will be well again! We assume that our first, biggest problem is our situation—what has been done to us, happened to us, caused our trouble. We are both the victim and the hero. Since external trouble and real enemies abound, this narrative premise appears attractively plausible. Plenty of families and nations have achieved a measure of unity and success by headlining external threats. Any internal weaknesses or evils are secondary and can be heroically overcome or sidelined. Self-questioning has little role in the stories that appeal to us.

The stories that attract us most can hide in tacit affections. They offer a big story that makes meaning of all the other stories we meet. Some well-loved, well-hidden stories' metanarratives:

- *Victimhood.* "Bad things always happen to me." Even more hidden: "God did it; he's not as good and strong as he's made out to be."
- *Cynicism.* "Everyone has a selfish reason for what he does." Except maybe me.
- *Perfectionism, hoop jumping.* "I am omnicompetent." Or I should be. Or I could be, with a little more effort. I must triumph, so it will be counted in my favor.
- *Entertainment-ism, boredom.* We collect good memories, earn easy significance, or just distract ourselves. When it works.
- *Blame-ism.* "If those people would only do right . . ." It's not that hard!
- *Blame shifting.* "I'm depraved because I'm deprived." "She's a good person who makes bad choices." "It isn't really my fault." Since tough circumstances cause bad behavior, we can prevent it by fixing circumstances.

Each of these appealing story lines shares the three plot elements of Satan's lie to Eve, as if to say, "You're the hero; you'll have a happy ending; your biggest problem is your situation, which God runs. Badly." Movies and novels, news sources, even computer games market stories featuring these same basic plot elements, weaving these unholy narrative features with others for complex and powerful appeal.

## Pop Messiah: A Favorite Story in Jesus' Day

Religious Jews in Jesus' time put a lot of stock in stories about the promised Messiah that followed these three main threads: you're the hero, you'll have a happy ending, your big problem is outside yourself in the situation, mostly Roman bad guys. These Messiah stories were not made up but formed in a long tradition of prophetic interpretation.[8] Messiah is the most important Jew; he brings a Jewish victory over their oppressors; he blesses his people with freedom, with plenty, and with prominence among the nations. He certainly does not die!

John the Baptist knew and loved this story, and he knew and loved Jesus. When Herod jailed John, John was puzzled over how long he stayed there and stayed there. The story wasn't unfolding according to plan. Seeing that Jesus' story was not following the "victory over the bad people" plot line that ought to have released John from prison, John sent his disciples to ask Jesus, in effect, "Where did I go wrong? Are you not the Messiah? Where did this story go off track?" (Matt. 11:2–3).

Peter, likewise, knew that no death should ever come to the Messiah, only victory, and assumed Jesus knew the same story he knew. Peter even chewed Jesus out for mentioning his death. "'Never, Lord!' he said. 'This shall never happen to you!'" (Matt. 16:22). We all, even religious people, love stories made up of Satan's three main themes.

## The Story of Self-Denial

As the story of perpetual personal pleasure, heroism, and imminent victory directs glory to us, so also the narrative of asceticism and self-denial directs glory to ourselves instead of to God.

- "Human commands and teachings . . . indeed have an appearance of wisdom, with their self-imposed worship, their false humility and their harsh treatment of the body" (Col. 2:22–23).
- "When you fast, do not look somber as the hypocrites do, for they disfigure their faces to show others they are fasting. Truly I tell you, they have

---

8. Eduard Lohse, *The New Testament Environment*, rev. ed., trans. John E. Steely (Nashville: Abingdon, 1974), 188–96, esp. 192.

received their reward in full. But when you fast, put oil on your head and wash your face, so that it will not be obvious to others that you are fasting, but only to your Father, who is unseen; and your Father, who sees what is done in secret, will reward you" (Matt. 6:16–18).

Notice here that the two stories of fasting are played out before two different audiences—people and God—and have two different aesthetic endings, a reward from people or a reward from God.

Self-denial can serve self-interest. One may abstain from wine in order to be seen as morally superior. One may always shop at secondhand stores, buy the cheapest car, and abstain from all luxuries to gain the moral high ground. One may live by nonbiblical rules and standards to appear righteous to oneself or to other people.

- "They forbid people to marry and order them to abstain from certain foods, which God created to be received with thanksgiving by those who believe and who know the truth. For everything God created is good, and nothing is to be rejected if it is received with thanksgiving, because it is consecrated by the word of God and prayer" (1 Tim. 4:3–5).
- "Do not let anyone who delights in false humility and the worship of angels disqualify you. . . . Since you died with Christ to the elemental spiritual forces of this world, why, as though you still belonged to the world, do you submit to its rules?" (Col. 2:18, 20).

## Short Stories

Sin breaks and takes out of context whatever it touches. This sinful impulse breaks up the stories we prefer. We fragment the metanarrative of God's story into numberless short stories of our pleasure, rightness, and purpose; we prefer short-term gratification, and we love shorter and shorter stories. "Of some sinful pleasure, [mortals] say, 'Let me but have this, and I'll take the consequences.'"[9] We lose patience. We ignore our bit part in the story God is unfolding. We do this by substituting an arbitrary ending—soon—for his final eschatology. We also substitute our own arbitrary beginning for God's creation and the obligations it implies.

- We prefer winning the argument to edifying our opponent.
- We prefer correcting our children's behavior to training their hearts.
- We prefer gratifying our tastes over discipling them.

---

9. Lewis, *Great Divorce*, 67–68.

We like to carve our short story out of God's long one.

Marriages degrade from "till death" to "as long as love shall last" to serial boyfriends/girlfriends and, unchecked, to one-night stands. We start a new relationship; we move to a new town; we find a new cause. Escape through any means begins to run together; escape itself becomes more important than what we're escaping to. Some seek comfort in freedom from obligation and find only free fall.

## Compartmentalization

We separate what we believe from what we like and from what we want. Our siloing leads to internal conflicts. We do things for pleasure (aesthetics) that are clearly impractical and that perhaps even violate our conscience (ethics). Our loves are inconsistent; our desires conflict. "One Part Be My Lover,"[10] and then there's the other part. "What causes fights and quarrels among you? Don't they come from your desires that battle within you?" (James 4:1). We compartmentalize, separating our loves from our beliefs and our will to do good, then suffer with the resulting mess of internal and external conflicts.

We seek to resolve internal conflicts by putting one value above the others. This should not surprise us, since we come from a long, long heritage of subordinating one suspect human faculty to another, preferred one. In the Age of Enlightenment, rationalists elevated reason and truth to resolve conflicts with feelings and with practical power. The Romantic Movement elevated beauty—aesthetics—over truth and goodness in order to rescue humanity from the dehumanizing rationalism of the Enlightenment. The Industrial Revolution followed power and productivity at the cost of beauty and truth; "form follows function." Each sounded like a good idea at the time, and none alone can deliver the goods.

## Cultural Quirks

Contemporary popular culture decontextualizes truth, beauty, and power. We treasure our freedom to choose and pursue individual aesthetic satisfaction, obscuring what should be our shared ethical commitment to defending our weak and marginalized neighbors. Our passion that every [blank] life matters forgets the truth that those we perceive as less just are also image bearers. We treasure knowing the truth, being right, then fail in love and compassion. Our to-do list trumps our study of truth and practice of making loveliness.

---

10. Bonnie Raitt, "One Part Be My Lover," *Luck of the Draw* (New York: Capitol Records, 1991).

All our cultural quirks show that we ignore God's glory and break up its triadic richness into component bits: siloed aesthetics, power, and truth. We love to be satisfied; we love power, including the power we only envy; and we love principles, abstract truth, the assured findings of modern science and fact checkers. We protect our control of each area from intrusion by the others.

Paul may have had people like us in mind when he wrote to Timothy, "The time will come when people will not put up with sound doctrine. Instead, to suit their own desires, they will gather around them a great number of teachers to say what their itching ears want to hear" (2 Tim. 4:3).

Such is the aesthetic appeal of the delicacies served up in our age through Twitter, Facebook, blogs, and websites. Follow the traffic and you will find what satisfies us.

The loss of the commerce driven by siloed aesthetics would cripple our culture. Someday it will: the merchants of the whole world, who "have grown rich from the power of her luxurious living" (Rev. 18:3 ESV), will lament just this crippling loss when the judgment comes. "The merchants who sold these things and gained their wealth from her [the great prostitute (Rev. 17:1, 18)] will stand far off, terrified at her torment. They will weep and mourn and cry out: 'Woe! Woe to you, great city, dressed in fine linen, purple and scarlet, and glittering with gold, precious stones and pearls! In one hour such great wealth has been brought to ruin!'" (Rev. 18:15–17). Our fascination with private indulgence cannot last.

## Church and Parachurch

Churches too fragment truth content from aesthetics, preferring one to another, or effectiveness takes the front seat. Some major on forms and aesthetics, often at the expense of doctrine; soaring architecture, glorious vestments, engaging liturgies can come to have freestanding value of their own, largely dissociated from biblical orthodoxy. Some focus on doctrinal purity, missing the meaning of forms in worship; beauty need not distract while we focus on the sermon. Some assume without saying so that it's easier to stay on track if we just start and stay with doctrinal truth taught in God's Word and ignore its stories, shapes, aesthetics, and the affections they are meant to stir. Some churches function on a techno-savvy, big-business model, highlighting the streamlined structure and effectiveness but short on beautiful intimacy with the Savior and clarity about his Word and promises. Many doctrinally careful churches make do in church buildings with low ceilings and bare, concrete-block walls, clothing the body of Christ in a jumpsuit: decent, orderly, but poorly suited for growing redeemed eyes for glory.

We in the Western church recognize that beauty can be powerful, even dangerous; we use it, and we take three steps backward. We attract the unchurched with music targeted to appeal to their existing loves. Do preachers craft sermons for truth or beauty or power but not for all three? We remember the noteworthy exceptions. In our sin, we never think that beauty's chief threat lies in us, in our affections. But in the Spirit, we start to notice and to hope.

A discipleship method that leverages people's aesthetic desires and habits to get to their reason has been tried. More than a thousand years of liturgical church used beauty and liturgy to correct and influence our minds, our beliefs. *Lex orandi, lex credendi*—roughly, "The law that is spoken in prayer is the law that will be believed"—still guides Roman, Episcopal, and Anglican churches.[11] Churches that relied on this discipleship model, for all its strength and appeal, also went astray in doctrine and ethics and invited Reformation. We know that right belief and true knowledge cannot save us from straying loves. But what advantage might we gain by reversing the order, putting loves above doctrine? Either way, the suggestion indicates we are on the right track in asking what the Scriptures teach about feelings. Having begun to learn Scripture's doctrine of aesthetics, and having begun our aesthetic repentance and renewal of our vision in the Spirit, we may profit from wholesome forms and liturgies and cultivate other good habits.

Many ministries and parachurch groups display results to stir giving, emphasizing effectiveness over truth and fittingness. Our seminaries reflect our doctrinal floundering, paying either too little attention to aesthetics or too much—often missing the connection to God's own beauty and his power to convert and shepherd our feelings. The rise among Bible scholars of literary approaches to the Scriptures generally assumes that literary forms are self-evident, having been well-established and recognized in literature as a whole, a valid parallel to Scripture, and so able to inform Scripture.[12] For all the riches that have flowed to the church through these approaches, we might look with equal warrant for a scriptural approach to literature.

We have stolen God's vision; we have broken what we stole; we have murdered God in our hearts. Yet he still speaks to us. He has come. He is here. We need his help.

---

11.   Frank C. Senn, *Christian Liturgy: Catholic and Evangelical* (Minneapolis: Fortress Press, 1997), 46.

12.   For example: Leland Ryken and Tremper Longman III, eds., *A Complete Literary Guide to the Bible* (Grand Rapids, MI: Zondervan, 1993), 20–23.

## READ, REFLECT, DISCUSS, SING————————————

1. Suggested reading: "The Weight of Glory," from *The Weight of Glory and Other Addresses* by C. S. Lewis.
2. Q1. Where have you seen a pleasure, even in something good, get the best of someone you love?
3. Q2. Where has your freedom suffered under the power of your love for pleasure? How is that going now?
4. Q3. What has your family or your church said about pleasure's power that has helped you to live and grow in freedom?
5. Sing: "When I Survey the Wondrous Cross," verses 3 and 4.

*Chapter 9*

# THE AESTHETIC CROSS

*It was the LORD's will to crush him and cause him to suffer. . . .*
*After he has suffered, he will see the light of life and be satisfied.*

—ISAIAH 53:10–11

The most ugly and the most beautiful event in history. Deeply aesthetic, evocative. Profoundly moving, full of brutality and horror, of love and tenderness. Called the passion for good cause. God intended it to look repulsive and ugly, but not first to us. It was for him to do and see. In this drama, God in Christ is the actor, and God the Father is the audience. The story went forward exactly as planned, with drama and power unimaginable. The crucifixion rang true to the Father. He has given us clues, though; the aesthetic fittingness of the cross appears most plainly to us in God's law. Jesus fulfilled the law's legal symmetry: an eye for an eye (Ex. 21:24). The punishment fits the crime: "When you eat . . . you will certainly die" (Gen. 2:17). He died. He paid sin's price in full.

He designed this story to show his glory, and its design is utterly brilliant. The crucifixion answers the Father's wrath about sin. The shameful death of his Son was the end of wrath, not the end of the story. Through extreme torment and real loss, he accomplished salvation. Jesus rose alive; this is the original of all the stories we love about the underdog who makes good and triumphs. The Father loves the story, because the Son *is* the story. He loves its hero: his own Son. He wrote the story and planned its glorious, satisfying conclusion (John 12:27; Acts 2:22–24; 4:27–28; Rom. 4:25; Heb. 2:14–15). Jesus will return in glory. Christ's resurrection and return in glory presents the sin of God's beloved people, my sin, to God's senses—his noetic, aesthetic, and ethical senses—through his crucifixion. This context alone makes the crucifixion satisfying. Can you see it? Those who see the cross as the only suitable context for our sin show this by living in Jesus' cross through ongoing repentance. The cross of Christ forms the centerpiece of God's drama, an aesthetic presentation that he wrote, starred in, and views as the chief audience. This display catches just the truth, the beauty, and the power he likes—his own. He presents it to himself, to the watching heavenly beings, and to all people of all time, rich in its form, reliable in its content, and powerful in its purpose. We focus here on the form of this story, especially on its troubling hinge, the crucifixion of Jesus the Christ.

God designed, arranged, and accomplished the crucifixion as the pivot in the larger drama by which he presents his bride to himself. In the crucifixion and in the anticipated wedding, we see the pre-fall co-seeing restored; God sees, Jesus sees with him, and we, the bride and the cloud of witnesses, co-see with them as well.

- "We know that the one who raised the Lord Jesus from the dead will also raise us with Jesus and *present us with you to himself*" (2 Cor. 4:14, emphasis added).
- "Christ loved the church and gave himself up for her to make her holy, cleansing her by the washing with water through the word, and to *present her to himself* as a radiant church" (Eph. 5:25–27, emphasis added).
- "They have washed their robes and made them white in the blood of the Lamb" (Rev. 7:14).

These white blood-cleansed robes bring to mind Aaron's bloodstained high-priestly garments; in both we are startled by blood as beautifying and cleansing. The priestly garments and the robes of the glorified ones please God as he sees the aesthetic excellence of this scarlet token of his Son's sacrifice.

The bridegroom, Jesus Christ, prepares his intended for her walk down the aisle. He stands on the dais to receive her. God the Father sees and deems her suitable, a proper bride for his beloved Son. Making her presentable to the Father took a lot! Only the Son's death in her place could do it. Jesus volunteered for his crucifixion[1] to make his bride, his church, beautiful enough for the Father to see and approve. She is the Son's true bride because he makes her so by his righteous life and by dying. "Jesus, thy blood and righteousness my beauty are, my glorious dress."[2] Here the co-seeing that was lost at the fall now makes her truly beautiful because her Maker looks upon her by the accomplished work of

---

1. "No one takes [my life] from me, but I lay it down of my own accord. I have authority to lay it down and authority to take it up again. This command I received from my Father" (John 10:18).

2. Nikolaus von Zinzendorf, "Jesus, Thy Blood and Righteousness," trans. John Wesley, in *The Trinity Hymnal*, rev. ed. (Suwanee, GA: Great Commission, 1990), 520.

the Son. The triadic shared vision is complete: Father's vision, Son's vision, and the cloud of witnesses' vision.

Christ's crucifixion, pivotal act in the great pageant, passes first before the Father's eyes—his audience, not ours. But "we have the mind of Christ" (1 Cor. 2:16), so we can share in God's seeing. God shares his seeing with his people in the Bible. In God's audience, we too can find satisfaction, including aesthetic satisfaction, in the crucifixion's gruesome, pathetic horrors. Courage, yes, in fullest measure, in the face of suffering. But the shameful suffering itself? Only when we see in it the mirror image of our sin does the ugly crucifixion finally make aesthetic sense. God saw it and was satisfied (Isa. 53:10–11).

## God's Long, Puzzling Story

Jesus' death forms the crisis of God's long, long story. This long story shows God's hatred of sin and his love for his people. Only this larger story can help us make sense of Jesus Christ's humiliating incarnation and ugly death. Although the end radiates with satisfaction beyond our imagining, its irregularities and unexpected changes of direction surprise us.

## The Puzzle of Aesthetic Inferiority

Isaiah, speaking for the Father, describes the Coming One in head-scratching aesthetic terms.

Who has believed our message
and to whom has the arm of the LORD been *revealed*?
He grew up *before him* like a tender shoot,
and like a root out of dry ground.
*He had no beauty or majesty to attract us to him,*
*nothing in his appearance that we should desire him.*
*He was despised* and *rejected* by mankind,
a man of *suffering*, and familiar with *pain*.
Like *one from whom people hide their faces*
*he was despised*, and *we held him in low esteem*.

Surely *he took up our pain*
and *bore our suffering*,
yet *we considered* him *punished by God*,
*stricken by him, and afflicted*.

But he was *pierced* for our transgressions,
> he was *crushed* for our iniquities;
the punishment that brought us peace was on him,
> and by his wounds we are healed.

—Isaiah 53:1–5 (emphases added)

Something must have gone badly wrong: the Lord's special Servant does not look glorious; he looks bad, degraded, shameful. Why? Is it just me, or does the Servant really look bad? What happened? Isaiah also offers us some clues that can help us understand what went wrong and give us further appreciation of the ugly crucifixion.

Isaiah builds on the Old Testament expectation that God's justice will be symmetrical—a form-based relationship of two matching sides, like the human face, having aesthetic qualities. God will bless obedience, but he will curse disobedience. His blessing is fitting for obedience, and his punishment fits disobedience. God will reward the obedient one, so the Servant's obedience should be repaid with blessing, especially by blessing that people can see. We meet this symmetry first in God's "When you eat from it you will certainly die" (Gen. 2:17), and again in Moses' "eye for eye" (Ex. 21:24); it is echoed in the psalmist's "Make us glad for as many days as you have afflicted us, for as many years as we have seen trouble" (Ps. 90:15).

In Isaiah's own writing—"Comfort, comfort my people, says your God. Speak tenderly to Jerusalem, and proclaim to her that her hard service has been completed, that her sin has been paid for, that she has received from the LORD's hand double for all her sins" (Isa. 40:1–2)—this last double payment may suggest a correspondence between crime and punishment that is like and also different. No payment by a human can directly measure up to an offence against an infinitely holy God. The double payment here suggests that their suffering is more than enough, even hinting that God himself has shouldered his people's unpayable debt by matching our crime with his punishment in a shocking but perfect symmetry.

Isaiah makes us wonder: does God's Servant really lack beauty and majesty, or does he embody beauty and majesty that we cannot see? Perhaps both. While our aesthetic vision has been damaged, God also deliberately hides his Servant's beauty and majesty, his aesthetic excellencies. The Father has deliberately concealed the perfections of his Anointed One during this strange part of the story, the season of his humiliation.

Since God hides his Servant's beauty, how can he blame us for missing it? I wonder. Jesus called the Emmaus Road disciples "foolish" and "slow to believe all that the prophets have spoken" (Luke 24:25) for failing to grasp exactly this, that the Servant's beauty and majesty were concealed only temporarily, and even then not completely. They knew Jesus, had heard him teach, had witnessed his miracles, even if they had missed his transfiguration.

We must conclude that our present dimness of sight that keeps us and others from falling to our knees and clinging to Jesus' feet arises partly from our own blindness and partly from God's concealing him from some people or at certain times. The Father intends this concealing as an act of kind patience, loving as he does the progressive revelation of his grand story. It is also one aspect of the Servant's complete, abject humiliation. Consider John's implied testimony that Jesus was crucified naked (John 19:23–24) in an ultimate humiliation typical of Roman crucifixions. Pilate meant his sign labeling Jesus the King of the Jews as an ethnic slap that stung the Jewish leaders (John 19:19–22), making Jesus' personal humiliation into a corporate one. Still, Isaiah, taking full account of the Servant's humiliation—including its gruesome capstone—calls his readers to see in it and beyond it a promise that the Servant's majesty and beauty would be revealed eventually. For now, his beauties are hidden, and we are born blind.

But the Servant of the Lord will fix both. Isaiah tells us how, though it makes no sense: "He will sprinkle many nations" (Isa. 52:15). The Lord's Servant will sanctify many nations by the very humiliation that he endures. We call to mind the glorious, gold-embroidered robes made to God's design for Israel's priests, and that these, for all their beauty, were unfit for their use until sprinkled with the blood of the sacrifice, marked permanently with bloodstains (Ex. 29:21). Many other things and people in the Old Testament were purified by similar sprinkling, but now we learn that the Servant will make the ugly, excluded nations pure and lovely by the very humiliation that his own people misinterpreted.

This is hard to believe, as Isaiah laments: "Who has believed . . . ?" (Isa. 53:1). Yet God is up to something, even though we cannot see it. God sees, and his seeing guides the whole story, as "before him" (v. 2) suggests: the Servant was weak, vulnerable, barely surviving, just as the Father had planned, just as the Father had envisioned him. Still, we puzzle over the Servant's so-so appearance. He looks like nothing special; he looks plain, unattractive.

Isaiah's focus on the Servant's ugliness, culminated in the humiliating cross, shows that God's pleasures and displeasures differ wonderfully from ours. The Father focuses his attention on the Servant—"he grew up before him"—and not on his people or anything pleasing about them, or even potentially pleasing. They are not attractive or intrinsically desirable in any way.

## Aesthetic Inferiority in Other Scriptures

Other Scriptures suggest a similar theme, suggesting that the Coming One will embrace aesthetic inferiority as a temporary means to greater blessing. Jacob chose the speckled and spotted goats and sheep as his pay. Even though Laban his father-in-law boss embezzled them all before Jacob could claim them, Jacob induced the remaining solid-color animals to bear lots of multicolor young, though these were considered inferior.

Boaz found surprising Ruth's appeal to him to marry her in order to redeem the family property and provide for his relative's family. What did he expect? Look: "'The LORD bless you, my daughter,' he replied. 'This kindness is greater than that which you showed earlier: You have not run after the younger men, whether rich or poor'" (Ruth 3:10).

Boaz thought Ruth had reason—probably her youth and beauty—to set her cap for a younger, more attractive man, and to appeal to him for protection. But clinching a deal like that would have left her mother-in-law and her family homeless and starving. Boaz saw that she was acting kindly toward them and also to him. As if he were to say, "Why would you want to be with me? You're so pretty, you could have done better." She appears to have set aside private aesthetic satisfaction and embraced instead aesthetic inferiority—choosing an older rather than a younger man—out of loyalty to family and to Israel's God. This unknown author enjoins us, with our Lord himself, "Watch for this theme to come up again."

Michal, first wife of King David, had a highly developed sense of aesthetics, chiefly for pageantry, classy clothes, and dignity. Call it excellence. She learned it growing up as daughter to Israel's first king, her father Saul. She also knew who should notice: the watching people, all the way down to the girls who served David's officials. David corrected her. God is the proper audience, though pleasing him will require even greater indignity before others than David has already achieved: "I will become even more undignified than this, and I will be humiliated in my own [or *your*] eyes. But by these slave girls you spoke of, I will be held in honor" (2 Sam. 6:22). David embraces aesthetic degradation, knowing it will result in honor, maybe later. Keep watching.

Jacob, Ruth, David, Isaiah, and others prepare us to recognize the Coming One by his plainness and by his repulsive humiliation and to go on looking for his marvelous appearance to come. We need such preparation: the aesthetic fittingness of the cross is concealed when we take it out of context. The cross is a horrible execution, made to look repellant, degrading, shameful, a deliberate aesthetic display designed to humiliate finally and utterly. Aesthetic meaning, like literary meaning, appears only in context. The context of the cross is God's entire story of redemption. The hidden beauty of the cross is revealed by the cross's correspondence to our sin. His punishment fits our offense, like a mirror image. Are we surprised? Did we know that the sins we treasure were that bad? Did we know they were all—*all*—paid for in Christ's death, including those we have yet to discover and confess?

Christ's humiliation and degradation, though complete in his person, persist in his body, the church. He calls his followers to walk with him in Isaiah's two themes: Christ's unimpressive plainness and his personal humiliation. Our Lord's call to aesthetic discipleship starts here, at the cross, and all our pursuit of beauty for God's sake (together with our wills and our beliefs) must first pass through this fire by aesthetic repentance and faith, and we must look to him for help to continue in repentance throughout this life, whatever satisfactions, accomplishments, and recognitions he may bring.

Watch where the story goes from here. The Servant will not remain humiliated, degraded. He will appear, revealing new meaning to the condemned sinner, joining the sinner to himself, the beloved Son, and making the sinner a beloved son or daughter, growing in loveliness, delight, and gratitude and growing in delighted awe for the Servant. We sing together, "Fairest Lord Jesus," anticipating his glorious appearance, when we will sing indeed!

## READ, REFLECT, DISCUSS, SING

1. Suggested reading: "The Dark Night of Faith: Luther's Theology of the Cross," chapter 5 of *Spirituality in an Age of Change: Rediscovering the Spirit of the Reformers* by Alister E. McGrath; "The Pleasure of God in Bruising the Son," chapter 6 of *The Pleasures of God: Meditations on God's Delight in Being God* by John Piper.
2. Q1. What passages in the Bible have turned your stomach? Why do you think the Bible shows readers ugly, repulsive scenes?
3. Q2. How have you coped with ugly scenes in your own life?
4. Sing: "Crown Him with Many Crowns," verses 1 and 2.

# Chapter 10

# FAIREST LORD JESUS

*All fairest beauty, heavenly and earthly,*
*wondrously, Jesus, is found in Thee!*
*None can be nearer, fairer or dearer,*
*than Thou, my Savior, are to me.*
—ANONYMOUS GERMAN HYMN,
"FAIREST LORD JESUS"

God the Father delights in his Son and is pleased to tell him so. "With you I am well pleased" (Mark 1:11; Luke 3:22).

God delighted in his creation because he delights in his Son. We explored in chapter 4 that God delighted right away in everything he had made because it all fit the Son perfectly, showing the perfection of the Trinity. All God's pleasure starts here; from this, his central pleasure, God radiates all his pleasure, and every true pleasure for people.[1] Since we, as God's people, have every good gift because of our union with Christ, Jesus Christ's approach to pleasure, in his words and his actions, compels our intimate attention.

Jesus alludes in his Last Supper prayer to the glorious mutual pleasure of the Trinity before the world was made. Jesus asks his Father to do the glorious work that they planned together from before the beginning: "Now, Father, glorify me in your presence with the glory I had with you before the world began" (John 17:5). The Father's complete pleasure with his Son before all creation will now reach even greater heights. Accomplishing their plan will mysteriously consummate their shared pleasure. Jesus says as much to his disciples: "The

---

1. See John Piper's excellent discussion of God's pleasure in his Son in *The Pleasures of God: Meditations on God's Delight in Being God*, rev. ed. (Colorado Springs: Multnomah, 2012), chaps. 1 and 6.

reason my Father loves me is that I lay down my life—only to take it up again" (John 10:17).

Jesus Christ gives this glimpse into the Father's very heart, declaring the reason the Father loves his Son. Who would dare say why another loves him? Any reason would risk sounding proud, as if one were to say, "He loves me because I'm so awesome!" Yet Jesus dares. His audacity has a goal: the Father's glory and our good.

Jesus explains that the Father loves the Son for what he does. We modern readers wonder whatever happened to unconditional love? Why doesn't Jesus say that the Father loves him for who he is? The Father loves the Son because of what he does? We would expect him to love his Son, to take pleasure in him, for his character as his Son, the eternal Word, and for their joy in each other before the story of redemption started. Jesus does not rule those out, but he says something different here, something that surprises us. God the Father loves the Son because of what he does, accomplishing every chapter in the story they planned out together long before. The Father's performance-based pleasure in his Son goes in perfect coordination with his pleasure in his Son's basic identity. Neither has priority, but they necessarily go together.

J. R. R. Tolkien, in his *Lord of the Rings*, develops Samwise's character as the story of the journey to the Cracks of Doom unfolds, step by step.[2] This hero's character cannot really be separated from the story of his deeds. In the same way, our Lord shows who he is by what he does. We might call these complementary views the portrait view and the story view. In linguistic analysis these perspectives are called the *synchronic* view, which views all times together (in Tolkien, seeing the hero's whole character), and the *diachronic* view, which shows the unfolding story over time (in Tolkien, the progression of the hero's actions). Theologians might find an echo of the inseparability of biblical theology's story (or, "History of Special Revelation"[3]) and systematic theology's detailed portrait. The great systematic theologian Richard Gaffin taught his students, "BT before ST," urging us to always study the biblical text first in context, then let the text shape our systematic conclusions.[4] And here we hear Jesus, in effect, telling his disciples the same: "The Father loves me because of what I do," as if he were to add, "because what I do shows who I am. But start with what I'm doing."

2. J. R. R. Tolkien, *The Lord of the Rings* (London: Allen and Unwin, 1968).

3. Geerhardus Vos, *Biblical Theology: Old and New Testaments* (Carlisle, PA: Banner of Truth, 1975), 14.

4. A repeated classroom theme of Richard Gaffin. As noted in chapter 5, biblical theology and systematic theology convene to guide and empower the third aspect of the theological triad, practical theology, and these three properly inform and enrich each other in pastoral practice and in the seminary training of pastoral candidates.

The close link between Jesus' character and his actions springs from pleasure, not from compulsion. Nothing drove the eternal Son of God to become a man and die. Rather he does whatever he pleases. Particularly, Jesus Christ does whatever pleases his Father.

## Aesthetic Jesus

Jesus takes a remarkable approach to aesthetics, to pleasure and pain, in what he says and in what he does. His approach traces the three-stranded cords we first noticed in our exploration of Genesis: truth, beauty, and power; content, form, and purpose; telling, showing, and doing; noetics, aesthetics, and ethics. Concerning Jesus' aesthetics, the Synoptic Gospels—Matthew, Mark, and Luke—feature especially what Jesus *does*, and John's gospel features especially what Jesus *says*. Together the gospel writers express the triadic, aesthetics-in-context character of Jesus' ministry. Let us examine a few highlights.

### *Jesus' Wilderness Temptation*

Chapter 5 noted the triadic nature of both Eve's temptation in the garden and Jesus' temptation in the wilderness. Both consisted in three aspects, one of which focused on aesthetics. The aesthetic aspect warrants further attention here.

Jesus Christ preceded his public ministry with a direct confrontation with Satan, right at the point of Adam's failure. He entered the strong man's house (Mark 3:27), facing Satan's temptation in the wilderness, a temptation noted in each of the Synoptic Gospels. Jesus, the second Adam (Rom. 5:14), shouldered the human trial Adam dropped, just where he dropped it: he submitted to temptation at his weakest and triumphed in weakness (imagine the weakness that must have followed his forty-day fast!).

Matthew and Luke detail three episodes of Jesus' temptation: stones to bread, pinnacle of the temple, kingdoms of the world. Jesus withstood all three temptations to fragment and master the Father's glory as his own. While we have noticed that the "kingdoms of the world" temptation corresponds particularly to aesthetics (chap. 5), the other two temptations are infused with aesthetic qualities. As in his temptation of Eve, Satan's temptation of our Lord offers a new vision of the object in view, a solitary view without the Father. Satan offered Jesus self-defined content, self-pleasing form, and self-serving power. These correspond to the three principal aspects of God's glory we saw in Genesis: the noetic, the aesthetic, and the ethical. Where Eve and Adam fell, Jesus stood.

The "stones to bread" temptation offers Jesus autonomy over truth content—autonomy that is, as in Eve's temptation, symbolized by food. The Father gave food for nourishment and also for delight. Even coarse, tasteless bread might have satisfied Jesus' hunger, but the appeal of its taste added weight to the temptation. Jesus knew that the Father had already made known his pleasure in the matter: "I give you . . . food" (Gen. 1:29). The Spirit had brought Jesus far from food, intentionally. To break this rule would break Jesus' participation in the Father's pleasure. Jesus would rather risk starvation.

Even though the "pinnacle of the temple" temptation focuses on power, it brings the temptation to the heart of Old Testament aesthetics; all the beauty and pageantry of Jewish worship centered here. Satan, like a film producer-marketer, has a plan for a show that will put Jesus' name in lights. Just one small shift in audience—from God to people.

In the "kingdoms of the world" temptation, Satan has dolled up these kingdoms to look a lot like Jesus' bride-to-be, his church, but with an appealing difference: consummation without suffering—no Father, no promise, no cross, no *purified* bride. These kingdoms are an attractive counterfeit, a loose woman. She is the wayward seductress of Proverbs 7:5; she is the great prostitute of Revelation 17:1. She has taken the time to make herself up, and she has timed her appearance to coincide with Jesus' weakness, enhancing the effect. She knows how to look great, if Jesus could be tempted to use his aesthetic senses independently. The price, though, is false worship. Aesthetic attraction is worship, and auto-aesthetic pleasure is idolatry. Jesus stood where we and our ancestors fell.

By this victory in the wilderness temptation, Jesus notifies Satan that the horrid hole in our duty to God, blasted so long ago, will be fully repaired. Satan cannot stop him; no, Jesus will stop Satan. Now, in his life and public ministry, Jesus builds something better than duty: God's glorious temple in his body, fulfilling noetic, ethical, and aesthetic righteousness for all his people.

One could discover much more richness here in the accounts of Jesus' wilderness temptation, but since we trace the aesthetic implications, we will look at only one more feature: the order of the temptations. Since the gospel writers shape their narratives, we may look for meaning in their forms. Luke lists the three episodes in different order than does Matthew. The "stones to bread" temptation appears first in both; Matthew lists the "pinnacle of the temple" temptation before the "kingdoms of the earth" temptation, while Luke reverses these. We may see in this variation of pattern an echo of the similar variation in the order of the aspects of creation we noticed in Genesis 2:9 and 3:6. We noticed similar variations in other biblical triads, a form that suggests the equality of the members.

## Jesus' Ministry Modes

Jesus' preaching starts with parables: "He did not say anything to them without using a parable" (Mark 4:34). He also acted powerfully: healing the sick, raising the dead, and providing bread, fish, and even wine. We see Jesus showing, doing, and then telling: "When he was alone with his own disciples, he explained everything" (Mark 4:34). Jesus' preaching begins with showing through parables, followed quickly by doing through miracles, and culminating in telling when he explained everything to his disciples.

In his parable of the talents—"bags of gold" in the NIV—Jesus shows that Eve's loss of shared vision with God will be restored. He quotes the king inviting the good and faithful servants to "come and share your master's happiness" (Matt. 25:21, 23). This is not an invitation to enjoy some portion of stuff the master likes to take away and enjoy alone; it's an invitation to participate in his very enjoyment. This delight Jesus offers his followers!

Zacchaeus's story in Mark gives a fascinating glimpse of aesthetics in Jesus' ministry. This man sacrificed his own appearance—climbing a tree looks as undignified as dancing before the Lord!—and abandoned any realistic prospect of meeting Jesus or having a conversation with him.[5] He did this on the chance of only seeing what Jesus looked like. Jesus accepted this little offering of self-humiliation and worship and entered, by this narrow aesthetics-only doorway, into Zacchaeus's whole life.

Jesus' ministry covers the full triad, all the aspects, of God's glory: word, image, and power. He appears in John's gospel as "the Word" (John 1:1) and in Paul's writings as "the image of the invisible God" (Col. 1:15). Jesus' own frequent references to his presence as the arrival of the kingdom of God, or the kingdom of heaven, suggest his kingly power, the completion of the triad of Jesus' identity. He is the truth, he is the beauty, he is the power. In all he does, he combines these. Each aspect serves also as a perspective on the others: the truth is lovely and powerful; beauty is strong and true; just power is also fitting, appropriate, and true. And fully personal. And now human!

As I write I listen to the jazz piano of Monty Alexander and his trio, noticing the drummer's astonishing precision and the power this gives the music.[6] I appreciate the tender sensitivity of the bass. In all, the fruit of long, long practice is shown in tight coordination, in making room for each other, in mutual support, and in the mutual pleasure these players take in each other and in the

---

5. I am indebted to William P. Smith for this insight, quoted in *The Heart of the Matter: Daily Reflections for Changing Hearts and Lives* (Greensboro, NC: New Growth, 2012), 326.
6. Monty Alexander, *Uplift* (South Orange, NJ: Jazz Legacy Productions, 2011).

music. What a great example of the mutuality of truth, beauty, and power! Such coordination points back to Jesus Christ, the Word, the image, the power of God.

He is the Word, the very truth himself. Every taxonomic list of species, every math equation, every meter reading, every summary of test results, every footnote, every dissertation depends on Jesus Christ just to be itself, whether true or false.

Moreover, he is the image of God—his symbol, his representation—and the fountainhead of every metaphor, every analogy, every simile, and a thousand other literary devices. He is the one true and perfect metaphor, an analogy so true to the original that the analogy itself shares the character, the divinity of the original, the Father. The story that reveals his character is likewise the original, the source, from which all stories are derived, despite all their imperfections, perversions, and lies. Every myth, epic poem, novel, screenplay, ballad, and narrative framework, every corporate logo, every joke takes its basic form from Jesus' grand original, the story of redemption. There is one perfect analogy.

John pays particular attention to the triadic character of Jesus' ministry and offers some firsthand insights on Jesus' approach to aesthetics. Look with me at a few excerpts. Jesus tells his listeners, "My teaching is not my own. It comes from the one who sent me. Anyone who chooses to do the will of God will find out whether my teaching comes from God or whether I speak on my own" (John 7:16–17). Here is a practical epistemology! As if to say, "I obey, therefore I know." Jesus' truth comes from the Father, the source of all truth content. In saying that those whose will aligns with the Father's will recognize that Jesus' teaching is God's truth, Jesus invokes the ethical aspect of his listeners to confirm the noetic aspect. These aspects are always integrated.

Jesus said to his detractors, "The one who sent me is with me; he has not left me alone, for I always do what pleases him" (John 8:29). Like Jesus' truth—always derived from the Father—Jesus' pleasure is also derived from his Father, shared with him. He does only what pleases the Father. In this, Jesus approaches pleasure as Eve should have approached it—by participating only in God's pleasure, the pleasure of "pleasing to the eye" (Gen. 2:9), the pleasure of "Behold, it was very good" (Gen. 1:31 ESV). That pleasure was not alien or inaccessible to Eve; no, she had walked in it for a while, in God's presence. So Jesus Christ enjoys the Father's presence: "He has not left me alone" (John 8:29). Here is pleasure indeed.

Jesus shows the close integration of three aspects of discourse and ministry in John 8:38: "I am *telling* you what I have *seen* in the Father's presence, and you are *doing* what you have *heard* from your father" (John 8:38, emphasis added). Three modes of communication—telling, showing, and doing—appear in rapid succession and are interdependent: telling, the noetic aspect; showing ("what I have seen"), the aesthetic aspect; and doing, the ethical aspect. Jesus returns to the start: telling ("what you have heard from your father"). These aspects always appear intertwined, even in their distortions. This can help us read better the various cultural expressions we face and produce daily.

## Jesus' Three Offices

Jesus fulfills Israel's three offices, instituted in the Old Testament with a promise of greater fulfillment in the future (Deut. 18:5; Gen. 14:18–20, Ps. 110:4; 2 Sam. 7:13–16, 1 Kings 2:2–4). He simultaneously holds office as Prophet, Priest, and King.[7] We discussed in chapter 6 that prophethood corresponds to truth content, priesthood to showing, and kingship to power. This correspondence, far from accidental, seals the immanent personhood of each of these qualities we have previously seen as abstract principles. Truth is a person. Power is a person. Beauty, likewise, is a person—our fairest Lord Jesus.

Jesus unites the three fragmented aspects of God's glory that got severed in our eyes, broken up in the fall and in the cultural disintegration that followed. He unites them by being, himself, their unity—Prophet, Priest, and King in one man. He shows this unity by what he does: his life, death, resurrection, and ascension. In his priestly office, he presents himself as a sacrifice to the Father in long-planned forms; he pursues the Father's pleasure instead of his own, suffering infinite wrath in a finite body. In his prophetic office, Jesus is the truth, speaking only the words of the Father. In his kingly office, he defeats Satan and destroys his work; he reigns with all authority; his kingdom will have no end. All is glory! In all these works, Jesus glorifies the Father, and the Father glorifies the Son.

Imagine all the libraries in all of history, filled only with profound, pious observations and rich wisdom, not just available but appearing all together, simultaneously. Got that? Now imagine all the dancing galaxies, the glorious mountain peaks and the surging sea, the most exquisite sculptures, the most striking and subtle paintings, the most stirring drama and dance, the most inspiring poems and novels, the highest-reaching orchestral music, the most poignant, joyous folk melodies, with a splash of holy rock 'n' roll thrown in just to keep us honest. Good. Now imagine the untamed lightning, the sea's tidal rush, with holy armies mobilized and deployed, powerful engines for good, just national governments, compassionate volunteer works, even church organizations, all with inner harmony and efficiency, all working well together in single purpose—power so orderly and unstoppable that our imagination has to stand on tiptoe

---

7. Charles Hodge, *Systematic Theology*, vol. 2 (Grand Rapids, MI: Eerdmans, 1995), 459–61; Wayne Grudem, *Systematic Theology: An Introduction to Biblical Doctrine* (Grand Rapids, MI: Zondervan, 1994), 624–29.

for a glimpse. Imagine all this truth, this beauty, and this power, presented at once in their full value and without confusion. Even this falls short of the truth.

And we cannot get tickets. Even if we could peek behind the curtains, we would badly mis-spin what we saw, as did the Pharisees who saw God's Son die, and mocked. We would be like intruders, trying to make sense of a 3-D movie without the special glasses—unless God himself invites us to share his private box, his reserved seat, the only seat in the house, and gives us his eyes to see. The Holy Spirit opens believer's eyes to the boundless treasure of the Scriptures' account of this holy, redemptive drama—Jesus Christ's amazing work as our great High Priest, our Prophet, and our strong King. The Spirit even brings us past the footlights into the very action itself, where he himself is always delighting in his work.

Jesus warns his followers that humiliation, loss, and suffering will come to them—all the negative aesthetics we avoid. Pleasures will come too: "No one who has left home or brothers or sisters or mother or father or children or fields for me and the gospel will fail to receive a hundred times as much in this present age: homes, brothers, sisters, mothers, children and fields—along with persecutions—and in the age to come eternal life" (Mark 10:29–30).

Looking again at Jesus' parable of the talents, note that his faithful servants will find a reward better than pleasant things: "Come and share your master's happiness!" (Matt. 25:21). God's faithful servants will enter, in Jesus, the very pleasure of God. God offers them far more than a portion of the good things he enjoys that we can enjoy privately. The master draws these servants directly into his delight! We imagine Eden's shared vision restored, but with more.

## Order in the Trinity: Jesus' Centrality

We have noted that wherever we see aesthetics, we should look for forms, and wherever we see forms, we should look also for aesthetics. So as we consider the Trinity, the bedrock and frontier of our knowledge, we can without fear consider the aesthetic implications of form in the order of the persons.

What aesthetic inferences shall we make of Jesus Christ's appearance as the second person of the Trinity? Clues arise in Scripture, in early creeds, in systematic theology, and in secondary literature. We have already seen that just as Trinity-like triads abound in Scripture, so they abound in theology. Many Christians have noticed that they abound likewise in life, in art, and in discourse in general. In all these, order is form, and form has aesthetic meaning.

The Father, first person in the Trinity, speaks the law, issues the Word; he originates all truth content. The Holy Spirit, third person, accomplishes all of

God's will. So the Son, the second person, occupies a position specially associated with aesthetics, with representations, with feelings, even with passions. He is "the Root and the Offspring of David" (Rev. 22:16), specially associated with sequence and narrative, with human history; he is "the bright Morning Star" (Rev. 22:16), ultimate of beauty, desirability, and radiance. Indeed, he is fairest!

## READ, REFLECT, DISCUSS, SING——————————

1. Suggested reading: "The Pleasure of God in His Son," chapter 1 of *The Pleasures of God: Mediations on God's Delight in Being God* by John Piper.
2. Q1. When have you delighted in the Lord Jesus himself?
3. Q2. What do you think about the apparent contradiction between the Bible passages "He had no beauty or majesty to attract us to him, nothing in his appearance that we should desire him" (Isa. 53:2) and "Take delight in the LORD, and he will give you the desires of your heart" (Ps. 37:4)?
4. Sing: "Fairest Lord Jesus," verses 1, 2, and 3.

# Chapter 11

# THE AESTHETIC EFFECTS OF REDEMPTION

*Be Thou my vision, O Lord of my heart . . .*
—EIGHTH-CENTURY IRISH POEM

## Joy!

We were made to share God's joy. After we had abandoned it and earned misery, Christ restored joy to his disciples, who passed his words to us: "I have told you this so that my joy may be in you and that your joy may be complete" (John 15:11). Joy has come now and is coming in fullness soon. Wonder of wonders, we will recognize and participate in God's eternal joy. In fact, we actually get started right now.

## Aesthetic Repentance

The transformation of our aesthetic senses from self-oriented and out of context, to God-oriented and integrated, comes to us immediately and gradually. The Holy Spirit speaks to believers through the Word-confirmed still small voice, pricking the conscience when we indulge in some self-centered, God-ignoring pleasure or pain. Conviction spurs us to repent, to turn to God and plead with him for forgiveness, cleansing, and a new love to replace the old one that must die. No aesthetic sense that turns away from the purging fires of Jesus' death and the Holy Spirit's conviction can grow godly, can grow true, sweet, good, strong.

We may scarcely recognize redeemed aesthetic eyes when they first develop. We might get twitchy about something we used to take sitting down. Perhaps we take less pleasure in things that used to delight us. Maybe our hearts begin to sing at a new loveliness. Our feelings are shifting. We get uncomfortable with something that used to comfort us. We may not call it this at first, but we grow to hate our sin. We respond by asking God, whose watchful eye we treasure more and more, for help, specifically for forgiveness and for new affections. All at once, and slow and gradual.

The eye of flesh perceives forms in themselves alone, opaque, seeking inherent qualities to use them for all sorts of human purposes, pleasure, motivation, persuasion, influence. We cry out to God for forgiveness and for new eyes. Our new aesthetic eye sees forms of all kinds and looks past them, through them. With Holy Spirit help, the forms we see and those we craft become translucent—light shines through them—allowing us to see God.

Stories, one of the most basic forms, depend for their basic narrative structure on God's great story of creation, fall, redemption, and consummation. The redeemed eye can see this, at last, although we often miss it. Images, the other basic form, we find redeemed as they reveal God's character. Still, images and stories have long led us astray; in their opacity, they become compelling myths, ideals, and character sketches. In our flesh, we love them that way, but the redeemed eye cannot stay comfortable in the flesh anymore. Our new discomfort, an aesthetic fruit of redemption, stirs us up more and more to pray for God's day-to-day help.

We are vulnerable to taking these images and stories at face value, seeing in them only themselves and missing the distortions. We used to like those distortions. This view, the opaque misinterpretation of the stained-glass window we discussed earlier, is in fact idolatry. We worship a picture, an image, a story, and the life-orienting meaning they give us, missing who God is and what he is saying and meaning.

Redeemed hearts can still worship these idols, but with at least three key differences. First, our idolatry—our love for false images and stories—has already been forgiven. Second, we worship idols less than we used to do as we grow in worship of the real God. Third, we grow in finding our identity in Christ, not in the idols.

Our Lord, in his compassion, knows that these idols, these pictures and stories, feel like part of us. When Jesus urged his hearers to gouge out their offending eyes and cut off their offending hands (Matt. 5:29–30), he was talking about our misplaced passions and about the words and actions that spring from them. He compared our love for our preferred images, our idols, to a precious eyeball; he represented our power to act on our loves with our right hand. These word pictures get us. We imagine the gouge or the chop and pull away in horror.

These are body parts; they are us. Jesus knows that we feel the same way about the pictures and the stories we use to make sense of our lives—our idols. Though they really are not us, they feel like us. Jesus knows how we feel, even while he warns us against the danger of following our feelings. Pluck it out! Cut it off!

## *Putting Off*

Jesus uses violent language—gouging out and cutting off—to depict repentance, warning us to expect to recoil at what he requires. Using similarly violent language, Paul orders Christians, "Put to death, therefore, whatever belongs to your earthly nature: sexual immorality, impurity, lust, evil desires and greed, which is idolatry" (Col. 3:5). Think of the lizard on the ghost's shoulder in C. S. Lewis's *The Great Divorce*.[1] The lizard represents the voices, the control, the story that has long ruled the life of the ghost, tormenting him and filling him with the fear of death. The ghost can scarcely bring himself to let the angel kill the lizard, but once killed, the dead lizard becomes a white stallion. Lewis catches here the transformation of our sordid passions into proper, strong, holy ones.

Paul pictures this in a less violent metaphor for the same transaction—changing clothes: "Put off your old self . . . be made new . . . put on the new self" (Eph. 4:22–24). Paul adds here two key features to this transformation: First, we "put off" so we can "put on." Our old love for stories and pictures, opaque and about themselves, dies to make place for us to love new pictures and stories full of God. Second, at the center stands a strange command: "Be made new." This command is passive but carries imperative force, as if to say, "As you were taught, this absolutely has to happen, and you must see to it. You simply cannot do it to yourself; it has to be done to you." We can only cry out to God for help. This is our repentance in which we put to death our perverse aesthetic judgments: our loves and our hates.

This repentance happens at a moment and in lots of moments after that, moments of prayer and heart searching. We can ask about the pictures and stories whose grip now makes us uneasy, "What do I love about this? What desire does this gratify? What am I taking out of its biblical context? Where am I siloing, focusing on pleasure or fear at the expense of truth? On pragmatics to the exclusion of truth? On doctrinal purity to the exclusion of affections, even of God himself?"

God gives us hope for this life of aesthetic repentance. We ask God to search our hearts for an inclination to a rogue story line, in which I play lead instead of God. Psalm 139's author may have had in mind just such bondage to a story when

---

1. C. S. Lewis, *The Great Divorce* (New York: Macmillan/Collier, 1946), 98–103.

he asked God, "See if there is any offensive way in me, and lead me in the way everlasting" (Ps. 139:24). What story line must be running for this indulgence to work? Like the psalmist, we need help to search for and destroy the affectionate protections around our favorite story lines; we need help to run to God for forgiveness and shepherding back onto the straight path. Help has come: even though offensive ways are in me, ways that I cannot see, God will put me in the way everlasting; I have asked him. God gives hope in Person.

No other hope will do. Let us not imagine that we can, having seen our misplaced affections, simply change our mind, deciding to believe and love differently. No, transformation of our feelings happens face to face with God our Savior or not at all. We run to him for help; we gouge out and cut off our misplaced loves and the habits of action that spring from them. We ask to be washed, cleaned, and for a new heart, new affections, in order to embrace ("put on") God's story, his knowledge, power, and love. That new heart can seek what God will ask of us.

## Putting On

Having "put off" our misplaced affections—a work in progress until we see the Lord—we ask how our new affections can stir us to love and respond to God, creation, and culture. We can now interact more faithfully with our surroundings and with all that people say and do, in the form of arts, media. We find remade loves, delights, treasures, hopes which correspond to our former false and death-dealing attractions but now feature a reoriented heart in relationship with the Creator. We fear different things, play to a different audience, delight in and desire with joy and peace. We take refuge and seek shelter in a Person, not a distraction. We are profoundly not alone.

We can "put on" Jesus' love for the story he and the Father wrote together before the beginning of the world, in which God appears as hero, viewing and relishing the story even as the beloved Son enacts its most awful moments. We can love God's power in place of our own, God's character in place of fantasies of our own opaque heroism. We can view heroes of the faith transparently, as they show God's goodness and power in their weakness.

God alone opens our eyes. He does this by regeneration and keeps doing it in us by the Holy Spirit, through ongoing repentance and faith. Ordinary Christian discipleship will include aesthetic repentance. All the effects of sin on our affections, all the aesthetic effects of decontextualization and self-glory, objectifying beauty, trying to take the God labels and glory arrows off the lovely thing so we can have it to ourselves—all these must die so we can see. We cannot limit our use of TV and digital devices enough to work this inner transformation.

We cannot learn or study our way into this change. We will know the truth, but we cannot cram our way to redemption. We must obey, but we cannot be intentional enough for this. This is personal. This is a conversation with God. We ask; we count on his promises. We take the next shaky step, reaching out our hand.

## Aesthetic Transformation

Scripture is full, full, full of aesthetic transformation—pictured, recounted, commanded. Consider an example. Isaiah describes and commands aesthetic transformation: "Come, all you who are thirsty, come to the waters; and you who have no money, come, buy and eat! Come, buy wine and milk without money and without cost. Why spend money on what is not bread, and your labor on what does not satisfy? Listen, listen to me, and eat what is good, and you will delight in the richest of fare. Give ear and come to me; listen, that you may live. I will make an everlasting covenant with you, my faithful love promised to David" (Isa. 55:1–3).

As if God were to say, "Thirsty? Hungry? Yes, come to me. Why go after all the usual garbage? I know you love it, but it never nourishes; it doesn't even taste that good. (You have known this for a long time, haven't you?) Of course you can't afford it! That's the point. I give freely to all who come to me. So turn, listen to me, and come to me. This is a matter of life and death. You are going to love this, and best of all, we will be together. And all this delight is going somewhere: because I will promise to love you, you will have a job to do, working out your place in my big story, my plan to bring the whole world right again."

The transformation of our affections is already under way. We are going to relish what God gives. God is giving his people new tastes so we can delight in real goodness, find nourishment, and get busy with God's work with him. More and more, we will see with God, sharing *his* tastes.

What will our redeemed affections feel like? Jesus shows us who we will be when we are joined to him, and what we will do, and how we will feel. As we have seen, Jesus' life forms a triad that includes aesthetics fully reintegrated with the other primary aspects of God's glory we saw in Genesis—truth and power. Jesus *said* nothing on his own authority, but only as the Father told him; *did* nothing according to his own will, but only what he saw the Father do; *pleased* not himself, but only his Father. Jesus presented his unified human life to the Father, who saw him and said, "I am well pleased," an aesthetic observation that summarizes his whole response to his Son, now the new man Jesus.

Jesus, who enjoyed with the Father, before all worlds, pleasures beyond our imagining, also pioneered the transformation of our sabotaged sense of pleasure. He did this by putting the Father's pleasure first, ahead of his own: Jesus found pleasure in the Father's pleasure, even when it meant his present humiliation and suffering. To these, he responded with the passion they deserved: he scorned them (Heb. 12:2). He also reunited the fragmented expression of God's glory, restoring to their proper, God-centered unity truth, beauty, and power: Jesus, the prophetic Word of God, the priestly image of God, and the kingly power of God, lived and died and rose as one man, uniting the severed parts of human discourse into one man with one purpose: God's glory.

We can see with God, because Christ has joined us to himself in mysterious union. This includes our aesthetic seeing, our satisfactions. We become dissatisfied with ourselves[2] and with our hopes for ourselves and satisfied with him. We become thankful. In a small way, we see what God himself sees: God's glory in the content, form, and power of his creation. We see this same glory as the proper goal of our own work, and value these three aspects equally. We see Jesus, the pinnacle and fountain of delights, present with his people now. He opens to his people a world of pleasures now and a future of divine delights: "In your presence there is fullness of joy; at your right hand are pleasures forevermore" (Ps. 16:11 ESV). God's redeemed ones are motivated no longer by a burning desire or need but by a burning sense of fulfillment, leading to a new, assured longing for the culmination still to come.

Let us pass in review these aesthetic effects of redemption.

Jesus Christ restores the primacy of the Father's seeing, a primacy Adam and Eve humanly shared for a while.

- "I always do what pleases him" (John 8:29).
- "'I have food to eat that you know nothing about. . . . My food,' said Jesus, 'is to do the will of him who sent me and to finish his work'" (John 4:32, 34). Jesus says, in effect, "I get as much nourishment and satisfaction from doing my Father's will as I would from a good meal."
- "Come and share your master's happiness!" (Matt. 25:23). Not just a gift of the same kind of things your master enjoys, for you to enjoy on your own, but an actual co-participation with the master in his enjoyment!
- "Christ . . . through the eternal Spirit offered himself unblemished to God" (Heb. 9:14). The offering was unblemished, aesthetically perfect; God the Father is Jesus' intended audience for his crucifixion.

---

2. Cf. John Calvin, *Institutes of the Christian Religion*, ed. John T. McNeill, trans. Ford Lewis Battles, Library of Christian Classics (Philadelphia: Westminster, 1960).

- " *'Eloi, Eloi, lema sabachthani?'* (which means 'My God, my God, why have you forsaken me?')" (Mark 15:34). Presenting his death to the Father, Jesus mourns aloud to the Father their loss of fellowship as his Father turns away (even though they planned this long before). Only in the hope of resurrection can our Lord endure this otherwise unbearable, inconceivable wrenching of the Trinity's eternal unity.
- "I will tell them plainly, 'I never knew you. Away from me, you evildoers!'" (Matt. 7:23). Jesus, appointed Judge by the Father Judge, restores God's primacy in the very nature of judgment and redemption. He does not say here that the evildoers did not know God; rather he says that God did not know them.

Jesus reunites his people's sense of truth, beauty, and power, which we discussed among the aesthetic effects of sin shown in Genesis 1–4. No more pleasure without truth, often masquerading as entertainment. "Art for art's sake," autotelic art, has become for the Christian a thing of the past. We discussed in chapter 10 that Jesus does this reuniting first in himself, joining in a single man God's three offices for Israel's leadership. He unites these especially in his death. In this, he frees his people and sets a pattern of humiliation, suffering, and weakness now, on the way to honor, delight, and power at a later great day. Meanwhile he comforts us by his presence (2 Cor. 1:3–4) and by his promises (John 17:13; 2 Cor. 12:8–10; 2 Peter 1:3–4).

Jesus restores transparent vision to all who seek him, reversing the objective, opaque meaning so natural to the self-guided eye. This new eye sees everything differently in the light of God.

## General Aesthetic Effects of Redemption

How does the gospel reshape our passions? We enter territory here both new and familiar. But Jesus occupies every inch, our Shepherd and Redeemer. This will work.

Our redeemed eyes will see all creation as transparent, showing God through everything. Each beauty, each twisted distortion, finds its meaning in the eye of God, as it points back toward himself in creation and forward to himself in redemption. We will know God more and more by what we see in ordinary life.

### Disgust

With the transformed eye, we see ourselves first as repulsive, a gratingly bad fit with God's holiness; only punishment would complete the picture, finishing the story fittingly. "There you will remember your conduct and all the actions by which you have defiled yourselves, and you will loathe yourselves for all the evil you have done. You will know that I am the LORD, when I deal with you for my name's sake and not according to your evil ways and your corrupt practices" (Ezek. 20:43–44). We have reason to expect God to deal with us according to our evil ways. Against this expected, aesthetically fitting ending, God's redemption surprises as thoroughly as it pleases, like the very best sort of joke. Amazingly, we *laugh*; this transformation came to us in our waking coma; our eyes have been regenerated. We respond by turning and believing, by repentance and faith. Times of refreshing come from the Lord (Acts 3:19)!

We pursue no longer only our own private indulgences, personal pleasures; instead we become capable of Jesus' impulse, "I always do what pleases him" (John 8:29). We will not do this perfectly in this life, but it is now possible to not sin and rebel and live solely for ourselves. Sin no longer has undisputed reign over us (Rom. 6:12).

We who loved our idols find God attractive; we love him instead of loathing him. Plenty of putting the flesh to death remains for us, but the gospel yeast has entered this rat-chewed old dough, and it will grow and spread, creating a new lump of dough.

We loathe ourselves and hate our sin, as we saw in Ezekiel 36:31. This has nothing to do with the contemporary psychological problem of self-loathing, because godly self-loathing is infused with heightened appreciation to Christ for his love and forgiveness. Many of the joy-centered hymns and choruses of the late nineteenth- through early twentieth-century American evangelicalism presume a powerful conviction for sin, even some that make no mention of it. Against this backdrop, our redemption appears hilariously attractive. David Powlison, executive director of the Christian Counseling and Educational Foundation, has said that a good doctrine of sin is the doorway to joy, as our forgiveness and redemption is so full of freedom and delight.

## Pleasure

In Christ our addiction to our private pleasure is dead, despite attempts at self-resurrection. Our impulse to self-indulgence or selfish self-denial has lost a bit of its luster. Many habits of heart and hand linger, but we can put out with the garbage our passion for our own pleasure, power, and authority, entertaining instead a growing passion for his pleasure, his power, his authority.

Because we are in Christ and have the Spirit, we please God (Rom. 8:8–9); we can share in his pleasure with us, free at last from the habits of cultivated self-loathing and its twin, inflated pride.

We share God's pleasures even now: "Come and share your master's happiness!" We actually begin to enter the divine delight. Not uniformly, but really and growing. The reader may know quite well what is meant here or may have to search his experience for clues—a worthwhile search. God's promise has already begun to come true, and more, much more, will come later.

We share Christ's sufferings. We used to suffer alone: solitary pain sometimes marked by isolation, hopelessness, blaming God or man, seeking refuge where it could be found. At times we enjoyed the solitude, whether for quiet to cope, or for pride, self-pity, or to enjoy imagining ourselves courageous and innocent. But now we can see our sufferings as a participation in Christ's sufferings (Rom. 8:17–18); we are not alone and our pain is not meaningless. God intends some suffering in our present redeemed aesthetic experience. This suffering, though no less sharp than that of nonbelievers, we share with Jesus, the beloved Son who bore the chastisement of our peace. Because of this, we find our suffering is saturated no longer with pride, despair, and anger, but with comfort and hope that stir us up to cry out to him for relief and help. God's redemptive story of suffering and delight contrasts with our story of private, solitary pain in its flavor as much as in its Person; the same pain, though familiar, now feels different; Jesus is the star sufferer. Far from disappointing us, these changes lift our spirits, and our voices in prayer.

## *Comfort*

Praise be to the God and Father of our Lord Jesus Christ, the Father of compassion and the God of all comfort, who comforts us in all our troubles, so that we can comfort those in any trouble with the comfort we ourselves receive from God. For just as we share abundantly in the sufferings of Christ, so also our comfort abounds through Christ. If we are distressed, it is for your comfort and salvation; if we are comforted, it is for your comfort, which produces in you patient endurance of the same sufferings we suffer. And our hope for you is firm, because we know that just as you share in our sufferings, so also you share in our comfort.

—2 Corinthians 1:3–7

Comfort is aesthetic. But God's comfort stands aesthetics on its head. Comfort comes to people who are used to suffering alone, from people who are suffering with Christ. It draws them into a new way of suffering, a way of shared suffering that brings comfort. This comfort spreads. It has spread to us and will keep on spreading through us.

This comfort includes hope. We hope for our adoption as sons and daughters, the redemption of our bodies—an intimate, physical, and sensate dynamic that stirs our inward groaning, and also patience. We believe the story God promised, so we hope; that hope is aesthetic, both physical and affectional. "We ourselves, who have the firstfruits of the Spirit, groan inwardly as we wait eagerly for our adoption to sonship, the redemption of our bodies" (Rom. 8:23).

The otherwise incongruous overlap of groaning and patience shows that we "get" the new story we are in; it makes sense of present groaning and suffering by God's presence and by his promise that we are heading toward very good things, toward him. Though it sounds strange to us now, part of these good things includes satisfying the whole creation's longing when we, God's children, are eventually revealed to free God's creation from its bondage to frustration and decay (Rom. 8:19–22).

## Holy Indignation

Aesthetic regeneration also brings godly discomfort. Paul notices and approves these effects: "See what this godly sorrow has produced in you: what earnestness, what eagerness to clear yourselves, what indignation, what alarm, what longing, what concern, what readiness to see justice done" (2 Cor. 7:11).

The redeemed aesthetic gets us worked up about important events in real life, about situations that cry out for all that we can do to fix them. Violations of social justice, once opaque to us and man-centered, become translucent. We can see God himself as the first victim, the great liberator and the just avenger. Release from oppression becomes all the more precious as we see it also symbolizes release from sin's bondage. God's promises energize our prayers, action, and patience.

God's people find a new pleasure in seeing sin defeated—the sins of others as well as our own. All the psalms that speak about the psalmist's enemies actually refer to real people. We can also read these psalms with new groaning and new delight by reading the psalmists' enemies as our sins.

## Peace of Conscience

Various witnesses speak of this peace, many in frankly aesthetic terms. One of the most famous, John Bunyan, describes his character, Christian, as "glad and lightsome" when he got free from the burden of his sin at the cross.[3]

- "How much more, then, will the blood of Christ, who through the eternal Spirit offered himself unblemished to God, cleanse our consciences from acts that lead to death, so that we may serve the living God!" (Heb. 9:14).

---

3. John Bunyan, *The Pilgrim's Progress* (New York: Grosset and Dunlap, n.d.), 49.

- "Let us draw near to God with a sincere heart and with the full assurance that faith brings, having our hearts sprinkled to cleanse us from a guilty conscience and having our bodies washed with pure water" (Heb. 10:22).

## Time

We now love a story a billion times bigger than the private little melodrama we once entertained; we love its hero. We find ourselves in it and grow to love our new, better role. These roles have higher dignity, higher drama. This improvement goes far beyond mere delayed gratification, beyond the promise of better pleasures later if only we wait. Those would still be private indulgences. Instead God himself inhabits the present and the future of his people's restored, dynamic aesthetic senses. He is giving us himself, and also his own taste buds to appreciate his overflowing, overwhelming sweetness. "Taste and see that the LORD is good" (Ps. 34:8). This comes incrementally, haltingly, and yet really.

More will come: "I consider that our present sufferings are not worth comparing with the glory that will be revealed in [or to] us" (Rom. 8:18). Both stories live in us: one resisting death, the other sure to beat it but suffering setbacks. The inward battlefield is the first and most important theater of culture wars.

God's people's affection for time changes. Where once our present pleasures, expectations, demands, and disappointments occupied our full attention, hope in God's future goodness now grows out of his promises and out of every incremental fulfillment, every token of God's kindness. How had we missed so many of them? Our gratitude grows. We thank God, we hope in God, in our pain and deprivation we cry out to him. Even when hope lags and stumbles, God is with us, himself, the Holy Spirit as comforter. While these effects remain incomplete for now, they are real and they grow.

## Specific Aesthetic Effects of Redemption

**Pleasure in God begins and grows.** God's free people can see God and enjoy him. "Take delight in the LORD, and he will give you the desires of your heart" (Ps. 37:4). We fear him, and we fear his judgments; we are in awe. We can see creation and see God reflected through it. We can delight in creation for his sake. God's people can hate evil, no longer as an abstraction but as a blot on his holiness, a demand for his justice. Our pain, humiliation, and misery, no longer solitary, draw us closer to God in Jesus Christ, whose sufferings we now share.

**Sensitivity grows.** Our feelings, once blunted, numbed, dulled, awaken; he replaces our hearts of stone with hearts of flesh (Ezek. 11:19; 36:26). We feel comfort, longing, deep sorrow, ardent concern, and great joy (2 Cor. 7:7).

We rejoice with the happy and mourn with the grieving (Rom. 12:15). When a friend is weak, we feel weak (2 Cor. 11:29). We love sincerely, hate what is evil, cling to what is good; we are devoted to one another in love, fervent in zeal, joyful in hope, patient in affliction (Rom. 12:9–12). Jesus gives his joy, and it is full (John 15:11). Quickly and gradually, we find our delights grow, our revulsion grows, our horror at evil and cruelty grows as we see them through God's eyes and for his sake. We're satisfied and more; our cup overflows.

**Gratitude grows.** We grow in contentment and gratitude (1 Tim. 6:6–8; 1 Chron. 16:7; Ps. 100:4; 2 Cor. 4:15; etc.). As our gratitude grows, demands and the sense of entitlement shrink. We can share God's pleasures and disgust and can grow in these. Contentment is both a redeemed affection and an aesthetic discipline. Likewise holy disgust. The unredeemed cannot know lasting contentment.

**Translucent vision grows.** God's people grow to treasure God as Beholder, who sees what is good, true, and beautiful as it reflects his holiness. We see God through more, and we see more through God's eyes; this about-ness grows precious to us. We will better see him in all things, see everything by him and for him, see him before all things and holding all things together, and through Christ reconciling all things to himself (Eph. 4:15; 1 Cor. 1:16–20).

**Self-centered seeing diminishes.** Our old sense of entitlement finds a new enemy in us. The Holy Spirit will win, and we take courage. Instead of myself or another person as God's replacement in the role of chief seer, who deserves all the indulgences and pleasures I can afford or that I merit by performance, we long to please the Lord, and we will long for this still more.

**Objectification and subjectification diminish.** Our impulse to grasp truth, beauty, and goodness per se reverses. Our fierce loyalty to our personal preferences begins to walk back. We find growing delight in God-centered connections of God's truth with his beauty and his power. We rejoice more in God's story and less in our own, not even in mere metanarrative as such. We can also rejoice in every distant echo of God's grand redemptive story in the stories of our surrounding culture, noting with the similarities the key differences of hero, setting, threat, resolution, and goal.

**Context grows.** We grow less and less comfortable with our habitual compartmentalization of the various aspects of our life and loves. Our impulse to objectify each aspect into a component for mastery grows unquiet, unsustainable. In particular, our willingness to sacrifice truth and goodness for personal pleasure comes under increasing challenge from the Holy Spirit, speaking through the Scriptures. We live more with God as our own context.

**Pure sexual affections begin and grow.** Our beloved sexual autonomy, which maximizes our treasures—pleasures of body and soul, convenience, personal dignity and self-worth, mental health—and minimizes persons, especially children and God, will diminish. We turn instead toward God-centered sexuality—redeemed passions in his context—full of gratitude and joy, reflecting his glory and his preferences. All questions and struggles about sexual identity and preference pivot here, from inward-directed to godward-directed. God redeems and moves us toward his intention, his pleasure, his beauty. All of us will, in redemption, grow twitchy with sexual autonomy and turn away from it and toward a creaturely sexuality that reflects the Creator, a redeemed sexuality that honors the Redeemer. Fornication and adultery, whose longings we once could only hope to suppress, can actually lose their sheen. Sexual union, previously opaque in its surface value, can grow transparent—like, yet unlike—revealing behind it God's transcendent love for his people, Christ's coming wedding to his intended bride, and our calling to represent his story in our own, whether in contented singleness or in delighted marriage.

**We measure creation by God instead of by ourselves.** We who once wondered if we could get enough (we couldn't) have now stopped measuring God's gifts by our own demands and expectations. Instead of measuring God's provision by our own desires, quantifying his divine bounty in created units of measure, we now thank God for his superabundance. "Command those who are rich in this present world not to be arrogant nor to put their hope in wealth, which is so uncertain, but to put their hope in God, who richly provides us with everything for our enjoyment" (1 Tim. 6:17).

Suffering, likewise, we once measured by our own perceived capacities, saying, "I cannot bear this; this is too much for me." "I don't deserve this." "I am at the end of my rope." In redemption, we look to our Christ, whose sufferings we share. He sends us only what works for our good, even when it is excruciatingly difficult or feels like the fire. He is with us and "will not let you be tempted beyond what you can bear. But when you are tempted, he will also provide a way out so that you can endure it" (1 Cor. 10:13).

## My Testimony to Some Aesthetic Effects of Redemption

I write here of my own experience, so this section is neither Bible study nor an attempt to organize ideas in a systematic theology. Rather I recount my story, testifying how God has changed my aesthetic sense in my relationship to my wife.

When Sharon and I met, I appreciated her considerable—one might say objective—beauty. When I grew to love her, though, my long-held expectations objected. I imagined tall and blonde; she was a short brunette. I was hip; she was straight—culturally conservative. I grew up with folk music; she grew up with opera and musical theater. I rode my bike everywhere; she drove her car. I grabbed a snack under a tree; she went out to lunch. Though I loved her, she seemed rooted in the culture I was trying to escape; I could not see my way clear to marry her. I told her so, to my shame. God in his kindness changed my mind, my will, and my affection. Though I had spoken rashly, she accepted me and my marriage proposal.

As our years together unfolded, my appreciation of her beauty sometimes faltered, again on account of my presumption of objective beauty standards. God has gradually and graciously turned my heart away from impersonal ideas to the woman he has given me. I see my darling is lovelier than ever, thinking I see clearly what is really there. My lady, on the other hand, attributes the beauty I see in her to God's redemptive work in my eyes, my redeemed taste. Either way, her beauty actually grows. Yes, a ripening, but more than ripeness appears to my eyes; rather her beauty appears to me cumulative, adding later beauty to earlier, so that her present loveliness now seems so radiant, complex, immeasurably rich, that sometimes I can scarcely bear to look at her, or to look away from her. Thankfully, my capacity to delight in her grows too, and my gratitude. I suppose beauty may eventually fade with age, but I'm willing to wait.

## Redeemed Aesthetic: Eyes for God

The Redeemer gives us eyes to see God himself as the most beautiful of all, revealed in a thousand ways through his creation, as interpreted by his Word. But not all at once; no longer static, objective, and absolute, our sense of beauty becomes dynamic. We no longer look to the best beauty we can see or imagine as ultimate. While a thousand delights are ours now in Christ, he will give still more. "'What no eye has seen, what no ear has heard, and what no human mind has conceived'—the things God has prepared for those who love him—these are the things God has revealed to us by his Spirit" (1 Cor. 2:9–10).

We see created things now, by the Spirit, and we will see more later as we grow in Christ, and more still when we enter his presence and see him as he is. Until then, our aesthetic sense remains limited and hampered by sin. Both of these, the hampering and the limitation, come to us by the design of God, who loves, apparently, the incremental unfolding of his purposes, the gradual revealing of his glory.

The exhortation in the letter to the Philippians to think on what is true, honorable, pure, lovely, commendable, on excellence, on things worthy of praise, reflects Paul's radical transformation and the radical transformation of those he loves—people who, if not transformed, could think of nothing but the false, dishonorable, impure, repulsive, blameworthy, inferior, worthy of reproach. Of course, we can still think on these things, but our new ability to think on good things leaps off the page in Philippians 4:8–9. Our aesthetic senses have been redeemed and are being redeemed.

## Redeemed Eyes on Our Surroundings

Because God's people see all creation in him, we can see first our own distortions of his glory and find reason to repent, receive, and give thanks. We can also cast a redemptive eye on our culture, seeing its distortions against the backdrop of the created perfection like we see our own. We can also appreciate in every cultural expression those wonderful truths that persevere, distorted or not, in various forms. We can see what most artists know intuitively and practically: despite the theory, art simply cannot be for art's sake alone. Aesthetics cannot be truly isolated and pure; always there is a point to be made, an effect on the receiver, a transaction. Content, form, and power still point, however distantly, to God's triadic glory, even in the most sordid stuff. All stories, even the deceptive ones, work with borrowed capital, concocting variations on God's original redemptive epic.

Because our Savior feels things, we feel them too. Jesus wept (John 11:35); he was deeply moved (John 11:38); he longed for the well-being of those he cared about (Matt. 23:37); his love was supreme (John 15:13). We can share in his affectional responses.

"Go throughout the city of Jerusalem and put a mark on the foreheads of those who grieve and lament over all the detestable things that are done in it" (Ezek. 9:4). God's own remnant sees the abominations God sees, and their passionate revulsion is aroused. They hate it, and this very hatred, though apparently inarticulate, sets them apart as God's own people. God spares them from the destruction that comes on the city's other inhabitants.

Our loves and hates can grow like our God's. So the psalmist can say, "Take delight in the LORD, and he will give you the desires of your heart" (Ps. 37:4). God satisfies the new desires he gives, and draws us into his own disgusts.

- "I say of the holy people who are in the land, 'They are the noble ones in whom is all my delight'" (Ps. 16:3).
- "Let those who love the LORD hate evil" (Ps. 97:10).
- "Who despises a vile person but honors those who fear the LORD" (Ps. 15:4).

Jesus Christ has an open ear, and "my ears you have opened" (Ps. 40:6). His people have open ears in him, even before they are aware. They hear what they once missed, what others miss: "He who has ears to hear, let him hear" (Matt. 11:15 ESV). The singular masculine pronoun points to Jesus in his spectacular singularity; he is the one who hears, and in whom all his people, men and women, first hear God's Word with delight and will hear more.

## Redeemed Aesthetics of Creation

Creation, once opaque, becomes translucent. God's people see more, far more, than abstract truth, beauty, and goodness in God's rich creation; we see God's beauty, his truth, his goodness. We can see these even in their conspicuous absence and distortion, in creation's danger, its futility, and the decay of our own bodies and of those of our loved ones.

The redeemed eye can see creation's value in God's eyes, as it belongs to him and shows him: "Since the creation of the world God's invisible qualities—his eternal power and divine nature—have been clearly seen, being understood from what has been made" (Rom. 1:20).

## Redeemed Aesthetics of Society

We read that God rules in sovereign providence in all that occurs; the redeemed eye can see God's beauty, truth, and power even in the tawdry and grotesque, the lie or half-truth, the oppressive use of power—sometimes in its contrasts, sometimes in his phenomenal promised redemption, sometimes even in the comfort of the cleansing of his sure judgment or almost unbelievable mercy. This intimate view stands close to the suffering, even to the oppressor. We can see this because, since we love a longer story and so believe God's promise to punish and to redeem, we find comfort that he takes passionate, holy interest in all he has made. He will see it right again, even at stunning cost.

God made the world for his glory, so his redemption of the world means glory to God in each detail, in each moment. Of course each chromosome, each species, each person means itself, but it means itself only because it means more than itself; it means him. The inherency of creation's meaning does not spring from objectivity; the inherent meaning of creation and of society presents no difficulty to the redeemed eye. Instead redemption presents rich, satisfying explanations of that meaning. Beauty is an aspect of all meaning, for God's glory always has three intertwined aspects. So he calls his people to keep looking for and working for his beauty with his truth and his power. Meaning is in context, context is glory, and God is context for all his creation. Glory belongs to God.

## Redeemed Aesthetics in the Church and Parachurch

Churches and seminaries with a redemptive theology of aesthetics will connect better our knowledge of doctrine with our love for Christ and his story. Since Scripture speaks in forms and about forms, as well as in truth content and ethics, devout aesthetic training of pastors can support better the aesthetic discipleship of all members. We remember that forms, by stirring our affections, are meant to motivate, while truth content and doctrine direct our motion with proper limits and corrections. God's models motivate; his morals delineate. Taken together, in the Word and in the world, they bear fruit that will last.

Our newfound abhorrence for our own sin helps us love our neighbor, especially the tricky one. We who hate our sin and look to Christ for improved habits can take a similar approach in loving and helping others, with humility. We may find help here for understanding the godly hatred that puzzles us from the Psalms.

- "In whose eyes a vile person is despised" (Ps. 15:4 ESV) characterizes the person God draws close. God changes his eyes, his vision.
- "I hate those who cling to worthless idols" (Ps. 31:6).
- "Do I not hate those who hate you, O LORD? And do I not loathe those who rise up against you? I hate them with complete hatred; I count them my enemies" (Ps. 139:21–22 ESV).

Since despisement and hatred are feelings, or have feeling aspect, we notice these passages with a jolt, first because this hatred is pointed at a people rather than at evil deeds. We remember God's command to love our neighbors. Let us remember that our own sins are to be hated first; we are the vile person, we are God's enemies unless he has mercy. He can and he has. He can have mercy on others who deserve hatred.

Aesthetically based outreaches and ministries of the church and parachurch organizations might consider more closely the Christ-centered connection of truth with beauty and delight. Instead of asking, "What will attract the people we hope to reach," we can ask, "What appeal can attract those among these people whose existing tastes have a germ of attraction to God? What appeal can stir this attraction?" Jesus used this approach, broadcasting his parables to all his hearers, knowing he would reach only those with new tastes: "He who has ears to hear, let him hear" (Mark 4:9 ESV). Such redeemed aesthetic criteria do not constitute a new ground for legalism in the church or the parachurch; rather they constitute a fresh hope for exploring the fountain of redeemed delights, to which the Lord may awaken anyone at any time.

## Redeemed Aesthetics of the Future

God's people have long rejoiced at the defeat of their enemies. Miriam led the Israelite women in a dance and song of rejoicing when Pharaoh's army was destroyed in the Red Sea; the women who greeted Saul and David upon the defeat of the Philistine army sang, "Saul has slain his thousands, and David his tens of thousands" (1 Sam. 18:7). All the Psalms that call for a new song of praise to God do so in response to the King's victory over his enemies.[4] The Israelites' conquest of Canaan under Joshua's leadership, completed by David, prefigures Christ's conquest of his people's sins. Matthew records Gabriel's connecting these dots when he appeared to Joseph in a dream: "You shall call his name Jesus [Greek for Joshua], for he will save his people from their sins" (Matt. 1:21 ESV). Just as the first Joshua saved his people from their enemies, so also the last Joshua, Jesus, will save his people from their enemies, their sins.

God's people will take joy in this salvation as they never could before they were saved.

God's people will also find a new pain, a holy dissatisfaction, a tension that never would have found a resting place in their emotions before the Holy Spirit brought new life. We will find our unconfessed sin a stone in the shoe or worse. We will find unpunished sin in others out-of-joint, a tension, requiring relief in prayer (Psalm 73). Our growing appreciation of God's justice and mercy transforms our response to injustice, oppression, and the need for repentance.

Like yeast, this new vision grows from the barely noticeable to suffuse the whole conscience, swelling with life. All God's people grow in vision, seeing as time unfolds more and more of Christ's beauty and majesty. Others see less and less of whatever glimpses may have come to them. One can get a general sense of whether a person sees or doesn't by watching which way his or her vision grows over time.

We are not in charge of the growth or degeneration of our vision. Rather God's gift of seeing *anything* either increases our grace or increases our guilt for failing to appreciate and repent.

---

4. Tremper Longman III and Daniel G. Reid, *God Is a Warrior* (Grand Rapids, MI: Zondervan, 1995), 45.

# Redeemed Aesthetics of the Final Judgment

Pleasures play a prominent role in prophecy of the end times. All the luxuries of the great whore Babylon (Revelation 18), pleasures seized in rebellious defiance of God, will fall in ruin, destruction, and torment. These examples should startle us with their familiarity.

> The merchants of the earth will weep and mourn over her because no one buys their cargoes anymore—cargoes of gold, silver, precious stones and pearls; fine linen, purple, silk and scarlet cloth; every sort of citron wood, and articles of every kind made of ivory, costly wood, bronze, iron and marble; cargoes of cinnamon and spice, of incense, myrrh and frankincense, of wine and olive oil, of fine flour and wheat; cattle and sheep; horses and carriages; and human beings sold as slaves.
>
> They will say, "The fruit you longed for is gone from you. All your luxury and splendor have vanished, never to be recovered." The merchants who sold these things and gained their wealth from her will stand far off, terrified at her torment. They will weep and mourn and cry out:
>
> "Woe! Woe to you, great city,
>> dressed in fine linen, purple and scarlet,
>> and glittering with gold, precious stones and pearls!
> In one hour such great wealth has been brought to ruin!"
>
> —Revelation 18:11–17

All the delights and treasures of our God-defying hearts, and of all worldly cultures, from Adam and Eve to Lamech's three sons and all the way to the end, find their place in this Babylon. All her punishment, the destruction and loss of her luxuries and sexual immoralities, together with the loss of power represented in all those lost sales and the judgment on the market driven by appetites for luxuries and oppression, all her deprivations and even her terrifying torment, have their own aesthetic aspect. It forms a fitting wage to her aesthetic sins, the symmetrical closing to the tale. A heavenly voice commands it, and for just that reason: "Give back to her as she has given; pay her back double for what she has done. Pour her a double portion from her own cup. Give her as much torment and grief as the glory and luxury she gave herself" (Rev. 18:6–7).

This command comes to God's people (vv. 1, 6), who God expects will see and appreciate the judicial symmetry between the whore's luxuries and her judgment, with its aesthetic fittingness. Since it concerns them, God gives them the strange privilege of obeying his command by throwing Babylon down in disgrace. A psalmist anticipates just this strange privilege. "May the praise of God be in their mouths and a double-edged sword in their hands, to inflict vengeance on the nations and punishment on the peoples, to bind their kings with fetters, their nobles with shackles of iron, to carry out the sentence written against them—this is the *glory* of all his faithful people. Praise the LORD" (Ps. 149:6–9, emphasis added).

This glory, this privilege, is not presently ours; in fact, we probably see it not as a privilege but as a thing to be avoided. I recoil at the thought, knowing my own appetite for pleasure enough to tremble. I dislike even the idea of violence or vengeance, and I love many fine people who do not now love and trust Jesus, but find him distasteful. Yet in many Scripture passages that promise God's coming judgment and our role in it, God speaks to comfort us. I gather that our comfort, like the judgment promised, waits for a future time. Apparently, God will further change our aesthetic senses so that we will take satisfaction in seeing his judgment of the wicked, even in participating in it. Here are mysteries too deep for us.[5]

## Redeemed Aesthetics of the New Jerusalem

Only transformed aesthetic senses will glimpse and desire the eternal glories of the coming kingdom of God. As our aesthetic senses are redeemed, we will find God's promises for our future more and more desirable. We will be better able to imagine and hope in the coming kingdom. God is fitting us for heaven; the promised glories will be fully accessible to God's people. Delight will be ours and will remain mysterious.

All the delights we know in this present life—food, rest, love, comforts, friendship—will in their translucency make the delights of the heavenly kingdom somehow familiar. Our Lord intimates this familiarity to the faithful thief on the cross: "Today you will be with me in paradise" (Luke 23:43). God's people "feast on the abundance of your house; you give them drink from your river of delights" (Ps. 36:8). Every wonderful good thing in the eternal kingdom will be familiar to eyes that have grown to see God in them in this life.

The coming glories will also be strange, mysterious. "In your light we see light" (Ps. 36:9) suggests that God's radiance will illumine light itself. This surpasses our understanding. The scale and proportion of the New Jerusalem

---

5. Notice that God addresses his declaration through Ezekiel, "I take no pleasure in the death of the wicked" (33:11), only to the wicked among his own covenant people, not to wicked people outside his covenant.

seem bizarre: an enormous cube with gates of pearl, each as big as the state of Ohio. (Only think of the oyster!) Though familiar, the delights of God's eternal kingdom surpass our imagination.

God will wed the familiar delight to the mysterious, in himself: "'What no eye has seen, what no ear has heard, and what no human mind has conceived—the things God has prepared for those who love him—these are the things God has revealed to us by his Spirit'" (1 Cor. 2:9–10).

God is with us, and he is beyond us. He alone will interpret delight to his people in his eternal kingdom, by being with us. God calls *himself* Abraham's "very great reward" (Gen. 15:1). The delights we recognize, those for which we hope, are ours as he is ours and we are his. Simple pleasures, scintillating delights, all flow from God because God is whole, holy, and he will be with us then in an intimacy we can believe without fully grasping.

And yet grasp we will, apparently: Jesus, after his resurrection, cautions Mary, "Do not hold on to me, for I have not yet ascended to the Father" (John 20:17). We cling to him now in the Spirit because he has ascended. We will cling all the more earnestly when we "see him as he is," and so come to be like him (1 John 3:2). Mystery and familiarity of the fully restored aesthetic will meet, and will come to us, in the returned person of Jesus Christ.

## READ, REFLECT, DISCUSS, SING

1. Suggested reading: "Artistry in Christ," chapter 4 of *Voicing Creation's Praise: Towards a Theology of the Arts* by Jeremy S. Begbie; "The Gospel Solution to Idolatry," chapter 5 of *The Things of Earth: Treasuring God by Enjoying His Gifts* by Joe Rigney.
2. Q1. Tell about an example of how your tastes and preferences change as you grow in the grace of Christ.
3. Q2. Our tastes also change as we grow older. How has grace changed you even more than age? Where do you hope to see God's grace change your tastes in the coming two years? How can you pray about this?
4. Sing: "It Is Well with My Soul."

# Chapter 12

# VISION REDEEMED AND REDEEMING

*Naught be all else to me, save that Thou art!*
—EIGHTH-CENTURY IRISH POEM

How shall the redeemed eye interact with all that comes into view? Our interaction consists in our interpreting and responding to our situation. Our surroundings, everything we see and hear, everything we smell and taste, come through God's providence. Jesus encompasses this broad category in his metaphor: "It is not what goes into the mouth that defiles a person, but what comes out of the mouth; this defiles a person" (Matt. 15:11 ESV; also in Mark 7:15–23). By "what goes into the mouth," he signifies our situation; by "what comes out of the mouth," our interpretation of it and response to it—"making something of the world."[1] We do culture, either defiling ourselves or working in building the culture of the kingdom of God.

God began making something of the world, first by giving form to the formless heaven and earth that he created, and then by seeing its goodness. He called and enabled Adam and Eve to make something of the world with him, but they rebelled and walled him out of their cultural interaction. Now that Christ has restored us to sharing the Father's interpretation and response, we do not lead; we follow. We leave at the door any presumption that making something of the world is properly a purely human work. Rather, cultural interaction is a human work because God works it first and we bear his image; Christians now respond, making something of the world, because our eyes are redeemed and we no longer pretend autonomy.

---

1. Andy Crouch, *Culture Making* (Downers Grove, IL: InterVarsity, 2008), 23.

God changes our taste buds when he regenerates us, first for God's Word. The Bible that once repelled us grows tolerable, then sweeter, richer. Isaiah casts this whole-life transformation in aesthetic terms, using the food metaphor that reminds us of "good for food" in Genesis: "Why spend money on what is not bread, and your labor on what does not satisfy? Listen, listen to me, and eat what is good, and you will delight in the richest of fare. Give ear and come to me; listen, that you may live" (Isa. 55:2–3).

God changes his people's taste so they can delight in the richest of fare instead of working for what does not satisfy. The transformation of our aesthetic sense comes from God. Once begun, it grows. This growth governs the entire path of cultural interaction, since Christians come to make meaning of our surroundings in the same way we make meaning of Scripture. This transformation of interpretation, while as simple as eating an ice-cream cone, acquires a richness of nuance and perspective, full of love that fills life.

I see the first real snow just now, falling on our rain-starved north Sierra mountains—a travel nuisance, of course, but most welcome. As we thank God and pray for more, we remember that God shines the power of his Word through the snow and rain. He gives this insight in poetic form. The precipitation we prayed for that he sends today accomplishes the good he intends for his creatures and points to his Word.

> As the rain and the snow
> > come down from heaven,
> and do not return to it
> > without watering the earth
> and making it bud and flourish,
> > so that it yields seed for the sower and bread for the eater,
> so is my word that goes out from my mouth:
> > It will not return to me empty,
> but will accomplish what I desire
> > and achieve the purpose for which I sent it.
> > > —Isaiah 55:10–11

This snow I see, infused by God's Word with metaphoric richness, now shows God and his Word. All three aspects of God's glory come into play here; the truth of God's Word comes with full power to do all God wants. It comes in a common Hebrew literary form, the two-line grouping most prominent in poetry but salted through all other types of biblical Hebrew literature.

Isaiah's poetry conveys the about-ness of rain and snow, pointing to God's powerful Word. Although this brief mention offers no details of the truth contained in God's rain-like Word, this truth is depicted together with its power ("it . . . will accomplish") and beauty in its poetic form—content, purpose, and form in triadic fullness, just as we saw in the creation account. Our redeemed, Bible-guided eyes can see new connections in every direction. In these few verses, we catch a backward glance at the creation story and a forward glance at the completion of many of God's words that awaited fulfillment. This fulfillment includes the revelation of his Word in person, which John mentions with the "in the beginning" (John 1:1) that suggests the Genesis creation account. We could go on, but you get the idea. Redeemed eyes on Scripture and creation see the glory arrows in more and more.

## Redeemed Interaction

The new eye begins our redemptive interaction by seeing what we encounter, no longer according to our autonomous vision, but sharing God's vision. We cannot see to the bottom as God does, but our depth perception can grow, through new birth and growing up. God sees everything in its proper context. This context includes the story and the cultural categories of creation and redemption taught in Scripture.

We have made special note of the first three chapters of Genesis, just to start on the right foot with passions. Only when we discover what passion is can we notice its distortions. Genesis teaches that what a thing is originates in how God sees it. We glimpse from a distance the innocence of Adam and Eve's shared perception with God, including pleasures. God is the first seer, revealing our distorted seeing. We are incapable of aesthetic objectivity and of objective knowledge and objective ethical goodness, not just because we are finite or even because we are fallen. We are incapable of objectivity of any kind because this precious presumption was never valid. We were never made for objectivity, whether about truth or beauty or goodness. Now in our redemption, God calls us back to share, even more richly than Adam and Eve shared, in his divine subjectivity. We are called to this shared truth, love, and goodness.

## Scope and Horizons of the Redeemed Eye

We can look for content, form, and purpose in everything people do and say, because all we say and do glorifies either God or his creatures. That glory is always triadic. We can look for the glory arrows; where are they pointing? Whose glory is in view? Whose glory hoped for or sought or credited? In a work, these arrows show up on three horizons, a triad of triads: the intention of the author (what he believes, loves, and wills), the character of the work (its content, form, and purpose), and the interpretation of the viewer-experiencer (his presuppositions, pre-affections, and predispositions). We always find the same three aspects, visible to greater or lesser extent in every word, deed, making. Discourse is always the ascription of glory, though a work may emphasize one aspect of glory over others. In popular music, for example, form and its aesthetic properties seem to take center stage, often leaving truth content in the background.

Even a slight misunderstanding in conversation reminds us that our meanings differ. Communications consist in at least three horizons: what the author meant, the properties of the communication itself, and the interpretation given that communication by the reader, listener, viewer, toucher, or eater. Each requires careful consideration, but we will pay especial attention to seeing—to interpretation. The interpretive task has particular importance for us who find ourselves surrounded by media, when we ask, "Can I see this redemptively, or should I look away?"

The redeemed eye has great freedom, to be used in wisdom. Paul argues for our freedom, defending it to Timothy against pietistic cultural externalists by sketching its conditions: "They forbid people to marry and order them to abstain from certain foods, which God created to be received with thanksgiving by those who believe and who know the truth. For everything God created is good, and nothing is to be rejected if it is received with thanksgiving, because it is consecrated by the word of God and prayer" (1 Tim. 4:3–5).

With transformed eyes, we will see and respond to everything we behold, visible and invisible, in five basic steps.

1. Know the truth that applies to this object; consider together the three aspects of glory in terms of the object's creation, and identify the object the work glorifies.
2. See the object's reference to God.
3. Thank God for this reflection of his character he gives for our benefit. He saw creation good, so we can see bits of goodness even here. This work borrows from God's glory, though with distortions; we can see the goodness through the distortions and thank him for its reflection of his goodness (even in his redeeming or judging).
4. See the object according to God's Word, including its prohibitions.
5. Pray for greater insight, wisdom, sound affection, and love for others. This may include asking God to search our hearts for the misplaced emotions, beliefs, and practices with which we have responded, so that we may pray for forgiveness and better eyes.

Notice that this pattern of Christian cultural engagement is neither a principle nor a system of principles; it is relational. God brings us into his new covenant; he talks to us by the Holy Spirit speaking through the Scriptures, enabling us to reply, thanking him and making our requests known. He hears and answers. Christians are called to reject no created thing for which they can thank God. Wisdom from Scripture and fellow Christians will direct us to avoid areas of weakness or deceitful desire (Eph. 4:22).

## Aesthetic Discipleship

Aesthetic discipleship is a Christian privilege and duty. God enables and expects us to acquire godly tastes, his tastes. He commands affections.

- "Delight yourself in the LORD" (Ps. 37:4 ESV).
- "Rejoice in the wife of your youth. . . . Let her breasts fill you at all times with delight" (Prov. 5:18–19 ESV).
- "Hate evil, love good" (Amos 5:15).
- "Love must be sincere. Hate what is evil; cling to what is good. Be devoted to one another in love. Honor one another above yourselves. Never be lacking in zeal, but keep your spiritual fervor, serving the Lord" (Rom. 12:9–11).

Yet this runs contrary to the premises of our hearts and of our day. We treasure our feelings just as they are, imagining they cannot be changed. What we desire, we soon "need," then demand. The evolution requires no change to our affections, only bloating. We protect our feelings against all challengers, expecting them to serve us. Instead, soon enough, the servant becomes the master, and we serve them. So the project doesn't work as hoped. That doesn't stop us. Only Christ can redirect our feelings and tastes. This he does by regeneration and our constant repentance and by all the ordinary graces and disciplines of the Christian life. In Christ, we change from needers to thankers, sanctified through discipline, because God works gradual sanctification in us. We grow in contentment. We suffer more faithfully. Watch the general direction of change, thank God, and press on.

King David says, in his prayer of repentance, "You delight in truth in the inward being" (Ps. 51:6 ESV). Such truth exceeds the objective facts, the data we collect and store. He who is true calls us to become true as he is true. Likewise, believers in Jesus are called to *become* beautiful, not just to grow in our ability to recognize and appreciate beauty. We gain the counterintuitive beauty of the blood, of weakness. Our Redeemer calls us to grow strong, even strong through weakness for now. He does this by uniting us, mysteriously but really, to himself.

The new person has ears and can obey the Lord's command, "Let him hear." He sees with transformed eyes, loves good and beauty with refreshed passion, hates evil with renewed fervor, beginning with our own sin. Everything is different. We know this, and we also discover gradually renewal's full extent, in our practical aesthetic discipleship. In the first place, aesthetic passions no longer stand alone, competing for our attention against truth and goodness; although we may be messed up, we know that properly these three always go together. That will lead us to better questions than we were asking before.

With our old eyes, we saw our passions, and all aesthetics, in a story of one chapter. We could ask only, "Is this good or bad?" "Do I like it or not?" "Should everyone like this or not?" Even asking, "What intrinsic properties has God placed in his gifts?" still reduces the aesthetic story to a single chapter. Any aesthetic story in one chapter remains essentially static. Without the narrative arc of creation, fall, redemption, consummation, it refers to nothing beyond itself.

The redeemed eye, informed by Scripture and opened by the Holy Spirit, can see aesthetics in a God-centered story of four chapters: creation, fall, redemption, consummation. With the first chapter, creation, we are asking, "What should I be like? What did God make, and how did he see and respond? Where does that put me?" Here we find our concepts and definitions. We find that all saying and doing was meant to be about God and his glory and that, even twisted and fragmented, discourse is always about someone's glory.

With the second chapter, the fall, we are asking, "What went wrong?" We have already noticed how our disordered passions press in on us: how they catch us, almost against our will. Even when they serve us, we serve them. Only by knowing the creational purity of God's glory can we begin to notice the distortions of sin. Then we can recognize in our present experience various kinds of perversions and disintegrations that attack our affections and our reasons for loving them just as they are—the aesthetic effects of sin.

With the third chapter, redemption, we ask, "How can I change?" "What has Christ done and promised to keep doing to redeem those distortions and disintegrations?" "How has his life, death, resurrection, ascension, and vow to return in glory accomplished just what our bewildered and tawdry affections need in order to join together with each other and with God?"

With the fourth chapter, consummation, Christ's return in glory comes into view. This remains mostly mysterious, but God has given us enough solid clues that we can anticipate confidently some of the solid hope he offers for a final restoration of our aesthetic slavery and solitude.

All discourse retains many basic aspects of God's glory revealed in creation; even twisted and fragmented, the basic aspects cannot be undone, only damaged and perverted. God, working in redemptive history, restores these in individuals, in families, and in the church.

Although the Christian eye can affirm the creational value, wisdom about our weakness and sin can help us avoid cultural mousetraps. You are probably not called to try to interact redemptively with works and media in which you have faced habitual temptation. Still, staying away from it will be an act of wise obedience, not an act of self-protection against the harmful effects of bad input, as if no other defense were possible for others. The separatist approach, common among pietists and many contemporary Western evangelicals, focuses on antithesis, assuming that cultural media has all the power and will infect and hurt you if you get close. This position rests on static, one-chapter aesthetics; it pays little to no attention to our interpretive eye or to how God can change it in Christ. H. Richard Niebuhr calls this "Christ against Culture."[2]

With a new, redemptive-historical view of aesthetics, we can now abandon the many other popular approaches to media and feelings:

- Feelings (aesthetic responses) are neither good nor bad; they just *are*.
- Feelings cannot be changed but form an inviolable part of our humanity.
- Feelings are inherently good; they shouldn't be challenged.
- Feelings are inherently suspect; if it feels good, it must be dangerous.

Instead we can take a pre-affectional approach to feelings of all kinds. This approach to aesthetics reshapes the questions we'll ask of any aesthetic or artistic work, process, or undertaking, and of our own feelings, so we can interpret them according to the kingdom of God. No longer "Is this a Christian work? Is the maker a Christian?" but "What of God's glory remains in this? What in this does God affirm? What can I affirm with him? What does he challenge? What does he call me to challenge, in myself by repentance or in another person or in the culture broadly? How can I love God and my neighbor right here? What message does it intend as truth? What power does it practice or honor? What ethics are in view here? What must be true about God for this message to work? Where does this work borrow from God's glory? How can a redeemed eye see this redemptively? What does God intend here?"

We have seen that Scripture argues for a pre-affectional approach to aesthetics, as it argues for a presuppositional approach to truth content and a

---

2. Richard Niebuhr, *Christ and Culture* (San Francisco: HarperSanFrancisco, 2001), 45–82.

predispositional approach to ethics. Forms, their aesthetic properties, and our aesthetic responses to them are always infused with worship, always turning us toward God or away from him. So we must repent of our selfish, isolationist, fragmented, and compartmentalized view of aesthetics. Only God can change us, reshaping our loves and preferences, our aversions and disgusts, to share increasingly with his own.

## Examples

Now we can glimpse bits of sunlight glowing red and blue through patterns of colored glass. Let us look more closely at some individual pieces to explore a redeemed cultural interaction. We will consider a few examples, individual works, and even forms—the building blocks of those works. We examine forms here to show that, just as truth can never be rightly understood as generic but always points to God or to some false object of glory, so also the conventional shapes of discourse always point in many ways to God's glory or to the glory of some created object.

First, the redeemed eye will interpret all it sees using the same triadic hermeneutic we learn from Scripture. Scripture teaches more than doctrine; the redeemed eye also learns and practices how God sees, how he interprets.[3] Because these changes are personal, the Christian again sees with God rather than autonomously. We learn a redemptive interpretation, a redemptive hermeneutic. We remember that the Christian will find in everything something to affirm and, in everything but Scripture itself, something to redeem. We remember as well that although all things are lawful or permissible to us, not everything is beneficial or constructive (1 Cor. 10:23); where sin has left us weak and vulnerable to temptation, each of us needs safeguards against our sinful habits.

Using the interpretive story of creation, fall, redemption, and consummation, the Christian eye will find in everything something to affirm, though with caution fitting to the distortions. Those distortions we are called to notice and perhaps to challenge, sometimes avoid, or even suppress in the public interest, remembering that their danger points beyond the distortions in the work to the misplaced loves of human viewers.

### *A Modern Story Example:* **Winnie the Pooh**

How might a Christian interact with A. A. Milne's classic work?[4] First, what can we affirm? Consider three simple observations: First, it's a story, and a series of stories that form a whole, a lot like God's great story. Second, the characters

---

3. Westminster Confession of Faith I, IX, from *The Trinity Hymnal*, rev. ed. (Suwanee, GA: Great Commission, 1990), 854.
4. A. A. Milne, *Winnie-the-Pooh* (New York: Dell, 1970).

often act foolishly and selfishly, but the author deals tenderly with these foibles, and the other characters love the selfish fool. "Silly old bear," says Christopher Robin about Pooh, expressing his patience and love. This patience and love arise from an pre-existing, unshakable relationship, much like a covenant. Third, external threats look bigger at first than they turn out to be later. Where do the glory arrows point? They point to the treasure of loyalty, and through it to the same loyalty and kind patience that the author shows to Christopher Robin. The Christian eye can affirm much more here.

What in Milne's book does God's eye challenge? In reading these stories to our own children, not much. Stories can ask questions and suggest answers. We need not make much of God's nonappearance in this story. Still, the mom or dad reading this aloud to their small child will remember that all human loyalty springs from and points back to God's covenant loyalty to his people and teach this in other ways to their children.

## A Principle Example: Plato's Truth, Beauty, and Goodness

Plato's three principles of human philosophy—beauty, truth, and goodness—correspond closely to the three aspects of God's revealing his glory mentioned in Genesis. The redeemed eye can affirm this, recognizing this correspondence to the three aspects of God's glory—capital borrowed from God.

Plato and his heirs depersonalize these into principles and ideals, not acknowledging that these three aspects constitute the perfections of God's glory, inherent to the Godhead and revealed in creation. We tend to assume that any right-minded person would recognize these principles, and many do. This assumption implies that at least the best human minds work fine, and that sin has no effects on the faculties that recognize truth, beauty, and goodness—our cognition, our feelings, or our will. More than this, God's appreciation of his own glory has no place in the Platonic formula. Plato's light shines on human culture, and with his help we recognize bits of red, amber, and blue glass. Only the redeemed eye can see God's glory shining through these bits, and with it the very culture of the Trinity.

## A Hybrid Example: Story as Principle

We love stories; that is why they move us so powerfully. Every story borrows its narrative form from God's story of creation and redemption, often called redemptive history. Their debt is real, even if the human story glorifies equivocal values or features an ambivalent redeemer.

Myths and other stories attract us so strongly that most ancient cultures identified themselves chiefly by their myths, usually weaving origins with the compelling narrative frameworks that give meaning to every component of ordinary life. We love stories in which we have the meaning and control that we want, even if it means we serve some god—some objective value—in order to get what we want. In this, we differ little from the Canaanites, who offered sacrifices to Baal, even cut themselves, pressuring him to do what they wanted (1 Kings 18:28).

For all our pride, we differ little from these early pagans; our stories aren't all that different from ancient Near Eastern myths, Greek and Roman myths, Nordic myths. Every movement embraces a defining myth. The turn-of-the-sixteenth-century myth of human progress toward world peace exploded in the poison gas shells of the First World War. Communism has a compelling story of class struggle, culminating in perfect equality. The Darwinian story implies progress, constant improvement in an eternal, God-free continuum.

We love these myths because they offer us appealing plot premises. Any happy ending, any redemptive story, can win our affections. Even the dystopian novels and movies that have spiraled to popularity depict bad circumstances as the setting for occasional heroism. Video games tantalize us with the hero role and with the feeling of control, mastery, or accomplishment.

## A New Testament Story Example: The Messiah Story

The apostle Peter, like most of his friends and neighbors, loved a Messiah story: the one he had in mind when he tried to stop Jesus from talking about his death, because that's not the way the familiar Jewish Messiah story is supposed to go. Messiah is supposed to show up, trounce his enemies, reward his friends, and set up his reign over a restored Israel and a perfect world. No humiliation, no death, must come to Messiah, according to this story. Peter hadn't made it up; this story was widely popular during the surge of messianic expectation in Judea during the century before the start of Jesus' ministry. John the Baptist loved this story even though he had announced Jesus as the Lamb of God. He expected Jesus to move against the Romans at least enough to get him out of Herod's prison, and he sent his disciples to Jesus to ask, "Are you the one who is to come, or should we expect someone else?" (Matt. 11:3).

This popular story closely resembled the story with which Satan tempted Jesus: no suffering, no humiliation, no death; go directly to the throne, do not pass through the valley of the shadow of death. Who wants a story with suffering, humiliation, and death? Not Jesus; he made it clear as he pled with his Father for any other way. "Father, if you are willing, take this cup from me." He prayed for obedience, and he obeyed: "Yet not my will, but yours be done" (Luke 22:42).

Jesus obeyed because he loved his Father and he loved his people. He also loved the story he and the Father had planned together before the world, even though that story had brought him to the eve of his great passion. These loves meet in the long, long story of redemption, aimed at the eternal glory of God. This consummately lovely story stirred our Lord to persevere through his Father's dark wrath and the agonies of the garden, the flogging, and the cross, because he saw the story that Eve rejected, the story from which Satan tried to dislodge him, the story that Peter missed; he clung to it in love and hope. He suffered its depths that he might win its even greater heights. "For the joy set before him he endured the cross, scorning its shame, and sat down at the right hand of the throne of God" (Heb. 12:2). Even in the seat of honor, our Lord waits patiently for his coming triumph: "Sit at my right hand until I make your enemies a footstool for your feet" (Ps. 110:1). He embraced the story, though it led through his death and protracted delay. What a hero!

Jesus draws his people into his story, and by his death gives us power to kill our impatience, our lust for the stories that spring up so naturally in our fallen affections. He helps us delight in his story as he has revealed it in the Scriptures. He helps us wait in hope, even as we groan (Rom. 8:23–25). In our repentance, we recapitulate Jesus' death and resurrection; we walk in his story. Repentance takes place only in a time sequence. We leave our own story and enter God's. We understand ourselves and each other in terms of this redemptive story.

## The Story of Sorrow Now

Our new passion for God's story leads also to sorrow. The story turns a blind corner, even seems to go off course. When the great story Jesus showed John on Patmos seems to go astray, John knows the story should not go this way! He responds passionately. "I wept and wept because no one was found who was worthy to open the scroll or look inside. Then one of the elders said to me, 'Do not weep! See, the Lion of the tribe of Judah, the Root of David, has triumphed. He is able to open the scroll and its seven seals.' Then I saw a Lamb, looking as if it had been slain, standing at the center of the throne" (Rev. 5:4–6).

The new story remembers forever the hero's death, marked by his appearance. John saw, in his great vision of the Lord's return, a lamb "looking as if it had been slain" (v. 6). His death appears forever in memory; his reign is the greater for it, marked by his present position, "standing at the center of the throne." The great story is reaching its climax. Worship around this throne has this story strongly in mind, as the four living creatures and the twenty-four elders sing a new song to mark the King's victory: "You are worthy to take the scroll and to open its seals, *because you were slain, and with your blood you purchased for God persons from every tribe and language and people and nation*" (Rev. 5:9, emphasis added).

Ezekiel, among many Old Testament saints, finds himself in the grip of passion over the warnings he must prophesy. He first finds that the scroll, written with words of lamentation and woe, tastes sweet in his mouth, sweet as honey (Ezek. 3:3). Still, as the Spirit carries him to the scene of his prophetic ministry, he goes "in bitterness and in the anger of my spirit, with the strong hand of the LORD on me" (v. 14).

The redemptive story that grips God's people always carries these two themes: unlooked-for pain and great joy. God does not call his people to embrace mere delayed gratification, pie in the sky; he calls us to embrace death on the way to new life, to embrace God himself in Christ's death and resurrection. Our natural passion for story longs for the happy ending in which the hero overcomes by his strength, brains, courage, possibly in spite of weakness and opposition. The story of triumph *by means of* weakness and opposition has less appeal. Still less appeal has any narrative that points out our sin, our passions gone bad, our inability to get there from here. We're in God's story, but it's not about us. God's story is first and best, and it leaves plenty of room, with guidance, for the creativity of the redeemed eye.[5]

## Navigating Complex Media

More tricky but still on the same path, the movie you saw last week was good in some ways and bad in others—good directing, some weak acting, engaging story but disappointing cinematography—a complex read, but we can think about the movie and its intrinsic characteristics. The way we see the movie is not that different from the way we see the sunset.

The redeemed eye, the faithful interpreter, can approach the complexities of human cultural statements with the same approach we learned in Scripture. Movies, books, songs, news, even weather stations appeal to our affections: they speak for us, telling us what we want to hear, expressing our feelings; they also speak to us, informing and steering our feelings and actions. These media form a sort of modern secular priesthood, saying what we want to say to our peers and speaking into our lives with new context, new meaning.

How does he call me to respond here? How do I respond now? Love it, hate it? Why? To what affections does this appeal? What discipleship steps are called for? Three perspectives—three horizons, glory arrows, God's presence—begin our conversation and our work. First, consider the work's meaning along the

---

5. For more on this, see J. R. R. Tolkien, "On Fairy-Stories" in *The Tolkien Reader* (New York: Ballantine, 1966), 3–84.

three horizons already mentioned: what did the maker mean, what does the work convey in itself, and what meaning does the receiver make of it?

Second, remember to look for glory arrows. All communication consists in claims of beauty, truth, and power. These claims always attribute glory to something. What does this work glorify? A person, a group, an ideal, a product? Cell phone instructions, classical music, casual remarks, every sort of human communication can be mapped on the three aspects of glory we learned in Genesis. We can keep all three in mind, even when one aspect gets special emphasis. These imbalanced emphases usually indicate some form of siloing, an attempt to make one aspect more important than the others. Consider church worship music: the best hymns and choruses usually feature strong doctrine and strong poetic and musical quality; those that sacrifice doctrine for strong aesthetic experience, like those that overload on theology without much attention to the meaning of forms, lift one aspect of glory above the others. These songs' distorted emphasis distorts God's glory. We have explored the doctrine of this glory in earlier chapters and found its pinnacle in Jesus Christ, whose three offices have equal importance.

Third, remember God's providential hand. God is up to something. What does God mean by this? Probably, judgment and redemption both come into play in some fashion.

We, the redeemed, can now make our daily aesthetic choices with God and others in mind—personal choices like what clothes or music to buy, or shared ones like how to craft a persuasive report, what movie shall the family watch this weekend, what carpet color in the church foyer, what songs for the worship service, what word pictures to illustrate a sermon, what phrase to translate a Bible passage. No longer do we consider only aesthetic properties, hoping to create a particular impression for the target audience. No longer do we consider only the assumed aesthetic sense of the target audience. Now we can not only ask what our target audience loves and prefers at the moment; we can consider what God loves and what they would love, as their taste buds are redeemed. The apostle Paul mentions this strategy in a vivid aesthetic metaphor: "Thanks be to God, who in Christ always leads us in triumphal procession, and through us spreads the fragrance of the knowledge of him everywhere. For we are the aroma of Christ to God among those who are being saved and among those who are perishing, to one a fragrance from death to death, to the other a fragrance from life to life. Who is sufficient for these things?" (2 Cor. 2:14–16 ESV).

Some people catch a whiff of sweetness and recognize Christ by smell;[6]

6. "Quelle est cette odeur agréable?" a seventeenth-century French Christmas carol, asks, "Whence is that goodly fragrance?" meaning the birth of Christ!

others get only a stench. We cannot anticipate someone's reaction. God mysteriously regenerates some, giving them new taste, smell, sight, hearing, and touch. With others, he waits. We grow to love God's power to show his glory this way.

The redeemed eye makes aesthetic decisions about beauty and distortion, pleasure and pain, but no longer in isolation. We keep truth more and more in mind, and rightness, justice, fairness, not in themselves but as God sees them. We keep his pleasure in mind. Our pursuit of pleasure gets its doors blown off. It's all about God's pleasure, not my private delights. We share the beauty of God with him, and with brothers and sisters, together with pain and hardship. We can affirm biblically that meaning is in context. One might even say that meaning is context, and context is glory. This equation gives one small glimpse into Paul's mysterious remark, "so that God may be all in all" (1 Cor. 15:28).

God reveals himself in everything, so God's people can make God-centered meaning from everything, even when we take redemptive liberties with the work of others. Jesus has given us some initial pointers. "They have received their reward," he says (Matt. 6:16), as if to add, "and they're not going to like what's coming." The Pharisees love a truncated story, one that goes for the quick payoff but omits the coming punishment their hypocrisy deserves. They have taken everything out of context, but God will restore it in judgment.

Every crime will be punished: "It is mine to avenge; I will repay," says the Lord (Deut. 32:35). God will reveal horrible oppressions as against himself, since the oppressed bear his image. He will repay either with eternal fire or upon the person of his Son, should today's oppressor become tomorrow's penitent, as in David's case.

This creative interpretation, redemptive hermeneutic, follows the pattern we learned from Scripture. First, look for truth content, aesthetic form, and ethical purpose; these of course will inform each other. Second, locate the four principal chapters of redemptive history: creation, fall, redemption, consummation.

God's people can reinterpret what we see with great freedom, exercised in wisdom. We need not fear cultural contamination more than we fear the sins of our own hearts. Because these are already forgiven in Christ for all believers, we have strong motivation to ask him for help. If something we see seems inherently good rather than referentially good, we can ask, "Why does this attract me?" If it seems dangerous, we can likewise ask, "What corrupt lust in me does this appeal to?" Christians have no need to blame the culture, the media, at least not first. The lusts of our own heart are quite enough to keep us busy, careful, diligent, patient, and in touch with our Lord. In him we are advancing, overcoming evil with good.

Our mind's eye sees pictures and stories always, and always with a feeling response. We have discussed some stories that thread the beads of our lives into meaningful sequences, powerful to command our love and hatred. These mental pictures and stories that we love and hate predispose us to look for them among the images and tales that surround us—in effect, to click the "Like" icon, buy a movie ticket or book, read a news magazine, or follow a sports team.

The redeemed eye can look at and respond to almost anything, guided by wisdom that takes our weaknesses into account. The redeemed eye has great freedom to engage in anything and interpret God's value in it. In work created to mean only itself, to be opaque, a Christian with eyes to see can trace some threads of meaning back to the first Maker himself. Even the ugly and sordid, the unjust and oppressive, seen through eyes that God's people share with him, point backward through the horrid distortion and decontextualizing to God's created good, and forward to Christ's glorious return.

The redeemed eye must always be the repentant eye—the gouged-out, dead, and resurrected eye. We would be glad to presume (I would, anyway!) that our impulse reactions are always just fine, that no changes are needed in our judgments. My gut instincts about music and lyrics are just fine, pretty reliable. God help me. I need God's eye. "We have the mind of Christ" (1 Cor. 2:16); "To the pure, all things are pure" (Titus 1:15).

The redeemed eye will see all increasingly in context. Consider our culture's classic example of decontextualization: sex. When we focus on its pleasure as simply our own, we mistake a shared God-created union for a commodity, an "it" that we, alone, can "get" or "have." We minimize the accompanying truth content of sexual union's covenant meaning of God's love for his people in the context of spoken vows. We minimize the power of sexual union to create oneness and little people. Whether in media, imagination, or a bed, we take sex out of context and so distort beauty, meaning, and purpose.

Siloing is over. The dividing wall between the arts, technology, and science is crumbling. We already knew that the entertainment media always has a message built in—information and ethics. But we can receive redemptively as well as building, making, and speaking. God is building his eternal kingdom through us, through our cultural interactions. He calls us in redemption to notice aesthetic statements and expect them to be accompanied by truth statements, premises, assumed truths, as well as ethical judgments and ascriptions of power. Beauty for beauty's sake, beauty for the sake of our private enjoyment alone, is dead. Our impulse to seek it arose from our rebellion; our delight is now shared in Christ with the Father, who gives us all things richly to enjoy.

Solitary pleasures are over, at least as private indulgences. We have known all along, intuitively, that pleasure is always greater when shared; the clues are everywhere, from marriage to celebrations, from hospital visits to sympathy cards—feelings are better when shared. Watching a movie in a theater, or even with a few good friends, is better than seeing it alone. When you invite a guest to supper, you hope to take pleasure together. We will look for ways to share the pleasures God brings us, according to his calling. Shared aesthetic is culture, and we are building a culture of shared heavenly values; of Christ-honoring, God-centered treasures of truth, power, and beauty that spill over from his uncontainable glories to his guests.

Yes, a new and better picture, a better story—Christ's story. He has called us to put on his pictures and story. He gives us better eyes, his eyes, to replace those we gouged out. With those eyes, we can see the thousand reflections of God's pictures and stories everywhere, in all media. Consider, when you encounter a story line that seems twisted, unpleasant, or includes unwelcome elements like drugs, sex, violence, bullying. The redeemed eye can recognize in a perverted story the twisting of God's original story. Every story ever crafted, pious or ugly and anywhere between, finds its source in God's great story of creation, fall, redemption, and consummation.

At last we can see light. The plywood is pried off the rose window; the light of the sun shines again through sparkling glass images. We can see creation as it was meant to be seen—glorious in itself because it refers to God. We can appreciate what others say and do, including all that we once called art, in all its layered value, good and bad, and comprehend it in its context in God's redemptive story. This light, this eye-opened way of seeing, we may call a redemptive hermeneutic. The Christian eye judges the work in view in all three aspects of God's glory (truth content, aesthetic form, and ethical purpose) and locates it in God's great story, including its four major chapters (creation, fall, redemption, and consummation).

Because this light shines brighter over the whole course of our lives, the much-vaunted culture war properly starts in our own hearts. My call to Christian apologetics, even cultural apologetics, begins in my affections and my beliefs and in my church. We can help others answer their intellectual objections to the faith only as we answer our own, from God's Word. We can serve others with goodness and beauty through ongoing aesthetic repentance and faith, through the Holy Spirit's transforming work. We may not have made much progress, but as we move toward God instead of away from him, lights come up, hope blooms, and promises begin to come true. Meaning-connections of every true sort sprout and spread. Complex media—even Creation itself—grows transparent, referential; glory radiates through created things to God.

We close our consideration of redeemed aesthetics with a note of comfort. Jesus assures his followers that they will always recognize his voice, as sheep recognize their shepherd's voice (John 10:3–5). Sheep simply recognize the signature vibrations, like voice recognition software. Not much content, mostly form. Even though sheep's grasp of truth brings them, and us, little credit, still the form of the Good Shepherd's voice will bring us home.

## READ, REFLECT, DISCUSS, SING————————————

1. Suggested reading: *The Great Divorce* by C. S. Lewis; "Rhythms of Godwardness," chapter 6 of *The Things of Earth: Treasuring God by Enjoying His Gifts* by Joe Rigney.
2. Q1. Where have you seen God glorified in something made by a non-Christian?
3. Q2. What have you made that glorifies God, for non-Christians to see?
4. Sing: "Be Thou My Vision."

# Chapter 13

## GLORIOUS THINGS
### Restoring Godly Aesthetics to Doctrine and Culture

> They feast on the abundance of your house;
> > you give them drink from your river of delights.
> For with you is the fountain of life;
> > in your light we see light.
>
> —PSALM 36:8–9

We here broaden our conversation beyond our focus on aesthetics to consider its proper place in theology, culture, and in some basic Christian structures. We will consider some examples, which can help set direction for faithful conversations to come. First, an illustration from my own experience to illustrate the need and map the territory.

When Sharon and I started full-time music performance work, we hoped to use the power of song to help Christians live more consistently with their beliefs; we took that as an informal mission statement. We hoped to arouse people to new love for God and his doctrines through their existing love for music. We sang hundreds of concerts and talked with many, many people after those concerts. We made many good friends.

As years unfolded, we discovered that the power of music did not work as uniformly as we had hoped. People responded to it differently, according to the loves and beliefs they brought with them when they came to the concert. We found that people need no help to act according to their beliefs; people always act the way they believe. We discovered that professed beliefs are real beliefs only as they are lived out. This conclusion drew us back to the familiar gospel dynamic, reliance on the Holy Spirit working through God's Word to change people's beliefs, and even to change our affections.

Those years taught Sharon and me that music is not just a little better than teaching and cannot alone give the extra nudge toward God; no stories or pictures can. No appeal to capital-T truth can; no method or technique can. Scripture has been teaching all along that only the Holy Spirit, working through all these and other means, can overcome people's resistance to God—resistance of the mind, the affections, or practical habits. The godly power of music and of story, or of anything aesthetic, springs from the Spirit's work to transform our affections. Aesthetics' power to pull us closer or drive us away always, always speaks to a heart that has in its nucleus a love of God or a hatred of him.

To review: Scripture teaches us, especially in Genesis, that God created to declare his glory and that creation reveals his glory in three equal aspects. This triad consists of content, form, and purpose, corresponding to God's character, God's glory (revealed in creation's forms and in the story of creation and redemption), and God's powerful will. Though these went astray in our rebellion, the basic architecture of communication did not. All of human life consists in these three aspects and their various articulations. In whatever we do or say, we ascribe glory in these three perspectives, either to God or to a created object, an idea, or a person. We communicate by ascribing glory to some object, and that glory always consists in roughly these three aspects, though we may emphasize one over another.

In our sin we can glorify only created things (Rom. 1:23, 25). What gets glory claims our worship (which is idolatry); whether objects, people, carved images, or stories that give our life the meaning we want. We treasure principles such as truth, power, and beauty as objective ideals and appreciate them without regard to God. These we employ individually to overcome or leverage the weaknesses we see in our practices in the other aspects, resulting in progressive personal disintegration.

The believer in Christ, no longer under God's judgment, pleases the Father. Discipleship brings reintegration of the severed aspects of glory as we more and more attribute that glory to God while seeing, living, and saying in him. Truth content, rich aesthetic form, and powerful purpose come together in Christ for those he saves and inhabits.

Just as our passions, arising in response to forms, cannot lead us to God any more reliably than can our minds, so we cannot rely alone on either truth (reason) or power (pragmatics, habits, liturgies)—the other two aspects of discourse that fill out the triad of God's glory—to rescue our pesky, sometimes treacherous emotions. When twentieth-century Christians relied on fact-based arguments to prove their faith, Cornelius Van Til, Christian philosopher and apologist, showed that truth by itself cannot stir people toward God, because non-Christian presuppositions always distort facts, often invisibly. He contended that all facts are always organized into connected systems that either assume God is true or commandeer God's truth while denying *him*. Unbelievers live with inconsistency, borrowing bits of God's system to organize the facts, while refusing him. Van Til found that we can know nothing unless God knows it first. He wrote, "God knows or interprets the facts before they are facts. It is God's plan, God's comprehensive interpretation of the facts that makes the facts what they are."[1]

Van Til draws our attention to the religious presuppositions that condition how we see the truth content aspect of God's glory. Adam and Eve had a godly presupposition about truth, sharing God's seeing with him. Then they spurned the seeing they shared with God, instead seeing glory by themselves and breaking it into pieces. Scholars reflect on the noetic effects of sin: sin's impact on our mind's ability to reason, know, and believe. Since sin has touched our whole interpretion, including our seeing and doing, we must also consider sin's aesthetic effects and its ethical effects.[2]

God restores sin's isolating, disintegrating effects for his people in Christ Jesus. In him we see revealed the noetic, aesthetic, and ethical effects of redemption. In our consideration of redemption's aesthetic effects for the believer, we note that God the Father, whose seeing makes truth what it is, also makes beauty what it is through his comprehensive delight in the Son.[3] The Son's perfections are translated into the creation, and it reflects him. God's enjoyment of creation's beauty as a token of the Son's beauty makes beauty what it is.

The proper Christian approach to aesthetics, then, starts with God's aesthetics. God calls and enables his people to make sense of pleasure and pain and passion—the entire aesthetic aspect of human life—according to the Father's delight in the Son, a pre-affectional approach. This Sharon and I observed during our touring years, though we didn't know the categories.

I had hoped the power of music would, by softening hearts to the gospel, prove that people's affections are precognitive. If so, we had hope of honing our craft enough to make an end run around cognitive defenses. I found otherwise and began to conclude that people's hearts will change only in repentance, which

1. Cornelius Van Til, *Christian Apologetics* (Phillipsburg, NJ: Presbyterian and Reformed, 1976), 7.

2. For a detailed look at the ethical effects of sin and redemption, see the ongoing work of the Christian Counseling and Educational Foundation (CCEF) in Glenside, Pennsylvania. www.ccef.org.

3. As noted in chapter 10; see Piper's thorough exploration in *The Pleasures of God: Meditations on God's Delight in Being God*, rev. ed. (Colorado Springs: Multnomah, 2012).

alone can transform our pre-affections. It might be argued that our music was not good enough for this. I will readily grant that our music may not have been *that* good, but I wonder if any music could be good enough. A larger problem in the human heart lies elsewhere.

The power of affections, stirred by forms and their aesthetic qualities, is a power to motivate, but motivation in itself cannot guide. God gives us his own picture and his own story to stir our affections and get us moving, his truth to set the handrails for our progress. Affections stir us but cannot guide, so must not work alone.

Our hunger for beauty can neither save us nor trash us. Just as we modernists have looked to the power of truth and doctrines to save us and found that our knowing needs first to be converted, so also our loves and desires must be transformed, brought under Christ through his cross.

## Love, Believe, and Obey the Son

A new affection springs to life in the heart of the believer: love for Jesus Christ, his character, his story. He loves us, so he teaches us. He teaches us in pictures and stories and in his presence. We love him, so we believe what he teaches. Like the disciples, we are close enough to ask him to explain matters that puzzle us. We also obey him. Although we often go astray, even our tiny shreds of Christian obedience show the Spirit of God at work.

Christians have a new presupposition: we presuppose that God is right and has spoken through the Bible, giving us his own system of thought. We have a new pre-affection with which to make aesthetic sense of creation's forms. We have a new predisposition by which we can obey and act or leave alone, according to the Father's will.

Groucho Marx spoke for us: "Those are my principles, and if you don't like them, well, I have others."[4] We too have others. Christians retain our old presuppositions, our old pre-affections, and our old predispositions, but God in his kindness has forgiven us, giving us the Holy Spirit and power and incentive to pursue the new ones with faith and repentance and with courage. We grow away from our old principles and toward Christ.

This unity of form, content, and purpose in the believing heart constitutes a radical new life. Calvin Seerveld, grappling with a similar Christ-centered reintegration of isolated aesthetics with the life of devotion to God, observes, "That *aesthetic obedience* is required of everyone by the Lord—artist or not—is

---

4. Echo from my childhood, confirmed by internet attributions, multiple sites, no details.

a thesis I am only beginning to probe with understanding."[5] The closer we come to Jesus Christ, the better we will understand the unity he personifies and into which he draws us. The biblical aesthetic is no longer autotelic, as "art for art's sake" has been described, but *theotelic*—all glory godward.

## Form, Image, Stories: What Importance for Interpretation?

Our new Christ-centered unity of affections, belief, and will informs everything we encounter and our responses. We need practice in considering form and aesthetics in the same breath that we consider truth content, and conversely. We have learned that our attitude toward God conditions the emotions with which we respond to anything in the daily life God sends us. If we are following the trail of biblical breadcrumbs aright, and the gospel initiates and requires a pre-affectional approach to aesthetics, then we must also expect to find that forms, as well as our affectional responses to them, point to God. We must look for God-centered referentiality in all forms, including literary forms. As we have come to expect no brute aesthetics, so, because form is linked to aesthetics, we must also expect no brute forms. Instead forms are always for God or against him. No literary convention is *only* that. Let us explore a few literary forms as examples and to set a course.

### *Interpreting Biblical Forms*

All creation moved from formless to formed under God's hand. All we have studied here—truth, beauty, goodness—are expressed or seen or experienced in meaningful forms. "Formless and empty" and dark (Gen. 1:2) are gone; God formed, filled, and lightened. Forms are the architecture of meaning; they signify distinction and sequence: truth is not a lie, blue is not red, and today is not tomorrow.

Our studies in the Genesis creation story brought us two key observations concerning God's glory that can help us read forms right. First, forms always go with truth and with powerful purpose. The three themes of God's glory always function in parallel. They constitute its inseparable aspects, not its parts. Remembering this, we interpret the Bible's symbols and other picture language not according to freestanding literary conventions alone; we look beyond the conventions in order to interpret them according to God himself as revealed in the text itself and in the Bible as a whole. The unity of truth, beauty, and power

---

5. Calvin Seerveld, *Rainbows for the Fallen World: Aesthetic Life and Artistic Task* (Toronto: Tuppence, 1980), 9 (emphasis in the original).

in the Scriptures also calls believers to interpret everything else according to this unity. This leans hard against our habitual isolation of aesthetics.

Second, each of the three themes always directs glory to God. No literary form has a life of its own; each points, when questioned, to some attribute of the Godhead. These forms are subject, of course, to perverse applications and interpretations; these the redeemed eye reads through Jesus Christ, the lens of God's redeeming story—creation, fall, redemption, consummation. Let me offer a few examples of how some forms can point to God.

## Story

Let us start with a familiar form. God reveals his glory through narrative form. God's story lends its shape to all stories. Jesus' parables follow certain narrative conventions—forms. God has purposes to accomplish through his story. Story depends on time or sequence, and time may find its origin in the Father-Son relationship.[6] The Son, the Word, is himself sent to accomplish the Father's purpose, as God says through the prophet Isaiah: "My word ... will not return to me empty, but will accomplish what I desire and achieve the purpose for which I sent it" (Isa. 55:11). Notice the verb tenses. God desires now, purposes now in the present tense, and his Word will accomplish it, future tense. Therein lies the Story, redemptive history. All other stories borrow their story form from the Father's relation to the Son, the mysterious inner workings of the Trinity.

Our Lord, in his earthly ministry, used stories with masterly skill and redemptive purpose. His followers likewise told stories. Peter told the story (Acts 2:14–41) of the recent events of Jesus' death, interpreting those events according to God's redemptive purpose, and his hearers were "cut to the heart" (v. 37). Stephen told the Sanhedrin their own story with such powerful glory arrows toward Jesus Christ that his hearers responded with emotion strong enough to murder him just to shut him up (Acts 7:1–60). Paul told the Athenians their own story, weaving its elements into God's larger one; some of his listeners moved closer, some backed away (Acts 17:22–34). God's story, the original, sorts out all the stories we enjoy, the God-loving from the God-defying; we can leave our own stories and rejoin God's grand redemptive story only through faith and repentance.

## Symbols

While the Bible is full of symbols, symbolism—together with its cousins metaphor, allegory, simile, type, and others—seems so universal to humankind

---

6. I am indebted to Dr. Vern Poythress of Westminster Theological Seminary for this suggestion, offered in private conversation.

in all cultures and times as to stand alone. Still, symbolism constitutes a form, so we may explore it for its divine origin. Where can we trace its origin, the first symbol, the first representation? God has a Son, his very image. "The Son is the image of the invisible God" (Col. 1:15). The eternal Son, the second person of the Trinity, incarnated as Jesus the Messiah, was from before all time the perfect representation of the Father, so perfect that he was fully the Father's equal in deity. Like all analogies and symbols, he is the same but different, corresponding in some respects yet fully himself, not interchangeable. While no other symbol can display such perfect correspondence, we must find no fault in symbolic meaning itself. In God himself we find the symbol's essence and source. With a nod to the medieval church philosophers who argued for God's existence by analogy with the existence of creation—the analogy of being—we find instead, in Scripture, the *being of analogy*.

Analogy and symbolism, then, stand alone not as self-existent literary forms but as forms whose meaning points to God. In all symbolism, we are to see that God exists in Trinity and that all symbols find their meaning in reference to this ontological symbol, Jesus Christ. Symbolism is capable, with infinite nuance, to stir affections and motivate as a direct statement alone cannot. Symbolism's divine origin reveals by contrast the abuses of symbolism throughout human culture and points to God's redemption.

## Chiasm

The Old Testament authors frequently wrote using an X form, arranging the elements of the second half of a passage in reverse order from the first half:[7] A, B, B$^1$, A$^1$. This literary form appears in large and small examples, and the story of Noah and the flood gives a widely recognized illustration. In the Noah chiasm, "But God remembered Noah" (Gen. 8:1) stands at the center, giving emphasis.

The form includes symmetry around a center point, a portrait view with corresponding sides, like the human face. It also includes progress, movement through time, the story view. The chiasm's combination of the synchronic and diachronic perspectives in a single form reflects God's character, always the same and always free to do whatever he pleases.

This brief exploration of literary forms for possible God-directed reference neither exhausts the mysteries nor makes a claim for accuracy. I offer it in the hope of adding encouragement to what seems a necessary caution against viewing any literary form as self-evident and freestanding—brute form—and

---

7. Leland Ryken and Tremper Longman III, eds., *A Complete Literary Guide to the Bible* (Grand Rapids, MI: Zondervan, 1993), 33.

of suggesting a direction for future study. We might refine our observations as we search for God's glory, which is revealed in Scripture's forms—together with their aesthetic value—as much as in Scripture's content and its power.

## Interpreting Creational and Cultural Forms

Having suggested a God-centered, glory-threading pattern for interpreting Scripture's forms, we can apply this same redemptive hermeneutic to creation's forms. Let us adhere to the general rule that we interpret our surroundings, including all discourse, according to the triadic shape of glory we see in Scripture. Not only have we learned from the Scriptures information about God—theology—we also see with transformed eyes, growing to recognize God in Christ through all of Scripture and in every created thing. These eyes were so important to Jesus that on the day of his resurrection, he spoke with strange harshness to the Emmaus Road disciples for their failure to read Scripture with just this Christ-centered redemptive hermeneutic (Luke 24). He had, after all, taught them just this sort of seeing during his ministry, applying it to Scripture and to everyday things—bread, wine, grass, flowers, birds. He taught his disciples, through the Scriptures, how to read both translucently. These Scriptures point to him in the way he directs, giving rich meaning to every stick and stone, every fence post and website. When they saw the risen Christ, they got it; and so will we, seeing Jesus, his world, and his story with Scripture-opened eyes.

## Restoring Aesthetics to Context

Here we consider aesthetics as redeemed, no longer as a compartment of life. The contrast between high art and popular culture is now reframed as competing styles of desire for competing objects of glory—idols. Now the aesthetics that touches life's whole scope is reintegrated as part of the glory we were made for—God's—along a human story made glorious in Christ's own. This will imply changes—healthy developments—in our daily living, changes in private and small group Bible reading, in pastoral care, in academic studies, in systematic theology, and in all we say, do, build, write, cook, sing, hear, see, and eat.

## Aesthetic Objectivity Is Not Enough

Form and pleasure are closely linked, but their link is indirect, personal, mediated, religiously qualified, and requiring redemption. I used to wonder, as a young Christian folk-rocker, why secular musicians always seemed to make better music than Christian musicians. They led the music industry, and that seemed fair; they were the best. Other Christian musicians of those days, eager to restore Christian voice in media, followed their lead along a parallel track. They developed Contemporary Christian Music (CCM), hoping to pull alongside the secular industry, measured by the aesthetic standards we shared with them. Many of us wanted to improve and, eventually, to write and perform with the best, for Christ's sake. How? The means seemed obvious: learn and master the proven musical and lyrical standards—objective aesthetics.

We assumed that people's aesthetic taste, particularly their taste for music, was more or less sound. We all do. You have your own personal concerns for taste, so substitute your own field for mine. I gauged aesthetic mastery as much by popular response as by my personal judgment. Yet Jesus' warnings against popularity lurked in memory, warnings that spoke of a greater difference than I had noticed between the loves of God's people and those of others.

We naturally assume that our tastes do not change, either with time or through the inner work of God, that aesthetic qualities are brute. I remember contemporary news stories about the Islamist extremists who killed themselves and thousands of others in the Twin Towers attacks. News reports said they indulged, the night before their death, in sexual pleasures forbidden by their religion. Real pleasure, they may have thought, remains real pleasure, and no inner effects of religion can change that—objective aesthetics.

## "Already/Not Yet" Aesthetics

Churches wrestle across this same turf in choosing worship music: "Should we offer people what appeals to them or what *should* appeal to them?" With aesthetic discipleship in mind, we must answer, "Both, and keep us moving." We take full account of what people love and hate and fear now, in order to notice and approach what Christ has done and to grow in sharing God's delights, his loves and hates—an "already/not yet" aesthetics.

To do this, we must take a clear-eyed view of the good in everything we see—in creation, in artistic works produced by nonbelievers, and in all sorts of work not usually considered art. We must also retain some sense of the antithesis between where we have come from and where we are going—between the flesh and the Spirit.

The Christian's task is not to integrate reason and affection and power, since they are already one in God. Our task is to repent of having torn them apart and to believe the health-giving gospel of Jesus Christ, who reunites them and restores us.

The redeemed eye builds the kingdom of God. We do this by inviting and building and practicing agreement as we grow in faithful life together. In building his kingdom, God builds his culture. Imagine sharing God's values! Our growing agreement with God about his glory, in its noetic, aesthetic, and ethical aspects, prepares us in real, mysterious ways to live in his coming eternal kingdom. Let us consider some cultural implications.

## Purposive Common Grace

Like our view of pleasure, the Christian doctrine of common grace also needs an oil change where it deals with the arts. Faithful Christian scholars and artistic makers and performers have long looked to common grace, partly to explain God's purposes in the aesthetic qualities of works of non-Christians and partly to defend those qualities against pietistic critiques. We have all heard, "This song's lyrics go against God's Word." Or perhaps, "This songwriter is probably not really a Christian." Or my favorite, "Rock music has a strong beat, and we all know what that means."

Common grace, properly conceived, has a purpose. Like Jesus' parables, it is telic: tending toward a goal or end. By common grace, God distinguishes people. As with the good and bad seeds mingled in the field in Jesus' parable (Matt. 13:24–30), God blesses mingled people alike so that their responses will show more and more clearly over time whether they are weeds or wheat. Sunlight, rain, earth, and passing time all look the same to all the young plants. Jesus' preaching, especially his parables, came to all in common. Some responded sooner, others later; some turned away sooner, some later; some followed slowly, some eagerly. This progressive distinction seems one point of Jesus' parables and of his common grace.

Common grace is not brute grace. It means good to wheat and impending judgment to weeds, but this distinction remains partially hidden for now. God's goodness to all without distinction has eventual distinction as its goal. God will finally and fully clarify the antithesis between flesh and Spirit, between goats and sheep, on his great day. For our good, he keeps this distinction hidden for now. We rejoice in his patience with us and with many we love.

Common grace goes off the rails when it disregards antithesis. Antithesis turns ugly when it tries to bring the final judgment into the present. We lose our way when we assume that works created by non-Christians can have less value or that any given non-Christian, whether author, sculptor, or dancer, will never turn to Christ. Christians who focus on antithesis tend to miss this one. Nor may we use common grace to validate misrepresentations in media or to imagine that God counts a work's goodness as the author's merit. Those who see common grace as static, brute grace tend to miss this.

Common grace is, as noted, telic grace, as it has a goal or end in view. This rejigged, dynamic understanding of common grace accounts for passages that link present glories, including the aesthetic, to the New Jerusalem. John describes it:

> The city does not need the sun or the moon to shine on it, for the glory of God gives it light, and the Lamb is its lamp. The nations will walk by its light, and the kings of the earth will *bring their splendor into it*. On no day will its gates ever be shut, for there will be no night there. *The glory and honor of the nations will be brought into it. Nothing impure will ever enter it*, nor will anyone who does what is shameful or deceitful, but only those whose names are written in the Lamb's book of life.
> —Revelation 21:23–27 (emphasis added)

While a casual reader might imagine that these are the very glories and art treasures accumulated over the course of human history, carried directly to the heavenly kingdom, the author makes plain that they are transformed by redemption; all the impurities of each work's planning, making, marketing, and interpretation must undergo the radical purification of the crucifixion, resurrection, and ascension of the beautiful Savior.

## Redeeming Art

The redeemed eye knows how to read artworks, and most artists know that art includes much more than aesthetic pleasure or discomfort; it includes assertions of truth content and accomplishes a practical purpose, even if that purpose is commercial. But we struggle with our own impulses toward private personal enjoyment, toward isolated aesthetics. Some philosophers support us in following Eve's isolation. Those who insist on "art for art's sake" or who find art as ideally autotelic,[8] and those who justify the inherent goodness of the delight of isolated "aesthetic contemplation"[9] may merely encourage our exclusion of God as seer and impede our redeemed vision of the unity of truth, beauty, and goodness in the glory of God.

The redeemed eye, now that it finds aesthetics reintegrated into all discourse, may find "art" a useless concept for Christian thought. We have seen that it

8. Madeleine Boucher, *The Mysterious Parable: A Literary Study* (Washington, D.C.: Catholic Biblical Association of America, 1977), 16.

9. Nicholas Wolterstorff, *Art in Action* (Grand Rapids, MI: Eerdmans, 1980), 173, 193.

cannot be clearly distinguished from nonart. Further, the concept adds nothing to the benefit, appreciation, and respect the affectionate Christian can give to works—songs, paintings, poetry, everything. Without it the redeemed eye can consider works, together with their aesthetic properties and people's various responses to them, more wholly, more redemptively, simply as what people say and do—often with tremendous God-glorifying creativity and expression.

We already know this intuitively. Artists over the centuries have lived and worked with a practical understanding that art involves far more than aesthetics. Artworks always communicate content with its forms, though sometimes badly; they always call for a response. Most working artists, critics, and Christian commentators will raise no eyebrow at the aesthetic reintegration we have discovered in Scripture, having learned it in their craft and practiced it right along. The God-centered implications of aesthetics may challenge us more pointedly, since each Christian's redemptive path passes through repentance on the way to God.

We in the church might find it worth our while to demystify "the arts" and "artists" as a breed apart from others. Reintegrating aesthetics in the church could restore to each person a sense of capability, calling, and responsibility to live before God's audience as a redeemed lover, not only a redeemed knower and doer. While drawing the whole church toward godward responses, the church receives particular aesthetic gifts and callings with heightened appreciation.

Art, no longer an isolated category turned in on itself, emerges to the redeemed eye as ordinary discourse with aesthetic emphasis. This does not flatten out artistic expression but celebrates varied giftings and skills while ascribing glory in all three of its aspects: content, form, and purpose. That glory will be directed either to God or, by means of ideals, principles, or conventions, to God's creatures.

Since all human communication carries the triad of aspects analogous to our Creator's communication, form and its delights cannot remain the unique province of art but must belong to everything people do and say, all we make and perform. The redeemed eye will look for forms and aesthetic qualities in everything, even what seems to fall outside the customary distinction of art.

Our tendency to isolate pleasure from other aspects of glory forms the heartbeat of popular media. Listen to the popular music of our age, and you'll hear our love for pleasure elevated to something approaching the ultimate.

Perhaps a more cultured approach appeals better? High art occupies center stage in most culture efforts, an agreeable common ground of value. Take in the theater, spend an evening at the philharmonic, peruse an art show, wrestle with life's joys and sorrows in a literary classic.

God calls us in his Word to read art and culture like we read the Scriptures:

triadically, with an eye for content, form, and purpose all together. Also, to read it looking for glory arrows. What's this about? Who or what is supposed to look good, look glorious? Our own hearts will be revealed in our attractions and revulsions, and with them the glorious gospel.

## Cultural Forms

I have mentioned some theological implications of bilateral symmetry. I hope to suggest a way for Christians to handle forms and their aesthetic properties in such a manner that they too are transparent, showing God himself in their very essence, not just as his gifts with stand-alone properties. Every aesthetic property points in some way to God, to his glory in creation and redemption. We'll briefly examine here the cultural form of marriage and its God-oriented derivation, meaning, and aesthetic properties. In a gender-fluid culture, consider with me a godward perspective on this controversial form.

We would do well to look at marriage, if indeed forms find their meaning in God. Marriage, a familiar cultural form, has fallen lately into some confusion. The Bible's teaching argues a form-based, aesthetic justification for the marriage of one man to one woman. The Bible depicts human marriage not as a freestanding cultural convention but as a symbol representing God's relationship with his people, a relationship rendered clearer by its comparison with Christ Jesus' coming wedding to his bride, the church. Like all analogies, the original is first and independent, the copy second and derivative. Human marriage always finds its meaning as it depicts God's covenant with his people. A husband represents God; a wife represents God's people. All human marriages distort this image in various ways, but still, any marriage between any one man and any one woman, though they be non-Christians, represents God's original with a certain formal accuracy.

Marriage between a man and a woman presents God through the husband, and his saints through the wife. Lovelessness, oppression, adultery, and other sins distort marriage's picture of God and his people. Still, the formal correspondence of this relationship remains intact. Every further deviation from this original picture misrepresents God still further, although the picture retains its basic about-ness. Adultery, so ugly in itself, lies about God and his people so heinously that God stirred many prophets to confront his faithless people by using adultery as a metaphor for false worship (Ezek. 23; James 4:4). So-called serial monogamy, in sequential marriages or live-in arrangements, fudges God's covenant love, which is exclusive and permanent. Extramarital affairs distort God's image still further: Could Christ be unfaithful, deceitful, covenant-breaking? Could he have many brides? Could the church have two Lords? He is absolutely faithful, and we can safely trust his consistent acceptance and love.

In Scripture, gender is not incidental nor optional; it is derivative and referential; gender reflects God's glory in the three aspects considered throughout this study. "Marriages" between any persons besides one man and one woman, even if affectionate and faithful, distort the Creator-creature distinction, a more basic and critical meaning than marriage itself. The "marriage" of two men implies that grooms are equivalent and interchangeable, symbolically proclaiming the deity of humankind, as if to say, "God and his partner consist of the same essence." Likewise, the marriage of two women declares that only brides exist, no bridegrooms; there is no God, and the true God is stripped of his deity and existence. The participants in such "marriages" may intend no such messages, yet the heavenly beings cannot fail to notice this message delivered through the vocabulary well known in heaven. The declaration of God's glory that he intends from every marriage is, in these "marriages," blunted, perverted, full of anti-God meaning, even though founded on deep human affection. God has already redeemed many people from such formal distortions, showing how strong, good, true, and beautiful he is. All of us, including the gender-identity communities, have formal, aesthetic reasons to look to the God of the Bible for help to reconsider our aesthetic impulses and demands for aesthetic autonomy.

All of us should find ourselves at home in churches with repentant sinners; we look to God to forgive our lust for isolated pleasures and have turned to God and found him merciful, patient, and strong.

## Interpreting as Context

We interpret Scripture, and everything else we encounter, in order to make meaning of it and respond with action. We may now contrive a definition of interpretation that takes account of aesthetics' role in God's revelation of his glory. Meaning is in context. Jokes illustrate the power of changed context to change meaning. Did you hear the one about . . .

A trooper, cruising the expressway in his patrol car, noticed a sedan rolling along at forty miles an hour, unsafe on a highway posted for sixty-five. When he pulled the driver over, he found a nun behind the wheel, and two others in the back seat. When the trooper asked why so slow, the driver replied, "I saw a sign for forty, so I was driving forty." With a smile, the officer set her straight. "Sister, the sign you saw said, 'Highway Forty.' The speed limit here is a little faster." He received his thanks and started to move off, when he noticed that the two nuns in the back seat were pale, sweating, clutching each other's hands, wide-eyed with terror. He turned back to ask what was wrong. The driver looked down and offered, "Maybe it's because we just left Highway One-Sixteen."

New context, new meaning. Perhaps this can explain Paul's strange saying, "The perishable must clothe itself with the imperishable, and the mortal with immortality" (1 Cor. 15:53). The new immortal context that will surround our perishable selves will transform them, making them imperishable. New context, new meaning.

The more context connections, the more glory. Reread a favorite book, rewatch a favorite movie, and discover new connections, new contextual links. Richness grows, and glory with it. Meaning might almost be said to be context with God, who connects everything to everything and of whom everything speaks, the most glorious of all.

Perhaps meaning *is* context, and context *is* glory; and truth, beauty, and power depend on each other in each visible thing as it points to God.

## Allegory

Allegorical interpretation of Scripture has gotten a rotten name through fanciful, unguided application. Scholars have largely set it aside, though literary approaches to the Scriptures have lately contributed much to scholarship through reconsidering what Scripture means by its use of allegory and other literary forms. If God's Word alone is to set the scope and direction for proper use of allegories, metaphors, similes, and all such comparisons, we may look to Scripture itself to guide and control their application. The making of meaning, including the meaning of literary forms, remains as always an ongoing discipline of the Christian faith, the unique province of "the church of the living God, the pillar and foundation of the truth" (1 Tim. 3:15), under the Scriptures.

## Symbolism and Scripture

Metaphor, simile, allegory, symbolism, and all their allies stand as strong meaning makers in the Scriptures, and also as a battlefield. We often hear the expression, "But that's symbolic" said about the Scriptures. This remark usually carries the subtext that symbolism is an inferior form of predication. Now, while symbolism can be used as a lesser way of saying something, we are right to ask whether a symbol is intrinsically inferior to the thing symbolized.

The liberal Protestants of the late nineteenth century interpreted much of the Bible as symbolical. They asserted, often wrongly, that its symbols do not mean what they would mean if taken literally. The conservative fundamentalists were ready to believe that the Bible meant what it said, so they asserted that the Bible was not symbolic. In so doing, they agreed with the liberals that symbolism is necessarily a weak way of saying things, an inferior means of predication, not quite the thing for serious theology.

Story and affections have been enjoying a popular resurgence among churches and Bible scholars in recent years—biblical theology, literary approaches, narrative theology, desire theology. This too can become imbalanced, chiefly through a pendulum swing: when systematics, dominant in the eighteenth and nineteenth centuries, falls from dominance, other organizing schemes take its place. Also, each system stands on conventions, whether literary forms or popular ideals and intuitions, that locate their authority outside the Scriptures. We may well be concerned that the surging battle over the dominant way to interpret the Bible cannot be won on these terms, or even in terms of balance. Where, then?

## Systematic Theology in Context

The theology we profess does not stand alone; it shows in what we do. When Sharon and I discovered that listeners always act as they believe, and changed our mission statement, we did not know how important this insight would prove. This connection between who we are and what we do comes to us straight from God. God always acts according to his character. If you want to know who God is, who he really is on the inside, watch what he does and listen to what he says about it. "The heavens declare the glory of God; the skies proclaim the work of his hands" (Ps. 19:1). Those with the eye of Christ can see it. Eyes drawn to see God anywhere, even everywhere, make true sense of the world. We must beware; any aesthetic quality—whether in music, graphic layout, or storytelling—that we consider merely intrinsic, self-referential, requiring no redeemed eye and so revealing nothing about God, becomes to us a principle, an ideal, a fact, an idol.

We have seen from our studies in Genesis 1–3 that God shows who he is by what he does, and sees (interprets) all things in reference to himself. In the same way, people show who they are by what they do (Matt. 7:17–18; Luke 6:43–44). This includes all sorts of acts and talk, everything we do that flows out of our own hearts through hands, feet, and mouth (Matt. 12:34; Luke 6:45).

Systematic theology, biblical theology, and practical theology belong together as perspectives on God and his work as revealed in his Word. Let us call them the portrait view, the story view, and the face-to-face view.

God's eye saw his creation at a moment (several moments, actually), in the portrait, always-this-way view. He recognized and affirmed its solid truth, as that truth reflected his eternal character. With his eye, God certified creation's truth content as an accurate reflection of his own solid truth.

He also saw his creation in a story view, in its length; he saw its flow through time from beginning to end. He loves and treasures its forms. It pleases him overall, though we read frequently of his momentary displeasure. The Father planned the story of redemption with the Son before they created anything. God likes the long view, the story view.

God saw creation up close; he was there by his Spirit, hovering. He was present in the creating Son. God is here; he likes the close-up, "in your face" view.

God takes these views—portrait, story, and face-to-face—simultaneously. This is a mystery, but it pertains to his deity and helps us know him in his eternity, unbound by constraint, always the same but never restricted, always immanent and always transcendent. He has something like this unity of views in mind, perhaps, in saying, "Am I only a God nearby . . . and not a God far away?" (Jer. 23:23). He takes a nearby view of unimaginable intimacy; he also takes the long view, far away in space and in time. Into his unified and personal view, he invites all.

Systematic theology, the articulation and development of doctrines, cannot be separated from biblical theology, the narrative perspective. Nor can these two be properly cut off from practical theology, the development of the ways and means of gospel application in daily lives. These, while unified, have different roles: biblical theology, better called redemptive-historical theology, comes first and is full of forms—literary forms, including story, metaphor, and immediate context. There lies motive power. Systematics, while guiding movement, may have less of biblical theology's power to stir affections, but it can guide good movement and check the bad. When these two are combined, practical theology results. To be its best, it must stay connected both to truth and beauty; truth is powerless without beauty, and beauty is rudderless without truth. Working together in the hearts of God's people, they produce preaching, teaching, witnessing, missions, face-to-face ministry, and faithful living of all sorts, including what we have called the arts.

## Poetry

One finds a similar unity of perspectives in good song lyrics. First, the poet works in time toward a work that will find expression when performed in time. The poet or lyricist who builds a rhyming poem finds himself occasionally working backward in time. One picks the word or turn of phrase with which one wants to end, then works earlier elements to prepare the way for it. If one element in a group exhibits slightly less strength or is in the least awkward, the careful lyricist will place it earlier in the pattern and save the stronger word or phrase for the end, where it will most gratify and be longest remembered. In this, the lyricist reflects God's use of time to create a story that has a really good ending.

The best songs pair strong lyrics with well-suited melody and arrangement, producing the most impact. The correspondence of words to music points to the unity of Jesus Christ, who is the Word of God and the image of God, as well as the power of God. He is the true Prophet, who brings God's Word; he is also the true Priest, who fittingly represents us to God and God to us. He is the King with all power and authority to do as he wills. He doesn't just use imagery and aesthetics to do this. He is the image of God; he is the very Son of Man. In himself, he pleases the Father so fully that one might even say he *is* the Father's pleasure. No wonder words and music, when they go together well, seem to connect better with the listener. The triadic pattern of discourse suits the triadic pattern in which we are made.

### Ordinary Objects

Redeemed aesthetic senses grow in patience, gratitude, referential transparency. Our Lord Jesus saw all around him transparently, referentially. Daily objects were about something, about his Father. He demonstrates this by his parables. Jesus was not only a wise poet but a faithful seer.

## Giving Thanks

We have it better than Eve did before her disobedience; because we are in Christ, God is always involved in our feelings. Every favorite snack, even a good read, a glimpse of distant mountains through the fog, are meant as pleasures shared with God. In Christ, we can say, "I always do what pleases him" (John 8:29). When we thank someone, we say we share the value he intends in the gift. We see and appreciate that value as he does, sharing his eye, his pleasure. So too, when we thank God for a meal, we tell him we receive the goodness in this gift that he sees and means for us.

Paul writes about redeeming food by thankfulness: "If I take part in the meal with thankfulness, why am I denounced because of something I thank God for? So whether you eat or drink or whatever you do, do it all for the glory of God" (1 Cor. 10:30–31). Thanking God glorifies him and sanctifies an otherwise questionable gift.

We Christians can make meaning of cultural media, and with it daily life events, by returning thanks to the maker or presenter, so far as possible. This requires wisdom, of course, but it is the same wisdom that we exercise already. One can hardly track down the owner of a billboard to thank him for brightening his day with a cheerful picture or message (should the occasion arise). Still, expressions of ordinary human gratitude, when appropriate, are always a fitting Christian response: applause at a concert, even the "Like" icon on Facebook.

We can thank a preacher for his sermon, even if it was not his best; we may not have been listening up to our best either. God calls us to thank him as a means of sanctifying his general gifts of food; I suspect that thanking people can have a similar good effect.

Thankful eating blossoms as we consider the future feast, prefigured in communion: the Lord Jesus invites his people to his table in a covenant meal in which we participate with him in real food and real drink that represent the bread and wine he shared with his disciples, as well as his own body and blood. Our Lord has said he will deny himself wine until he drinks again with his apostles, and we presume with us, when he returns in glory. Then he will eat and drink with us! "Truly I tell you, I will not drink again from the fruit of the vine until that day when I drink it new in the kingdom of God" (Mark 14:25).[10] The covenant meal appears throughout the Old Testament, and the New Testament depicts it in two horizons: the Lord's Table and the wedding feast. Both cry out for immense thanks!

Paul writes with a redeemed and clear-eyed view of creation:

> The creation waits in eager expectation for the children of God to be revealed. For the creation was subjected to frustration, not by its own choice, but by the will of the one who subjected it, in hope that the creation itself will be liberated from its bondage to decay and brought into the freedom and glory of the children of God.
>
> We know that the whole creation has been groaning as in the pains of childbirth right up to the present time. Not only so, but we ourselves, who have the firstfruits of the Spirit, groan inwardly as we wait eagerly for our adoption to sonship, the redemption of our bodies.
>
> —Romans 8:19–23

Glorious things are indeed spoken of the creation and of our God. We may broaden our view of creation, enjoying its natural beauty and also seeing through it the promise of its overall goal as God has planned it. For now, creation groans; we groan, waiting for our bodies to be redeemed, confirming that we really are God's sons and daughters.

I find myself a bit embarrassed to say much about the transparency, the about-God-ness, of creation. I know only what I see, I who began looking into

---

10. Remembering that Christ refused to use his power to make anything for himself alone, I wonder if our Lord Jesus anticipates drinking, when he returns, a wine that he makes for us; or, just maybe, he will drink and share wine we will make. Since I make wine, I hope that our Lord will at some time taste wine I will have made in glory! I have much to learn from him about this craft.

these matters as a young man and have now passed middle age. I write today from an older person's perspective, and from the sweetness of God himself that has increasingly come to me. I have been a knucklehead since my youth—ask my friends—and have not changed much. God has become gradually sweeter to me now than before. I have sought to show scriptural warrant for every major step in this development, and the Scriptures can neither change nor lie. I testify to its truth. I speak of glorious things. Let the reader read the Bible! "Delight yourself in the LORD, and he will give you the desires of your heart" (Ps. 37:4 ESV).

Scripture is sufficient—enfolding aesthetics in redemptive history—to lead God's people in personal discipleship, the redemption of our own inner culture. From this it will lead us, in God, into full engagement with our own culture and with others. My assessment features contemporary Western culture, particularly the bits I know of it, since most people I know and love live here. Greater riches will emerge as others develop these and other scriptural insights further and in other traditions.

The biblical model allows for great complexity and rich nuance. It fosters development, conversions, reversions, and patience. Christian discipleship properly assumes that God is Lord of culture, that he has cultural purposes and goals, that the difference between God's culture and that of the world is clear in principle but obscure in life. We will not always have culture wars; we will have complete shalom.

## READ, REFLECT, DISCUSS, SING

1. Suggested reading: "Practicing (for) the Kingdom: An Exegesis of the Social Imaginary Embedded in Christian Worship," chapter 5 of *Desiring the Kingdom: Worship, Worldview and Cultural Formation* by James K. A. Smith.
2. Q1. What delight did you once understand in one way, and now in another? Think or tell about how that change came about.
3. Q2. How has your love of God grown since you first knew you were his child? How has your love grown for what he has said and for what he has made?
4. Sing: "This Is My Father's World."

## Chapter 14

# Taste and See . . .

*Eh, the bonny man, the bonny man!*
—GEORGE MACDONALD, *MALCOLM*

Books come into our hands all at once, but reading them takes time, as its journey unfolds before our eyes. You have traveled some to get here, unless you have skipped to the end—I do that sometimes. I have written this in the same way, and it tracks my own unrolling story. I could not have skipped to this end, though.

## Review the Storyboard

We can locate these ideas best with a quick review. We have noted that human feelings and aesthetic satisfactions are rightly ours only because God has them first. We discussed the aesthetics of God's glory revealed in creation, that aesthetics constitutes one aspect of God's glory in an integral triad including also truth content and powerful purpose or will. The Genesis account of creation describes the seeing of this glory that our first parents shared with God, then lost. We have seen the damage of our isolated seeing, a close kin to blindness. We have blinded ourselves in our sin, and all our feelings are now out of joint, the good ones with the bad. Christ has restored them by forgiving us, healing us, and putting back together our fragmented feelings, beliefs, and wills in himself. These used to fight inside us, but he reunifies them by turning our eyes outside ourselves to the Father, through Jesus' death and resurrection.

The persuasive, motivating power of beauty—the beautiful form of God's revealed glory—consists not only in creation—the object we see, hear, taste, touch, and smell—but also in how we see them in our own desires, our own pre-affections, our own eyes. Although sin perverted our aesthetic perceptions, God still pours out revelation in creation and in his Word, for eyes to see that can. Only in Christ can any human begin to read aesthetic experiences rightly—with God and in his eyes. So the much-discussed power of beauty finally works good only for those who love God, whose eyes God has opened. Christians must credit God with the power and goodness to open the eyes of any sin-blind person at any time. That means we keep talking, keep working, keep praying, keep on with our callings, for his glory, leaving results to his providence. Although this may seem counterintuitive, I doubt there is another good way.

All aesthetic experiences, coming to us as they do through God's hands, tend to separate people into two groups: those who see God through them and those who do not. The difference lies in regeneration, the rebirth of the heart—our knowledge, affections, and will—by the Holy Spirit. He gives people ears to hear who scarcely know it, at least at first. These believe in the gospel. To them Jesus says, "He who has ears to hear, let him hear" (Matt. 11:15 ESV). Their response to the beauty of what they see and hear, smell, taste, and handle, as well as to its truth and its power, distinguishes them from what they were before God's touch and also from those as yet untouched by God's saving hand.

Unbelieving hearts experience everything without reference to God, evaluating by themselves, by their own judgment, "knowing good and evil" as Adam and Eve did (Gen. 3:22). Christians do this too, though not all the time. We see creation's truth content, its beauty, and its power either objectively—assuming we rightly evaluate—or subjectively—assuming that, right or wrong, our tastes are all that matters. The believing heart can see *with* God, though, perceiving him shining through that experience. Repentance and faith make sense of our desires, satisfactions, and sufferings. The beauty we love and the pain we fear do not make sense of these. Pleasure, love, affections, taken for their intrinsic value, form a poor path for our discipleship and often lead us far astray. We have a long way to grow; still, gusto for heavenly things has come alive in us, and we did not have it before. The power of beauty is the power of the cross. Repentance and faith bring us to true beauty. Beauty as an ideal does not bring us salvation; God uses his own beauty, his own truth, and his own power to bring us to himself.

Thus we have argued, "No brute aesthetics," meaning the redeemed eye can see light, can see God through the beauties of creation, even in its present bondage and through man-made works, as the unredeemed eye cannot. Of course, the redeemed eye does not see that light at all times, but our ability to see God at all, even share his delights—ever, at any time—shows that something new is happening. This is the kingdom of heaven Jesus described as the little bit of yeast a woman folded into a lot of flour (Matt. 13:33). The change, hidden now, will grow and show.

The difference between redeemed aesthetics and unredeemed ones constitutes no reason for me to stop singing songs for unbelievers, no reason for any artistic creator or performer to redirect his work one way or another; in fact, quite the reverse. Keep it up! Show! Tell! Do! God uses all sorts of means to stir the hearts of people to repent and believe.

"No brute aesthetics" only starts us moving. Because aesthetics spring from forms, there are no brute forms—forms that mean exactly the same to the unbelieving eye as to the believing. God shows his glory in his creation in forms. These forms that stir an affectional response show God's glory only to those with eyes to see it or to those God is calling by using those forms.

## Creation and Forms

Genesis mentions the unformed creation: "In the beginning God created the heavens and the earth. Now the earth was formless and empty, darkness was over the surface of the deep, and the Spirit of God was hovering over the waters" (Gen. 1:1–2).

The text makes no mention of God seeing the goodness of creation until he begins to give it form. That goodness he saw included the features mentioned of all the trees in the garden and of the two special trees; they had content, form, and purpose, comprising truth content, aesthetic value, and power to work. This text and others pushes us to associate forms with aesthetics. We discussed in chapter 5 that Augustine and Calvin link shapes with beauty and our feeling responses.

## God and Forms

God made creation to show his glory. What do creation's forms show us about God himself? Asking about form in God, we touch mysteries beyond our understanding, and yet we may well go forward where God has spoken. We risk using abstractions and jargon when discussing matters on the edge of our understanding, and we must make special effort here to use accessible words for these mysterious truths.

We must clarify first that by forms, we do not at first speak of physical forms. Moses reminds the Israelites in the Sinai wilderness, "You saw no form of any kind the day the LORD spoke to you at Horeb out of the fire" (Deut. 4:15). He warns them not to make an idol, trying to recapture the experience with pictures and stories of their own making. Words have shape, they have form—sentence structure, vibrating tones—so God warns the Israelites not to misuse forms, treating them as opaque, as masterable, and especially as a false picture for their idolatry. Form as such is not intrinsically wrong or inferior, but sinful people can interpret form wrongly, impersonally, or as a substitute for God himself.

Dorothy L. Sayers suggests forms in God's mind. "The implication is that we find the threefold structure in ourselves . . . and that it is in the universe because it is in God's Idea about the universe. . . . Further, that this structure is in God's Idea because it is the structure of God's mind."[1]

Is there structure in God? Has God revealed himself as having form? As we have seen, God has no physical form, barring the incarnation of Christ. Still, the few biblical references to God's form warrant examination. God distinguishes Moses from all Israel saying, "He sees the form of the LORD" (Num. 12:8). Paul highlights the humiliation of Jesus' taking humanity by describing his exalted essence as "in the form of God" (Phil. 2:6 ESV), so as to signify in this way Jesus' indisputable identity as God. A very few other verses make corresponding suggestions and hints, for example Ezekiel 8:1 and 2 Corinthians 4:4, 6.

Scripture's measured reluctance to mention God's physical form springs from the danger of idol worship. Still, the few references given suggest, first, that God reveals his glory in forms because God is formal and that he reveals his own form as a token of special intimacy. These matters occupy the very borders of unsearchable mystery, so we must walk with humility and caution. The Scripture frequently uses the language of forms, even if metaphorically, mentioning God's face, nose, arm, hand, back, feet, referring to his sitting, striking, standing, marching, fighting, speaking, seeing, hearing, weeping, being angry, laughing—all activities associated with physical form.

The Nicene Creed of AD 325 mentions structures in God, three forms in which God has shown himself, shapes of relationship by which God consists in himself. These three are the Trinity, the Begetting of the Son, and the Procession of the Spirit. I have emphasized by italics in the following text the words that indicate these relationship forms.

> *We believe in one God, the Father Almighty,*
> Maker of heaven and earth,
> of all things visible and invisible.
> *And in one Lord Jesus Christ, the only-begotten Son of God,*
> *Begotten of his Father before all worlds,*

---

1. Dorothy L. Sayers, *The Mind of the Maker* (New York: Harcourt, Brace, 1941; San Francisco: HarperSanFrancisco, 1987), 123.

God of God, Light of Light,

very God of very God,

begotten, not made, being of one substance with the Father;

by whom all things were made;

who for us and for our salvation

came down from heaven,

and was incarnate by the Holy Spirit of the virgin Mary,

and was made man;

and was crucified also for us under Pontius Pilate;

he suffered and was buried;

and the third day he rose again according to the Scriptures,

and ascended into heaven, and is seated at the right hand of the Father;

and he shall come again, with glory, to judge both the living and the dead;

*And we believe in the Holy Spirit, the Lord and giver of life,*

*who proceeds from the Father and the Son,*

*who with the Father and the Son together is worshiped and glorified;*

who spoke by the prophets;

and we believe in one holy catholic and apostolic church;

we acknowledge one baptism for the remission of sins;

and we look for the resurrection of the dead,

and the life of the world to come. Amen.[2]

The Nicene Creed speaks of the Trinity, falling as it does into three main headings, each concerning one person of the Trinity. Further, the Creed mentions the Son and the Spirit for their coequality with the Father. Thus the Trinity itself constitutes a form, a shape of relationship, in which each person appears coequal and coeternal. No priority can exist among the Trinity's persons in this unified perspective.

In the Creed's second formal perspective, the Father begets the Son. While the original Creed carefully clarified the distinction between begetting and creating, a later edition of this Creed added, "*eternally* begotten of the Father," as a further guard against any mistakes concerning the Son's eternality. This begetting is also called "filiation," from the Latin *filius*, son.[3] The tradition of the Son's eternal begetting persists in the Nicene Creed as printed in the Episcopal Church's *Book of Common Prayer*.[4] The Westminster Confession of

---

2. Nicene Creed, from *The Trinity Hymnal*, rev. ed. (Suwanee, GA: Great Commission, 1990), 846.

3. www.merriam-webster.com/dictionary/filiation.

4. The Church Hymnal Corporation, *The Book of Common Prayer and Administration of the Sacraments and Other Rites and Ceremonies of the Church Together with the Psalter or Psalms of David according to the use of the Episcopal Church* (The Church Hymnal Corporation: New York, 1979), 358.

Faith calls the Son "eternally begotten,"[5] and subscribing churches teach this today. If the reader finds "eternally begotten" puzzling or questionable, we can still find "begotten by his Father before all worlds," the translation of the original language, sufficiently time-free to distinguish this relational form.

These first two formal relationships of God—Trinity and filiation—prove the foundation for the two basic ways we understand anything. They give us two perspectives, inseparable yet distinct, that found our entire interpretive platform. First, the Trinity is eternal, never changing and always consistent. At the same time, the Father's begetting of the Son shows development, movement, and that God's eternal consistency consists in perfect freedom. The Father's begetting is not mutual; the Son does not also beget the Father. Begetting works only one direction. In the divine begetting, we find sequence; in sequence, we find the roots of time, itself a form. The Father's begetting the Son gives time a reference point and a launching point in God's unchangeable eternity. Only here do all stories start and finish: every narrative we have discussed and more, and most vitally the wonderful story of redemptive history that the Father and the Son planned together before all worlds.

This third relational form of the Trinity shows up in the Nicene Creed's third section as the Holy Spirit *proceeds* from the Father and from the Son. Even when we drop the "and the Son" in consideration of our Orthodox brothers and sisters, we can see that the Holy Spirit proceeds from the Father to be present, first among the persons of the Trinity and then with his creation.

The Spirit proceeds from the Father to be present with his formless creation: "The earth was without form and void, and darkness was over the face of the deep. And the Spirit of God was hovering over the face of the waters" (Gen. 1:2 ESV). In the second verse of the creation account, here is God, through the Holy Spirit, present with his creation face-to-face. This procession reveals one of God's highly personal forms.

## The Portrait: Looking at God

Think of an ordinary novel, like *Robinson Crusoe*. We meet the lead character, getting to know his personality. Though we learn more as the story goes on, all the new things we learn about him fit with all we have seen earlier; he seems roughly the same fellow at the end that we find at the beginning.

Paul the apostle has just such a perspective in mind when he describes what

---

5. Westminster Confession of Faith, from *The Trinity Hymnal*, rev. ed. (Suwanee, GA: Great Commission, 1990), 850.

God has shown us when he turned the lights on for us through salvation: "God, who said, 'Let light shine out of darkness,' made his light shine in our hearts to give us the light of the knowledge of God's glory displayed in the face of Christ" (2 Cor. 4:6).

Jesus' face presents the Godhead. He represents the Trinity in his face, fulfilling his three offices and presenting them, unified, in a single person. He is beautiful, majestic, awe-inspiring, even terrifying, in his person and most exquisitely in his face.

The portrait and the narrative always work together.

## The Story: Redemptive History

Crusoe's story pours out as we read the novel, full of his many mishaps, adventures, and resourceful adaptions. He makes progress, though with setbacks, and by the tale's end he lives among people again. He has accomplished much and learned much, which he has told us; we would not have heard these reflections without him. His story goes somewhere, even all the way to us, readers of his account as Defoe tells it.[6]

God has a story, because he *is* a story. The Father and the Son wrote it ahead, before they created the worlds. Jesus tells this story to the two walkers on the road to Emmaus in Luke 24. Though they mistake him for a stranger, he explains redemptive history: all the Law and the Prophets and all the writings of Scripture were about him. Although these two men had known Jesus before his crucifixion, they had missed this story and caught only the Pharisees' story: "It's over." These disciples failed to recognize Jesus before and after his crucifixion. Jesus changed that by teaching them, and they responded with a surge of feelings: "Were not our hearts burning within us while he talked with us on the road and opened the Scriptures to us?" (Luke 24:32). They also learned the truth he taught; they also acted, heading straight back to Jerusalem, maybe even feeling their way in the dark, to tell the others. The yeast is growing, the kingdom spreading!

In Defoe as in Scripture, we see the hero's character through his story, and his story rooted in his character. The portrait and the story perspectives cooperate. They exist and cooperate because of the forms inherent in God. The Trinity shows the coequality of the persons, while the begetting of the Son shows dynamic movement in the eternal Trinity. Both perspectives are true: the synchronic (all at once) and diachronic (through time). Theologians make theology in both perspectives: biblical theology traces the story of salvation through the

---

6. Daniel Defoe, *Life and Adventures of Robinson Crusoe* (Chicago: Rand McNally and Co., 1928).

gradual development of the Scriptures (diachronic), and systematic theology shows the consistent doctrines of God, always true every moment (synchronic). Both perspectives are true, and they work together.

These forms in God give us a framework for interacting with everything we see. When considering ordinary cultural media, imagine these two perspectives as the portrait view and the story view. All fixed media—photos, paintings, road signs, billboards, and many websites—come to us as a fixed image, a momentary appearance. We might take some time to study it, or move on after a glance. All moving pictures, including performing arts and books, unfold over time. We make sense of these only by the Father's begetting of the Son, the fountain of time. My special love, music, and all the performing arts, even ordinary conversation, consist only in time. Without the Trinity, we could make nothing at all of either the portrait view or the story view.

## Face-to-Face: The Presence of the Holy Spirit

How is God present with us? How does he come to us? The Holy Spirit is the intimate face-to-face presence of God. This third relational form of the Trinity shows up in the Nicene Creed's third section. In the creed, procession has nothing to do with physical creation but moves toward God's creation, carrying his very presence. The psalmist describes God's presence through his Spirit with his creatures.

> These all *look to you*,
>> to give them their food in due season.
> When you give it to them, they gather it up;
>> when you open your hand, they are filled with good things.
> When you hide *your face*, they are dismayed;
>> when you take away their breath, they die
>> and return to their dust.
> When you send forth *your Spirit*, they are created,
>> and you renew the *face* of the ground.
>> —Psalm 104:27–30 ESV (emphasis added)

Here again God appears face to face with his creation, through his Spirit. The Holy Spirit proceeds from the Father to come close to the world in Christ Jesus. In Jesus' Spirit-enabled presence, "the kingdom of heaven has come near" (Matt. 3:2; 4:17; 10:7). The Spirit came on Mary, uniquely present with her to cause her to conceive the Son as Jesus; the Spirit descended on Jesus when

John baptized him; the Spirit raised him from death (Rom. 8:11); Jesus ascended in order to send the Spirit to us (John 16:7). The New Testament overflows with the Holy Spirit as God's presence with his people, as Jesus promised. "If you then, though you are evil, know how to give good gifts to your children, how much more will your Father in heaven give the Holy Spirit, who is in you" (1 Cor. 6:19).

All human communication and all sorts of cultural media and delivery systems make sense to us only by this essential form of God, the Holy Spirit's procession from the Father and from the Son (or from the Father alone by courtesy). We can understand all communication, together with its distortions and misuses, only by the Holy Spirit. This singular role of the Holy Spirit may help us understand Jesus' puzzling words, "Every kind of sin and slander can be forgiven, but blasphemy against the Spirit will not be forgiven" (Matt. 12:31): by the Holy Spirit's procession alone is God present with us, so blasphemy against him closes off our only link.

God himself is the meaning of life; he is what life means, he is how it means, and he is the meaning. Thus Paul says, "From him and through him and for him are all things. To him be the glory forever! Amen" (Rom. 11:36).

## God's Forms in Bible Forms

The literary forms of Scripture teach Trinity and filiation. Consider scriptural groups of three. Interpreters through the ages have found it almost too simple to read the Trinity into these groups. We have noticed several here, first because they involved aesthetics or forms. The second iteration of the triad sometimes switches the order; usually the triad's first two elements are reversed. The trees in Genesis 2 have three properties, and the fruit in chapter 3 has corresponding properties, with the first two elements reversed. God promised in Exodus 33 to reveal his glory to Moses in three modes, and then revealed it in chapter 34—with the order of the first two modes reversed. Christ's triple wilderness temptations appear in Matthew 4, and then again in Luke 4, with the order of the first two elements reversed. Taken most simply, the author means that the order does not matter, because it signifies no precedence of one element over the other. By reversing the order, the author urges the equality of the elements of these triads. This repeated equality corresponds by analogy to the equality of the members of the Trinity. Forms in literature have meaning, because forms in God have meaning.

One common scriptural form should attract our attention here. Hebrew parallelism, long studied, was previously understood as a simple restatement. But recent scholarship suggests differently. Longman observes, "The new paradigm for understanding parallelism is development rather than equivalence. The biblical poet is doing more than saying the same thing twice. The second part always nuances the first part in some way."[7] Simply stated, in Hebrew parallelism, the second colon is the same and different. The parallel phrases are both true, and the second also adds meaning. Neither has prominence, but one comes first, giving rise to the other. They are not interchangeable, and one cannot reverse their order.[8]

Parallelism appears throughout scriptural genres, in narrative and other prose, and in the New Testament as well, not only in poetry. Its ubiquity tantalizes. Why? What is the point? We have argued that all forms somehow reflect not only God's design but also God himself. We have noticed one other scriptural form that may well reflect the relation of the members of the Trinity. In a similar fashion, the "A, what's more, B"[9] relationship between parallel lines shows a remarkable similarity to the relation of the Father to the Son—"development rather than equivalence." Again we must ask, which came first? "With a literary text, form is meaning."[10] Could this biblical form offer more value to the divine meaning of Scripture?

Scripture reveals further intriguing relational forms of God. Consider that Jesus is seated at the right hand of the Father.[11] Notice that Jesus, as the Lamb, also shares the Father's throne. "The angel showed me the river of the water of life, as clear as crystal, flowing from the throne of God and of the Lamb down the middle of the great street of the city" (Rev. 22:1–2). This is not a two-seater throne but a single one, for the Lamb sits in its center (Rev. 7:17). How can the Son sit at the Father's right hand while also sitting in the center of the Father's throne?

These two relations spring from the two we have discussed earlier from the Nicene Creed and give the same two perspectives, the portrait and the story. The Son's Trinitarian equality with the Father shines forth in his sharing his throne, while his position at the Father's right hand shows his filiation. Both relations are true eternally.

---

7. Leland Ryken and Tremper Longman III, eds., *A Complete Literary Guide to the Bible* (Grand Rapids, MI: Zondervan, 1993), 83.

8. "In the 1981 book *The Idea of Biblical Poetry: Parallelism and Its History,* James Kugel contends that the ways of parallelism are numerous and varied, far exceeding Lowth's limited three categories. He observes that the degree of connection between two parallel clauses may range anywhere from no perceivable correspondence to just short of a word-for-word repetition. He insists that the second, 'B' clause does not simply restate the first, 'A' clause. Instead, the B-line expands upon the A-line in a multitude of ways: reasserting, supporting, particularizing, defining, completing, or going beyond the first line." "Biblical Poetry" in *Encyclopaedia Judaica* by the Jewish Virtual Library (Detroit: Gale Group, 2007), www.jewishvirtuallibrary.org/poetry#BIBLICAL_POETRY.

9. Tremper Longman III, *How to Read the Psalms* (Downers Grove, IL: InterVarsity, 1988), 97–98.
10. Ryken and Longman, *Complete Literary Guide,* 17.
11. Ps. 110:1; Matt. 22:44; Luke 22:69; Acts 2:33; Rom. 8:34; Eph. 1:20; Heb. 12:2.

John locates the Word, the Logos, here called the only-begotten God, in the Father's bosom, using a Greek word rare in the New Testament—only five occurrences—and hard to translate: "No man hath seen God at any time, the only begotten Son, which is in the bosom of the Father, he hath declared him" (John 1:18 KJV). This Greek word *kolpon,* translated "bosom" in both the King James and the New American Standard versions, conveys in this context the greatest possible intimacy. This intimacy has a shape: the Son is in the Father's bosom, but the Father is not in the Son's bosom. Is this the same as filiation, that the Father begets the Son? John adds this phrase because it is not; this intimate relation means even more than filiation alone. It means an ultimate intimacy that remains ineffable, inexpressible. This ultimate intimacy may well show the Holy Spirit at work, establishing Father and Son in communion of perfect intimacy. John, who alone lay on Jesus' own bosom (John 13:23 KJV), gives us here his glimpse of mysteries beyond our understanding.

Other relations in the Godhead appear in Scripture. The Son is "the servant of the LORD" (Isa. 42:19); he is the Anointed One, the Messiah (Ps. 2:2). These relations consist within the Trinity and the filiation of the Son and express the content and power of their relationship more perhaps than they do the form of God's inner relations. The image (2 Cor. 4:4) and form (Phil. 2:6 ESV) relations we have discussed elsewhere. Jesus was "full of the Holy Spirit" and "led by the Spirit" (Luke 4:1); the Holy Spirit is sent by the Father in the name of Jesus (John 4:26); Jesus breathes on the disciples and says, "Receive the Holy Spirit" (John 20:22). These intimate relationships within the Trinity then become the face-to-face relationships of God's people as he is present in and with them.

## The Forms of God Orient God's People

God's forms for the relationship he builds with his people are sometimes confusing, but always intimate. In Psalm 16, King David says, "I have set the LORD always *before me*; because he is *at my right hand*, I shall not be shaken" (Ps. 16:8 ESV, emphasis added). While the right-hand location is familiar, the persons have traded; in this form, the covenant God of Israel is now at David's right hand. This shocking trade points to the Christ's coming incarnation, though in such a way as to mystify us. The psalmist revisits this startling formal relationship: "The LORD watches over you—the LORD is your shade at your right hand" (Ps. 121:5).

We face another puzzle: Where is God, in front of David or at his right hand? Is this one relational shape or two? Here again, the "before me" view of

God expresses his consistency, his character, while the "at my right hand" locates God in David's story, in time. The two perspectives work in harmony, and both indicate the Spirit's face-to-face intimacy.

## God's Delight

God the Father loves Jesus Christ: his character and his story. In our flesh, we do not. We love beauty that belongs to the end of the story, and any story that brings the happy ending into the present easily catches our eye. We love power now, not weakness now and power later. We love beauty now, not unattractiveness now and beauty revealed only slowly, and then with sudden completeness at Christ's return. We love pleasure now. We love to suppose we can learn everything now, at our initiative.

We craft our works with as much aesthetic excellence as we can, hoping to make the gospel attractive to the unsaved. Scripture shows Jesus in his mysterious plainness, weakness, and questionable authority, so that the regenerate heart that sees may recognize there the beauty of heaven rather than solely the beauties of earth. "Am I now trying to win the approval of human beings, or of God? Or am I trying to please people? If I were still trying to please people, I would not be a servant of Christ" (Gal. 1:10).

God's pleasures are stirred by an aesthetic dynamic that has no appeal for unregenerate tastes, unless God is revealing himself in order to draw. Presentations aimed at the aesthetic tastes of a heart that rejects Christ—at brute aesthetics—cannot please God, nor can we rely on the results in those they attract. Our God-oriented aesthetics aim to please him first and then be used by him for his purposes.

Jesus Christ's overwhelming beauty, power, and truth remain hard to see for now. Isaiah's description still applies to the Servant of the Lord in our time, between his first and second comings: "Who has believed our message and to whom has the arm of the LORD been revealed? He grew up before him like a tender shoot, and like a root out of dry ground. He had no beauty or majesty to attract us to him, nothing in his appearance that we should desire him. He was despised and rejected by mankind, a man of suffering, and familiar with pain. Like one from whom people hide their faces he was despised, and we held him in low esteem" (Isa. 53:1–3).

We all communicate, and many make a living at it, in media of all kinds. We generally evaluate our efforts by what people think and say about our communication; we welcome approval, especially the approval of many people, and can easily make that approval our chief goal. God calls us to seek his glory and kingdom first. He can give his favor to our words and our works, and he can withhold it. He calls us to present our work to his audience, an audience of one. This godward motive should not prevent us preparing the richest, truest, loveliest, strongest communication we can, nor from praying for God's help and guidance. Since our flesh leans the other way, yearning to master the medium to guarantee a positive response, we need each other to encourage us in clarity about audience. I need the help of my family, my friends, and my church to lean against my own desires and against the culture's pressures. We need God's grace!

## Cultivating Delight

We must add that, while conversion alone enables us to share God's vision with him, the regenerated vision will profit from meditating on God's pleasures[12] and by beholding beauty[13] and by yielding to its persuasive power.[14] In all this, repentance and faith form the internal dynamic of aesthetic discipleship.

While we speak here of aesthetic discipleship, we might better speak of the aesthetic aspect of a whole life of discipleship. In Christ, our feelings have come home, restored to unity with true belief and righteous will.

Christ will be back soon, and when he comes, his beauty, truth, and power will be revealed, no longer hard to see. A better day is coming! "Dear friends, do not be surprised at the fiery ordeal that has come on you to test you, as though something strange were happening to you. But rejoice inasmuch as you participate in the sufferings of Christ, so that you may be overjoyed when his glory is revealed" (1 Peter 4:12–13).

## "Taste and See That the LORD Is Good" (Ps. 34:8)

The Lord is good. God saw that his creation was good in Genesis, which uses the same Hebrew word for good. The psalmist knew he was using the same word, and it carries meaning as rich and full as we saw in Genesis: true, beautiful, powerful. God himself is true, beautiful, and powerful, so he creates to show these. We, with redeemed eyes, grow to see God's goodness through creation's goodness. Our restored vision opens our eyes to what we have called translucence, God's glory radiating through every created thing, visible and invisible.

---

12. John Piper, *Pleasures of God: Mediations on God's Delight in Being God,* rev. ed. (1991; Colorado Springs: Multnomah, 2012).

13. James K. A. Smith, *Desiring the Kingdom* (Grand Rapids, MI: Baker Academic, 2009).

14. David Bentley Hart, *The Beauty of the Infinite* (Grand Rapids, MI: Eerdmans, 2003).

The redeemed eye sees more than God's glory through these created things. These eyes see God himself, more and more clearly. The glory of God grows in our eyes as we see every event, every hardship, every gift, every created thing, as translucent, radiating God's own personality.

God's revealed Word must guide this translucency. Translucency is not allegorization, the awkward splashing of loosely guided meanings onto various Bible texts. The forms of God revealed in Scripture and in the forms of Scripture invite us to explore at length *how* Scripture conveys meaning in forms, and by that, how the creation likewise conveys meaning in forms—a scripturally regulated translucency. The Bible's richness in aesthetic matters deserves our best attention.

Most Christians have at least an initial experience with this. The psalmist invites us to reflect and pray as we look at the sky, asking and then seeing how "the heavens declare the glory of God" (Ps. 19:1). God's words and God's pictures go together as clearly as the Son's coeternity with the Father goes with his begetting by the Father. The eye so opened sees more fully, more richly, and, seeing more and more in creation, sees more delights, more sorrows, and more hope than before. This path of aesthetic growth—since it has God as its model, means, and goal—expands in inexhaustible riches of delight of all sorts, always a participation in God's delight in himself, seen in creation through redemptive history. Our earthly lives are not enough for this—only eternity.

To him who is able to keep you from stumbling and to present you before his glorious presence without fault and with great joy—to the only God our Savior be glory, majesty, power and authority, through Jesus Christ our Lord, before all ages, now and forevermore! Amen.

—Jude 1:24–25

## READ, REFLECT, DISCUSS, SING

1. Suggested reading: chapters 11, 12, and 13 of *The Dynamic Heart in Daily Life: Connecting Christ to Human Experience* by Jeremy Pierre.
2. Q1. What artistic media affect you most strongly? Which ones reach you less? Why do you think that is? Where have you seen exceptions?
3. Q2. How has your appreciation of God changed this year? Where do you need to look next? How can you talk to him about that?
4. Sing: "Holy, Holy, Holy!"

# Sources

These are sources I have consulted or quoted in the preparation of this book.

Alexander, Monty. *Uplift*. South Orange, NJ: Jazz Legacy Productions, 2011.

Alter, Robert. *The Art of Biblical Narrative*. New York: Harper, 1981.

Augustine. *Confessions*. Translated by Rex Warner. New York: Penguin, 2009.

Begbie, Jeremy S. *Theology, Music and Time*. Cambridge Studies in Christian Doctrine 4. Cambridge: Cambridge Univ. Press, 2000.

————. *Voicing Creation's Praise: Towards a Theology of the Arts*. Edinburgh: T&T Clark, 1991.

"Biblical Poetry" in *Encyclopaedia Judaica*. The Jewish Virtual Library. The Gale Group: 2008. www.jewishvirtuallibrary.org/poetry#BIBILICAL_POETRY.

Boucher, Madeleine. *The Mysterious Parable: A Literary Study*. Washington, D.C.: Catholic Biblical Association of America, 1977.

Brand, Hilary, and Adrienne Chaplin. *Art and Soul: Signposts for Christians in the Arts*. Carlisle, UK: Piquant/InterVarsity, 2001.

Bright, Bill. *Have You Heard of the Four Spiritual Laws?* Peachtree City, GA: Campus Crusade for Christ, 2007.

Brown, Francis, with S. R. Driver and Charles A. Briggs. *The New Brown-Driver-Briggs-Gesenius Hebrew and English Lexicon*. Peabody, MA: Hendrickson, 1979.

Bunyan, John. *The Pilgrim's Progress*. New York: Grosset and Dunlap, n.d.

Bustard, Ned, ed. *It Was Good: Making Art to the Glory of God*. Baltimore: Square Halo, 2000.

Calvin, John. *Institutes of the Christian Religion*. Edited by John T. McNeill. Translated by Ford Lewis Battles. Library of Christian Classics XX. Philadelphia: Westminster, 1960.

*Catechism of the Catholic Church with Modifications from the Editio Typica*. 2nd ed. New York: Doubleday, 1995.

The Church Pension Fund. *The Book of Common Prayer*. New York: The Church Pension Fund, 1945.

Clowney, Edmund P. "Preaching Christ from All the Scriptures," in *The Preacher and Preaching*. Edited by Samuel T. Logan, Jr. Phillipsburg, NJ: Presbyterian and Reformed, 1986.

Croegaert, Jim. "Why Do We Hunger for Beauty?" Meadowgreen Music Co./Heart of the Matter Music, 1989.

Crouch, Andy. *Culture Making: Recovering Our Creative Calling*. Downers Grove, IL: InterVarsity, 2008.

Defoe, Daniel. *Life and Adventures of Robinson Crusoe*. Chicago: Rand McNally and Co., 1928.

Edgar, William. *Taking Note of Music*. London: SPCK, 1986.

———. Introduction to *Christian Apologetics*, by Cornelius Van Til. 2nd ed. Phillipsburg, NJ: Presbyterian and Reformed, 2003.

———. *Created and Creating: A Biblical Theology of Culture*. Downers Grove, IL: InterVarsity, 2017.

Edwards, Jonathan. *The Religious Affections*. Carlisle: Banner of Truth, 1961, 2001.

Ellul, Jacques. *The Humiliation of the Word*. Grand Rapids, MI: Eerdmans, 1985.

Frame, John M. *Doctrine of the Knowledge of God*. Phillipsburg, NJ: Presbyterian and Reformed, 1987.

———. *Perspectives on the Word of God: An Introduction to Christian Ethics*. Phillipsburg, NJ: Presbyterian and Reformed, 1990.

———. *Theology in Three Dimensions: A Guide to Triperspectivalism and Its Significance*. Phillipsburg, NJ: Presbyterian and Reformed, 2017.

Gaebelein, Frank E. *The Christian, the Arts, and Truth: Regaining the Vision of Greatness*. Portland, OR: Multnomah, 1985.

Gaffin, Richard B., Jr. "Systematic Theology and Biblical Theology," in *The New Testament Student and Theology*. Edited by John H. Skilton. Nutley, NJ: Presbyterian and Reformed, 1976.

Gayford, Martin. "Duchamp's Fountain: The Practical Joke That Launched an Artistic Revolution." *The Telegraph* (February 16, 2008). www.telegraph.co.uk/culture/art/3671180/Duchamps-Fountain-The-practical-joke-that-launched-an-artistic-revolution.html.

Great Commission Publications. *Trinity Hymnal*. Rev. ed. Suwanee, GA: Great Commission, 1990.

Hart, David Bentley. *The Beauty of the Infinite*. Grand Rapids, MI: Eerdmans, 2003.

Hustad, Donald P. *Jubilate II: Church Music in Worship and Renewal*. Carol Stream, IL: Hope, 1993.

Jones, David Clyde. *Biblical Christian Ethics*. Grand Rapids, MI: Baker, 1994.

Keyes, Dick. "The Theology of Imagination." Cassette tape of his lecture at the L'Abri Conference, given in Atlanta in June 1983, published and distributed by L'Abri Fellowship in Southborough, MA.

Kuyper, Abraham. *Lectures on Calvinism*. Peabody, MA: Hendrickson, 2008.

———. *Wisdom and Wonder: Common Grace in Science and Art*. Edited by Jordan J. Ballor and Steven J. Grabill. Translated by Nelson D. Kloosterman. Grand Rapids, MI: Christian's Library, 2011.

L'Engle, Madeleine. *Walking on Water: Reflections on Faith and Art*. New York: Bantam, 1982.

Lewis, C. S. *The Great Divorce*. New York: Macmillan/Collier, 1946.

———. *Perelandra*. New York: Macmillan, 1944.

———. *The Screwtape Letters*. San Francisco: HarperOne, 2001.

———. *The Weight of Glory and Other Addresses*. New York: Harper Collins, 2001.

Lohse, Eduard. *The New Testament Environment*. Rev. ed. Translated by John E. Steely. Nashville: Abingdon, 1974.

Longman, Tremper, III. *How to Read the Psalms*. Downers Grove, IL: InterVarsity, 1988.

Longman, Tremper, III, and Daniel G. Reid. *God Is a Warrior*. Grand Rapids, MI: Zondervan, 1995.

McGrath, Alister E. *Spirituality in an Age of Change: Rediscovering the Spirit of the Reformers*. Grand Rapids, MI: Zondervan, 1994.

Milne, A. A. *Winnie-the-Pooh*. New York: Dell, 1970.

Mouw, Richard J. *He Shines in All That's Fair: Culture and Common Grace*. Grand Rapids, MI: Eerdmans, 2001.

Murray, John. *Selected Lectures in Systematic Theology*. Vol. 2 of *The Collected Writings of John Murray*. Edinburgh: Banner of Truth, 1977.

Myers, Kenneth. *All God's Children and Blue Suede Shoes*. Wheaton, IL: Crossway, 1989.

Niebuhr, H. Richard. *Christ and Culture*. San Francisco: Harper and Rowe, 1956.

Pierre, Jeremy. *The Dynamic Heart in Daily Life: Connecting Christ to Human Experience*. Greensboro: New Growth, 2016.

Piper, John. *Desiring God: Meditations of a Christian Hedonist*. Colorado Springs: Multnomah, 1986.

———. *The Pleasures of God: Meditations on God's Delight in Being God*. Rev. ed. Colorado Springs: Multnomah, 2012 (originally 1991).

Poe, Harry Lee. *See No Evil: The Existence of Sin in an Age of Relativism*. Grand Rapids, MI: Kregel, 2004.

Poythress, Vern Sheridan. *God-Centered Biblical Interpretation*. Phillipsburg, NJ: Presbyterian and Reformed, 1999.

———. *In the Beginning Was the Word: Language—A God-Centered Approach*. Wheaton, IL: Crossway, 2009.

———. *Symphonic Theology: The Validity of Multiple Perspectives in Theology.* Grand Rapids, MI: Zondervan, 1987.

———. "Multiperspectivalism and the Reformed Faith" in *Speaking the Truth in Love: The Theology of John M. Frame.* Edited by John J. Hughes. Phillipsburg, NJ: Presbyterian and Reformed, 2009, 173–200.

Rigney, Joe. *The Things of Earth: Treasuring God by Enjoying His Gifts.* Wheaton, IL: Crossway, 2015.

Ryken, Leland, and Tremper Longman III, eds. *A Complete Literary Guide to the Bible.* Grand Rapids, MI: Zondervan, 1993.

Ryken, Philip Graham. *Art for God's Sake: A Call to Recover the Arts.* Phillipsburg, NJ: Presbyterian and Reformed, 2006.

Sayers, Dorothy L. *The Mind of the Maker.* New York: Harcourt, Brace, 1941; San Francisco: HarperSanFrancisco, 1987.

Scarry, Elaine. *On Beauty and Being Just.* Princeton: Princeton Univ. Press, 1999.

Schaeffer, Francis A. *Art and the Bible.* Downers Grove, IL: InterVarsity, 1973.

———. *Basic Bible Studies.* Wheaton, IL: Tyndale, 1972.

Seerveld, Calvin. *Rainbows for the Fallen World.* Toronto: Tuppence, 1980.

Senn, Frank C. *Christian Liturgy: Catholic and Evangelical.* Minneapolis: Fortress Press, 1997.

Smith, James K. A. *Desiring the Kingdom.* Grand Rapids, MI: Baker Academic, 2009.

Smith, William P. Quoted in *The Heart of the Matter: Daily Reflections for Changing Hearts and Lives* by the Christian Counseling and Educational Foundation. Edited by Nancy B. Winter. Greensboro, NC: New Growth, 2012.

Snyder, Blake. *Save the Cat! The Last Book on Screenwriting That You'll Ever Need.* Studio City, CA: Michael Wiese Productions, 2005.

Tarnas, Richard. *The Passion of the Western Mind: Understanding the Ideas That Have Shaped Our World View.* New York: Ballantine, 1991.

Tolkien, J. R. R. *The Lord of the Rings.* London: Allen and Unwin, 1968.

———. "On Fairy-Stories" in *The Tolkien Reader.* New York: Ballantine, 1966.

Turnau, Ted. *Popologetics: Popular Culture in Christian Perspective.* Phillipsburg, NJ: Presbyterian and Reformed, 2012.

Turner, Steve. *Hungry for Heaven: Rock 'n' Roll and the Search for Redemption.* Rev. ed. Downers Grove, IL: InterVarsity, 1995.

VanGemeren, Willem A., gen. ed. *New International Dictionary of Old Testament Theology and Exegesis.* Grand Rapids, MI: Zondervan, 1997.

Van Til, Cornelius. *A Christian Theory of Knowledge.* Phillipsburg, NJ: Presbyterian and Reformed, 1969.

———. *Christian Apologetics.* Phillipsburg, NJ: Presbyterian and Reformed, 1976.

Van Til, Henry R. *The Calvinistic Concept of Culture.* Grand Rapids, MI: Baker Academic, 1952, 1979.

Vos, Geerhardus. *Biblical Theology: Old and New Testaments.* Edinburgh: Banner of Truth, 1948.

Walsh, Brian J., and J. Richard Middleton. *The Transforming Vision: Shaping a Christian World View.* Downers Grove, IL: InterVarsity, 1984.

Wolters, Albert M. *Creation Regained: Biblical Basics for a Reformational Worldview.* Grand Rapids, MI: Eerdmans, 1985, 2005.

Wolterstorff, Nicholas. *Art in Action.* Grand Rapids, MI: Eerdmans, 1980.

# SUBJECT INDEX

culture, human, 42, 48, 90, 180, 182–201
cynicism, 121

Dagon, 57
David, 53, 54, 57–58, 94, 133, 161,
    169, 212
decontextualization, 96, 179
degradation, aesthetic, 133
delayed gratification, 120, 176
delight, 116, 150, 213–14
desire, 100–101, 117, 118
diachronic view, 136, 208–9
discernment, 86
discipleship, 102–3
    aesthetic, 169–72, 190–91, 214
    model, 126
    personal, 201
discourse, 45, 85, 140, 168, 171
disgust, 150–51, 155
disobedience, 131
doctrine, 182–201
doing, 76, 81, 83, 85, 99, 137, 140
drug abuse, 119
Duchamp, Marcel, 40

Eden, 55, 63, 69–70, 81, 120
Eli, 94
emotions, 28, 60, 100–101, 184
end times, 162–63
Enlightenment, 124
entertainment-ism, 121
entitlement, sense of, 155
ethics, 85, 106, 124, 137, 141
    predispositional approach to, 172
    and redemption, 184
    and sin, 110
    triad, 75–76
Eve, 63–64, 80–81, 88, 89–90, 92,
    118, 121–22, 137, 140

evil, 63, 111, 115
excellence, 42, 43, 60
existential ethics, 75–76, 85
extramarital affairs, 194
eye, redeemed. *See* redeemed vision
Ezekiel, 51, 56, 176

face-to-face view, 197–98, 209–10
faith, 103, 104–5, 147, 203
fall, 170, 178, 180
fasting, 122–23
fears, 116
feelings, 20, 28, 31, 60, 90, 154–55, 160
    and art, 36–37
    God's involvement in, 199, 202
    hunt for consistent doctrine of, 32–33
    popular approaches to, 171
    sharing, 180
    as triad with thinking and doing, 73
"feelings first" model, 32
filiation, 206–7, 210, 212
final judgment, 162–63
flood, 54, 90, 91, 96, 188
food, 91, 138, 166
forms, 85, 178
    and aesthetics, 77–78
    biblical, 186–87
    and creation, 89, 204
    cultural, 194–95
    and God, 204–8
    interpreting creational and
        cultural, 189
    and meaning, 38
    and showing, 77–78
    as triad with content and purpose,
        70, 76, 79, 81, 83, 84, 92, 111,
        137, 158, 183
fornication, 156
Frame, John, 75–76, 85

# Scripture Index